M000309837

Praise for Aaron Friedberg

"A decade ago, Aaron Friedberg courted unpopularity with *A Contest for Supremacy*, a book anticipating the imminent failure of engaging China at any price. His warnings were demonstrably worth heeding. Now in *Getting China Wrong* he makes the case that the United States and other democracies still underestimate the struggle ahead. But this is no counsel of despair: instead, Friedberg articulates a multi-layered action agenda, arguing that the best form of defense could well involve a willingness to impose costs."

Rory Medcalf, Head of the National Security College, Australian National University, and author of *Indo-Pacific Empire*

"A telling account of how and why policy-makers, academics, and business embraced a form of engagement with China that proved to be a sincerely optimistic but hopelessly wrong gamble. A trenchant and accessible foray into the geopolitics of our time and our future."

George Magnus, Research Associate, China Centre, University of Oxford and SOAS

"In *Getting China Wrong*, Aaron Friedberg lays out a balanced and practical approach for managing relations with China. Most compellingly, he argues that liberal democracies must begin by taking their own side in this rivalry, making clear the stark differences of a future defined by the Chinese Communist Party. This book is essential reading for anyone seeking to navigate a multipolar world order."

Admiral John Richardson, USN (Ret.), 31st Chief of Naval Operations

"Friedberg's *Getting China Wrong* nails down half a century of mistaken American assumptions about China's future path. This essential non-partisan primer highlights the increasingly bold strategy of the Chinese Communist Party to defeat Western expectations."

François Godement, Senior Advisor for Asia, Institut Montaigne, Paris

"A splendid book with deep insights into the nature of the Chinese Communist Party dictatorship and an urgent message about the need to uphold and expand the liberal international order in Asia."

Nobu Kanehara, former Deputy National Security Advisor to PM Abe of Japan

Getting China Wrong

For Nadège
Ma chère femme, je te remercie pour tout.

GETTING CHINA WRONG

Aaron L. Friedberg

polity

Copyright © Aaron L. Friedberg 2022

The right of Aaron L. Friedberg to be identified as Author of this Work has been asserted in accordance with the UK Copyright, Designs and Patents Act 1988.

First published in 2022 by Polity Press

Polity Press
65 Bridge Street
Cambridge CB2 1UR, UK

Polity Press
101 Station Landing
Suite 300
Medford, MA 02155, USA

All rights reserved. Except for the quotation of short passages for the purpose of criticism and review, no part of this publication may be reproduced, stored in a retrieval system or transmitted, in any form or by any means, electronic, mechanical, photocopying, recording or otherwise, without the prior permission of the publisher.

ISBN-13: 978-1-5095-4512-4

A catalogue record for this book is available from the British Library.
Library of Congress Control Number: 2021946893

Typeset in 11.5 on 14 pt Adobe Garamond
by Cheshire Typesetting Ltd, Cuddington, Cheshire
Printed and bound in Great Britain by TJ Books Ltd, Padstow, Cornwall

The publisher has used its best endeavours to ensure that the URLs for external websites referred to in this book are correct and active at the time of going to press. However, the publisher has no responsibility for the websites and can make no guarantee that a site will remain live or that the content is or will remain appropriate.

Every effort has been made to trace all copyright holders, but if any have been overlooked the publisher will be pleased to include any necessary credits in any subsequent reprint or edition.

For further information on Polity, visit our website:
politybooks.com

Contents

Illustrations

Preface

Writing about contemporary China from the perspective of an American concerned with US and wider Western strategy towards that country is like trying to hit a very fast-moving object from the pitching deck of a ship at sea: both the target and the platform from which it is being observed are in constant, if irregular, motion.

This book was completed during the summer of 2021. Since that time, there have been a number of significant developments, many of which (like the US–UK–Australia nuclear submarine deal and Xi Jinping's recent crackdown on China's high-tech giants) are not discussed here. Between the writing of this preface (in the fall of 2021) and the publication of the book (spring 2022), there will no doubt be other noteworthy incidents and occurrences.

That said, the overall trajectory of events is already quite clear and, at least for the foreseeable future, nothing seems likely to deflect it. China is moving towards deepening political repression, expanded economic statism, and a more aggressive posture towards the United States, its partners and allies. Albeit belatedly and with an as yet insufficient sense of urgency and common purpose, the democracies have begun to face up to these facts and the dangers they pose, and to start the painful process of hammering out new policies with which to meet them. What remains to be seen is whether they can do so quickly enough to deter overt aggression while better defending their societies and economies against the subtler threats of penetration, manipulation, and exploitation.

As regards China, what has happened over the last several months is consistent with the broad patterns described here and with the overarching explanation offered for them. At home, the Chinese Communist Party brooks no opposition to its rule, claims for itself the authority to exert control over every aspect of social, political, and economic life, and uses that control to tighten its grip on its citizens and to build up the nation's coercive power on the world stage. Xi Jinping's recent directives extending ideological indoctrination down to the primary school level, cracking down on video games and pop culture, and reining in Alibaba, Tencent, and other nominally private companies are merely the latest manifestations of the normal functioning of China's Leninist political system.

Similarly, Beijing's stepped-up military pressure on Taiwan, dramatic test of a new type of hypersonic missile, and strikingly confrontational approach to dealing with a freshly elected US administration represent a continuation of trends that have become unmistakable over the course of the last two decades. As their assessments of China's relative strength have grown more positive, its leaders have pushed harder and more openly to reshape the world in ways intended to insure the longevity of their regime, first by reestablishing their country as the dominant state in eastern Eurasia, and ultimately by displacing the United States as the preponderant global power.

In his first year in office, Joe Biden sought to shed some of the crude and counterproductive aspects of Donald Trump's approach to dealing with China. As of this writing, however, Biden has continued in many respects to follow the main lines of policy laid down by his predecessor. At least in theory, his administration has accepted the need to reexamine the assumptions underpinning the entire US–China economic relationship, leaving in place for the moment most of the tariffs, export controls, and investment regulations that it inherited and even adding a few of its own. Top officials have also stressed the importance of shoring up the balance of power in the Indo-Pacific, both by strengthening US military capabilities and by working with allies and partners in the region and beyond.

Together with these positive indications, however, there are also some worrying signs.

Despite growing recognition of the harmful effects of China's predatory trade and industrial policies, there appears still to be hope in some quarters that these can be changed through the patient application of mild pressure and a few more rounds of what the chief US trade negotiator recently described as "frank conversations" with her counterparts in Beijing.[1] While Biden's advisors struggle to formulate an economic

---

1 Remarks as Prepared for Delivery of Ambassador Katherine Tai Outlining the Biden–Harris Administration's "New Approach to the US–China Trade Relationship," October 4, 2021.

strategy that better serves the nation as a whole, an assortment of industrial and financial groups are hard at work defending their particular interests, lobbying Congress and the executive branch to roll back some if not all of the restrictions put in place over the last several years, and urging Washington to get back to business as usual. Governments in all of the advanced democracies face similar pressures.

Having acknowledged the centrality of an intensifying military rivalry with China, the Biden administration has thus far been reluctant to make the public case for increasing defense budgets rather than holding them steady. This will become even more important as non-defense spending soars and debt rises. The absence of a clearly articulated and widely shared assessment of the nature and severity of the challenge has also contributed to problems in rallying support from other countries for a more unified effort to balance China's rising power and counter its growing influence. Beijing's heightened belligerence and Cold War-style "rocket rattling" seem intended in part to intimidate the democracies and discourage closer collaboration among them.

Instead of sounding the alarm, at least some in the new administration have appeared overly eager to improve the tenor of diplomatic exchanges with Beijing, and unduly optimistic about their ability to disaggregate the overall relationship into clearly delineated areas of cooperation and competition. The notion that the two powers can somehow agree on the rules of a more-or-less stable and "responsible" rivalry without first passing through a period of heightened tension and danger understates the intensity of the ideological and geopolitical forces at play.[2]

All of these concerns point to a deeper problem. Most Western observers now recognize that, despite years of intensive engagement, China today is far from the liberal, open, market-oriented, status quo power that many had expected to emerge. But acknowledging what China is not, and coming fully to grips with what it has in fact become, are two very different things. Without an adequate understanding of why past policies failed to transform the nation's Leninist political system, and absent a realistic assessment of its current strengths, weaknesses, and intentions, the United States and its allies will struggle to devise effective

---

2 "Readout of National Security Advisor Jake Sullivan's Meeting with Politburo Member Yang Jiechi," October 4, 2021.

counter-strategies. Persistent illusions about the depths of the regime's determination, the extent of its capacity for brutality, and the scope of its ambitions will result in more inadequate half-measures and more lost time. For the better part of the past thirty years, the democracies have gotten China wrong. They can no longer afford that luxury.

Aaron L. Friedberg
Princeton, New Jersey
October 2021

Acknowledgements

My thanks to Louise Knight of Polity Press for suggesting that I write a book on this topic. Louise and Inès Boxman were helpful and encouraging at every step along the way. Justin Dyer edited the manuscript with a deft touch. Margaret Commander found documents, tracked down citations, and generated graphs with alacrity and precision.

I am extremely grateful to Jacqueline Deal, Richard Ellings, James Mann, Stephen Rosen, Gabriel Schoenfeld, David Shambaugh, and Julian Snelder for taking the time to read the manuscript closely and for providing insightful comments and detailed suggestions. Needless to say, I alone am responsible for any errors of fact or interpretation that remain.

Most of all, I thank Nadège Rolland for her careful reading of every draft, for her help in locating and translating a number of Chinese sources, and for her enduring love, patient encouragement, and unstinting support in all things. I am the luckiest of men.

Portions of Chapter 6 draw from Aaron L. Friedberg, "An Answer to Aggression," *Foreign Affairs* (September/October 2020), pp. 150–64. Adapted by permission of *Foreign Affairs*. Copyright 2020 by the Council on Foreign Relations, Inc. *www.Foreign Affairs.com.*

Introduction

The history of the last half-century of relations between China and the West[1] can be briefly summarized. The United States and the other liberal democracies opened their doors to China in the belief that, by doing so, they would cause its system to converge more closely with their own. As anticipated, access to the markets, resources, technology, educational systems, and managerial know-how of the advanced industrial nations of Western Europe, North America, and East Asia helped China grow richer more rapidly than would otherwise have been possible. But trade and societal interaction did not yield the broader benefits for which the democracies had hoped. Instead of a liberal and cooperative partner, China has become an increasingly wealthy and powerful competitor, repressive at home and aggressive abroad.

When the Cold War ended in the early 1990s, the United States adopted a two-part strategy for dealing with China. On the one hand, in a continuation and expansion of policies that began twenty years earlier with the Nixon/Kissinger opening to Beijing, successive US administrations sought to promote "engagement": ever-deepening commercial, diplomatic, scientific, educational, and cultural ties between China and the West. At the same time, together with a collection of allies and strategic partners, from the mid-1990s Washington worked to maintain a favorable balance of military power in what has now come to be referred to as the Indo-Pacific region. While most non-Asian democracies did not participate actively in the balancing portion of US strategy, all embraced engagement, and especially its economic component, with vigor and enthusiasm.

The two elements of this dual-edged strategy were expected to work together. Balancing would preserve stability and deter aggression, even as China grew richer and stronger. Meanwhile, engagement would transform the country in ways that reduced the danger it might someday pose a threat to the interests of the United States and its democratic allies. By

1

welcoming Beijing into the US-dominated, post-Cold War international system, American policy-makers hoped to persuade China's leaders that their interests lay in preserving the existing order, adapting to its rules and adopting its values, rather than seeking to modify or overthrow it. Drawing China fully into an increasingly integrated global economy was also expected to accelerate its transition away from state-directed economic planning and towards a more open, market-driven model of development. Finally, US and other Western leaders hoped that by encouraging the growth of a middle class, the spread of liberal ideas, and strengthening the rule of law and the institutions of civil society, engagement would lead eventually to liberalizing political reforms.

Optimism on all of these counts reached a peak at the turn of the twenty-first century with Beijing's accession to the World Trade Organization (WTO) and its full, formal incorporation into the Western-built global economic system. The subsequent two decades – and, in particular, the years since the 2008 financial crisis – have been marked by a darkening mood and accumulating evidence that things have not gone according to plan. Instead of moving steadily towards greater openness and more reliance on markets, as most observers predicted and expected, Beijing has expanded its use of state-directed trade, technology promotion, and industrial policies. Despite the Chinese Communist Party (CCP) regime's ceaseless rhetoric about the glories of globalization and the wonders of "win-win cooperation," these policies now threaten the future prosperity of the advanced industrial nations.

Rather than loosen up, the Chinese party-state has cracked down on its own citizens, stifling the slightest hint of dissent, laying the foundations for a pervasive, nationwide high-tech surveillance system, and consigning at least a million of the country's Uighur Muslims to forced labor and concentration camps. China today is more repressive than at any time since the 1989 Tiananmen Square massacre and arguably since the Cultural Revolution of the 1960s.

Finally, far from becoming a satisfied supporter of the international status quo, Beijing is now pursuing openly revisionist aims: it seeks to displace the United States as the preponderant power in eastern Eurasia and hopes eventually to challenge its position as the world's richest, strongest, most technologically advanced, and most influential nation. In addition to eroding the advantages in wealth and material power that

2

the United States and the other Western democracies have long enjoyed, China now poses an explicit challenge to the efficacy, moral authority, and supposed universality of the principles on which their political systems are based. In the words of a 2019 report by the European Union, China is a "systemic rival" that claims to have developed "alternative models of governance" superior to those put forward by the liberal democratic West.[2]

Why did the policy of engagement fail to achieve its objectives? The simplest answer to this question is that US and other Western policymakers misunderstood the character of China's domestic political regime: they underestimated the resilience, resourcefulness, and ruthlessness of the CCP, misjudged the depths of its resolve to retain domestic political power, and failed to recognize the extent and seriousness of its revisionist international ambitions. Put plainly, engagement failed because its architects and advocates got China wrong.

Even before the Cold War ended, China's leaders believed that they were engaged in a life-and-death struggle with the democratic world, led by the United States. As viewed from Beijing, offers of engagement were merely a clever Western stratagem designed to weaken China by exposing its people to dangerous liberal ideas and unleashing societal forces that would lead eventually to irresistible pressures for political change. At the same time as they sought to subvert its system from within, American strategists were seen as aiming to contain China, preventing it from regaining its rightful place in Asia by encircling it with allies and forward-based military forces.

Faced with what it regarded as a deadly, double-edged threat, the CCP regime worked diligently to devise and implement a counter-strategy of its own. Highly flexible and adaptive in their choice of means, Chinese strategists have nevertheless been remarkably constant in their objectives. For over thirty years now they have found ways to exploit the opportunities afforded by engagement, expanding their nation's economy, building up its scientific, technological, and military capabilities, and enhancing its influence in Western countries, while at the same time maintaining and even reinforcing the Party's grip on Chinese society. As their strength and self-confidence have grown, China's rulers have begun to move from a largely defensive posture in world affairs to an assertive and even aggressive external stance. Albeit belatedly, in the last several years this shift has sparked concern and the beginnings of a more forceful response from the West.

Judged against their respective aims, Beijing's strategy has thus far worked better than that of the United States and its democratic allies. But the competition between the two sides is far from over. One reason why China has done as well as it has to date is precisely that its rivals have been so slow to react to its advances. Where Beijing has been fixed in its ends but flexible in its means, the democracies have tended to be rigid with respect to both, clinging to forlorn hopes and failed policies. If the liberal democracies can reset their assumptions and expectations about China, abandon their previous passivity and start to regain the initiative, the quality of Beijing's strategic reflexes will be put to the test. Confronted with a more alert and dynamic opponent, the CCP regime may be prone to seize up, doubling down on existing approaches in ways that could prove counterproductive and potentially self-defeating. Indeed, there are already some signs that this has started to happen.

Subsequent chapters will examine both sides of the complex, multi-dimensional rivalry between China, on the one hand, and the democracies, led by the United States, on the other.

The book's opening chapters focus on the United States, the architect and prime mover behind the policy of engagement, starting with an account of the policy's origins, from the latter stages of the Cold War to the debate over China's entry into the WTO at the end of the 1990s. Contrary to what some critics have claimed, engagement was not merely a fool's errand, a careless and self-evident blunder with an obviously unachievable aim; nor was it simply the handiwork of greedy "globalists" in search of profits. Rather it was the product of a unique set of historical circumstances that prevailed at the end of the Cold War. Chapter 1 describes the confluence of deeply rooted ideological beliefs, powerful material trends, and emerging interest group pressures that launched the United States on its quixotic campaign to reshape China's political system, economy, and grand strategy.

Chapter 2 lays out three sets of rationales for engagement offered by US policy-makers during the crucial decade of the 1990s. An examination of the historical record confirms that, despite some recent revisionism, a broad assortment of experts, officials, and political leaders did, in fact, argue that engagement would likely lead to China's economic and

4

political liberalization and its willing incorporation into the existing, US-dominated international order.

Three subsequent chapters will address the central question of why these expectations have not been met. Chapter 3 analyzes the Party's persistent anxieties about penetration and subversion, describes its unwavering determination to maintain its domestic political monopoly, and traces the evolving mix of coercion, cooptation, and ideological indoctrination through which it has been able thus far to do so.

As explained in Chapter 4, the CCP's preoccupation with power and its obsession with control are also essential to understanding the evolution of its economic policies. From the start of the process of "reform and opening up" under Deng Xiaoping in the late 1970s, CCP strategists have regarded the market as a tool of the party-state or, as one of Deng's colleagues put it, a "bird in a cage." While they have been willing at times to afford greater scope to market forces, contrary to the expectations of most Western observers, the Party's top leaders have never had any intention of proceeding down the path towards full economic liberalization. It should therefore come as no surprise that, in responding to the challenge of markedly slower growth, in recent years the regime has ignored the advice of most Western (and many Chinese) economists that it relax its grip, opting instead for policies that further enhance the role of the state at the expense of the market.

Chapter 5 will make the case that, as is true of its domestic political and economic policies, the outward-directed elements of China's grand strategy are also strongly shaped by the character of the CCP regime and its distinctive ideological worldview. Following the collapse of the Soviet Union, Beijing faced an international system that it saw as profoundly threatening, not only to its physical security but also to its very legitimacy. While for a time China lacked the power to challenge the status quo, the notion that it would want nothing more than to be accepted as a member in good standing of the existing regional and global orders was always fanciful. As their capabilities have grown, China's leaders have gone over to the offensive, pushing back at the meddlesome presence of US and allied military forces in their own backyard, challenging America's position as the preeminent global power, and seeking to neutralize the threat posed by the pervasiveness and continuing appeal of the liberal democratic ideals it espouses.

What comes through plainly in each of these three domains – political, economic, and strategic – is the consistency of the CCP's goals and the relentless determination with which they have been sought by successive generations of leaders. Since taking power in late 2012, Xi Jinping has felt emboldened to express those ends more openly and to pursue them more forcefully than his predecessors. Contrary to the way in which he is sometimes portrayed in the West, however, Xi does not represent a break from the past. To the contrary, he is following in the footsteps of his forebears and attempting to attain the same objectives.

For their part, the United States and its allies are presently suspended between a set of old policies that have not achieved the aims set for them and a new, not yet fully defined alternative strategy to guide their future actions. Before looking forward, Chapter 6 will look back one last time, examining the question of whether engagement's failure was inevitable and explaining why it has taken so long for Western policy-makers to acknowledge that it has, in fact, failed.

The democracies now find themselves confronted, not by a cooperative partner, but by a powerful and hostile state, deeply enmeshed in their societies and economies, and ruled by a technologically sophisticated, dictatorial regime that seeks to reshape the world in ways that are threatening to their interests and inimical to their values. This reality is unpleasant but it is also undeniable and must be faced. Continuing to engage with China on the same terms as in the past will help it grow even stronger and, instead of inducing positive change, such an approach will only strengthen the hand and encourage the ambitions of the CCP regime.

The book will close by laying out the main elements of a new strategy for meeting the challenge that Beijing now poses. Although there will be costs, the United States and its allies need to constrict engagement with China and invest more in the capabilities necessary to balance against its growing power. Abandoning the illusory post-Cold War goal of transforming the country by incorporating it into an all-inclusive international order operating on liberal principles, the democracies must focus instead on strengthening the sinews of a *partial* liberal system: an assembly of states that, whatever their differences, share a commitment to upholding and defending the rights and freedoms on which their societies are based.

1

The Origins of Engagement

During the climactic closing decades of the Cold War, US policy-makers viewed engagement with Beijing primarily through the lens of their ongoing competition against the Soviet Union. As the United States pulled back from its bruising defeat in Vietnam, the Soviets appeared to be moving boldly in the opposite direction. During the 1970s and into the 1980s, Moscow continued an ambitious, broad-based military buildup and launched a series of interventionist adventures of its own in Afghanistan, southern Africa, and Central America. Faced with these troubling trends, American strategists began to look for ways to enhance China's military, economic, and technological capabilities in order to build it into a more effective counterweight to Soviet power.

Working with Beijing required a revolution in American diplomacy. For two decades after the founding of the People's Republic of China (PRC), Washington had refused even to recognize its existence, clinging instead to the fiction that the Nationalist regime that fled to Taiwan after being defeated by the Communists in 1949 was the legitimate government of all of China. Following the first tentative, secret contacts in 1969, successive American administrations took a series of steps that moved Washington and Beijing away from intense mutual animosity and towards a close, albeit wary, strategic alignment against a common foe.

Starting with National Security Advisor Henry Kissinger's first visit to China in 1971, American officials provided their counterparts in Beijing with satellite photographs and other intelligence information about the capabilities and disposition of Soviet forces, and began to discuss possible contingencies involving a military confrontation with the USSR.[1] Together with these sensitive exchanges, Presidents Nixon and Ford also authorized the sale or transfer of limited numbers of so-called "dual-use" systems with both commercial and potential military applications, including satellite ground stations, civilian jet aircraft, and high-speed computers. In the wake of the Soviet invasion of Afghanistan in December 1979, Jimmy Carter added "non-lethal" military equipment such as transport aircraft, helicopters, communications hardware, and over-the-horizon radar systems to the list of items for sale. Seeking to strike a balance between countering Soviet power and upholding the continuing US commitment to Taiwan's security, four years later Ronald Reagan took a significant further step, approving the sale of weapons deemed "defensive" in nature, including torpedoes and both anti-tank and anti-aircraft missiles.[2]

Chinese planners ultimately proved less interested in buying military hardware than in gaining access to Western technology of all kinds. Within certain limits, the Americans were happy to oblige. Soon after Reagan's election in 1980, US officials indicated their willingness to relax controls on high-tech exports to China and to start treating it, as one put it, "as a friendly less-developed country and no longer as a member of the international Communist conspiracy."[3] In 1983, the Reagan administration announced that, for purposes of granting export licenses, the US government would henceforth treat China as "a friendly, non-aligned country." Among the commodities now deemed suitable for export were computers, integrated circuits, precision measuring devices, and semiconductor manufacturing equipment.[4] At the same time as it relaxed its own controls, Washington worked with its allies to synchronize national policies and ease collective export restrictions.[5]

According to one former State Department official, the "driving force" behind this loosening of controls was "overwhelmingly strategic, it had nothing to do with commercial factors."[6] As far as the US government was concerned, the object of the exercise was to strengthen China rather than to promote the fortunes of American companies. Still, the shift in policy was undeniably good for business. By the end of the 1980s, US high-tech exports to China (including both dual-use and purely commercial items) had increased in value by a factor of thirty.[7]

Technology transfer took other forms as well. Even before the resumption of formal diplomatic relations in 1979, the Carter administration agreed to permit several hundred Chinese students and scholars to attend universities and participate in research in the United States. These opportunities proved even more attractive than had been anticipated, and the number of visas granted for educational purposes more than tripled over the course of the 1980s.[8] During this period, a total of around 80,000 Chinese citizens came to study in the United States, the vast majority of them in science and engineering fields. In 1989, roughly 43,000 were still enrolled and another 11,000 had become permanent residents. The rest had returned to China to teach others, conduct their own research, and help rebuild a scientific establishment ravaged by years of political turmoil.[9]

American policy-makers took other steps to assist China in strengthening its economy and thus the foundations of its long-term national power. In 1972, the Nixon administration lifted a twenty-three-year embargo on all commerce with the PRC, clearing the way for an increase in bilateral trade from close to zero to over a billion dollars by the end of the decade.[10] In 1979, the Carter administration announced its intention to grant China most favored-nation (MFN) status, lowering tariffs on its exports to the same level as those imposed on any other trading partner.[11] Coinciding with the launch of Deng Xiaoping's program of economic "reform and opening up" in the same year, this enabled a further increase in two-way trade, which grew by an order of magnitude over the course of the 1980s.[12]

The Carter administration also helped China obtain much-needed capital by supporting its entry into the World Bank and the International Monetary Fund. In keeping with his preference for private enterprise, Ronald Reagan subsequently expanded the use of domestic institutions like the Export–Import Bank and the Overseas Private Investment Corporation to help finance the export of American products to China and to encourage investment there by US firms. As with its relaxation of restraints on technology transfer, these moves reflected the judgment contained in a 1984 National Security Decision Directive that it was in the nation's strategic interest to "lend support to China's ambitious modernization effort." In the words of a 1981 State Department memorandum: "[O]nly the interests of our adversaries would be served by a weak China that failed to modernize."[13] With significant assistance from the United States, China had begun its transformation from a poor and backward nation into a global manufacturing and export powerhouse.

For as long as the Cold War was underway, American policy-makers generally downplayed or ignored the repressive, illiberal character of the CCP regime. In a widely read 1967 article in which he made the case

9

for easing Maoist China out of its "angry isolation" and coaxing it back inside "the family of nations," Richard Nixon argued that "the world cannot be safe until China changes." It followed that, "to the extent that we can influence events," the aim of US policy "should be to induce change."[14] At least so far as its domestic institutions were concerned, however, once in office, Nixon explicitly rejected the idea of trying to change China. As he told Mao during their first meeting: "[W]hat is important is not a nation's internal philosophy. What is important is its policy towards the rest of the world and towards us."[15]

Despite significant differences in outlook, for all practical purposes, Nixon's successors followed a similar path. Jimmy Carter wanted to make the defense of universal human rights into the centerpiece of his foreign policy, and Ronald Reagan sought to rally the free world against the evils of Communism, but both ultimately bowed to the necessity of staying close to China in order to offset the greater threat posed by the Soviet Union.

As Deng's economic reforms began to unfold, it also became easier to believe that political liberalization could not be far behind. Following a 1984 visit during which the authorities censored portions of his speeches in which he discussed the virtues of faith and freedom, Reagan nevertheless concluded that China's embrace of markets meant that it was already merely "a so-called Communist country."[16] The president's optimism about China's direction was mirrored in shifting public attitudes. Even after the initial exchanges of the 1970s, a majority of Americans remained highly skeptical of a country that was just beginning to emerge from the ideological frenzy of the Cultural Revolution. With the normalization of relations, and the launch of market-oriented reforms, perceptions of China changed almost overnight. In 1978, 67% of those questioned in one poll regarded the country unfavorably, with only 21% expressing a favorable view. One year later, the ratio was almost completely reversed. By the spring of 1989, the figures were 72% positive and only 13% negative.[17]

If China was seen to be evolving in generally favorable directions, it was also still perceived to be poor and weak, and likely to remain so for some time. The prospect that it might someday pose a threat to the United States or its regional allies thus seemed doubly implausible. Nevertheless, from the start, there were occasional expressions of concern about what the future might hold. In a 1975 conversation with President Gerald Ford, Henry Kissinger mused of China that "in 20 years, if they keep developing the way they have, they could be a pretty scary outfit."[18] Asked in 1983 to assess the impact of proposed arms sales and technology transfers, the Joint Chiefs of Staff concluded somewhat more precisely that, while the risks were real, they were also still relatively distant. Intelligence experts expected that the People's Liberation Army (PLA) would take nearly a decade to fully absorb whatever new technologies it might acquire, meaning that the modernization of its ground forces would not "appreciably affect US and allied security interests through the 1990s," while improvements in its naval capabilities were "unlikely to have any significant impact on US forces in the region during the remainder of this century."[19]

Attempts to take a broader, longer-range view were few and far between, but there were some. In 1987, the Pentagon's Office of Net Assessment sponsored a study that aimed to project the worldwide distribution of economic capabilities twenty years into the future. The findings were striking: based on the size of its population and plausible improvements in productivity due to technological upgrading and market reforms, by 2010 China might have the world's second largest economy. If it began to invest even a small fraction of its newfound wealth in its armed forces, in two decades China could also "become a superpower, in military terms." Whether at that point Beijing's strategic interests would continue to align with those of the United States was an obvious but unanswerable question. Having highlighted the PRC's potential to transform the global balance of power, the report concluded prudently that "large uncertainties attach to China's future."[20]

Engagement 2.0

In the span of little more than two and a half years, a series of dramatic developments weakened and then swept away the foundations on which the policy of engagement had come to rest. The killing of over one thousand unarmed students in Beijing's central Tiananmen Square in June 1989 served as a brutal reminder of the CCP regime's continued, repressive character and cast doubt on facile assumptions about the inevitability of liberalizing reforms. Five months later, the Berlin Wall was reduced to rubble by another group of peaceful protestors, unleashing a wave of pent-up demand for change that would overturn Communist regimes across Eastern Europe, culminating in December 1991 with the collapse and disintegration of the Soviet Union. The primary justification for two decades of engagement – the claim that the United States needed China to help it balance Soviet power and win the Cold War – had suddenly been rendered obsolete.

It would not take long for an entirely new set of rationales to take shape, sustaining most, though not all, aspects of previous US policy and eventually gaining widespread, if not universal, acceptance. These rationales and the expectations derived from them will be discussed in detail in Chapter 2. In order to understand the logic that underpinned them, and to appreciate their emotional appeal and enduring persuasive power, it is necessary first to describe the unique set of historical circumstances, the distinctive confluence of events, ideas, and material interests, out of which they emerged.

Ideology: the American vision of a liberal international order

With the demise of the Soviet Union, the United States was suddenly the sole remaining superpower, with economic resources, military capabilities, and political prestige far exceeding those of any potential rival. What this meant to American policy-makers was not only that their own country was more secure, but also that for the third time in a century they had an opportunity and, as they saw it, an obligation to reshape the world in ways that would make it more peaceful and prosperous for generations to come. Their thinking about how to do this, and their vision of the ideal international system that they hoped to build, reflected principles deeply rooted in the nation's founding.

In 1919, and again in 1945, the United States had taken the lead in trying to construct what would today be described as a "liberal international order": a system made up of democratic states, bound together by trade, multilateral institutions, agreed norms of behavior, and a shared commitment to the protection of certain universal human rights. This vision was essentially an outward projection of the principles on which the American domestic political regime had been built: a belief in the primacy of individual liberty, and a set of rights and institutions meant to protect it, including representative government, private property, and the rule of law. The American design for an ideal international order also reflected the claims of the eighteenth-century philosophers of liberalism: that self-governing republics were less warlike than monarchies; that nations whose economies were organized around free markets and private property were more inclined to trade freely with one another than those pursuing the mercantilist schemes of powerful princes; and that trade itself was conducive to peace.

At the end of World War I, with Europe in ruins, Woodrow Wilson had tried to use the unmatched material strength and, in his view, the superior moral authority of the United States to reshape the entire international system along liberal lines. Wilson's plan called for overturning the autocratic regimes that he blamed for starting the war and replacing them with democracies, dividing Europe's multi-ethnic empires into self-governing nation states, breaking up imperial trading blocs, and instituting a world order based on free trade, freedom of navigation, open diplomacy, and mutual arms reductions. The entire system would be capped by a new kind of international institution, a League of Nations whose members would pledge to defend one another against aggression, regardless of the source.[21]

This scheme, sweeping in its scope and ambition, was quickly rejected as impractical and even dangerous, both by America's wartime allies and by Wilson's domestic political opponents. Nevertheless, as Henry Kissinger has pointed out, with the United States finally coming into its own as a world power, Wilson had managed to define a distinctive, liberal vision for its foreign policy objectives that "grasped the mainsprings of American motivation" and, in particular, the belief that the nation's "exceptional character resides in the practice and propagation of freedom."[22] Indeed, Kissinger writes: "Wilson's principles were so pervasive, so deeply related to the American perception of itself, that when two decades later the issue of world order came up again . . . America turned once more to . . . Wilsonian principles."[23]

At the start of World War II, President Franklin Roosevelt self-consciously echoed Wilson's rhetoric, declaring his intention to build a post-war world on the principles of self-determination, free trade, freedom of the seas, and a commitment to "life, liberty, independence . . . religious freedom," and "the preservation of human rights and justice."[24] Like

Wilson, Roosevelt also believed that, once the war was over, some kind of multilateral, collective security mechanism would be essential to keeping the peace. Hoping to strengthen the original design of Wilson's League, the president and his planners proposed that a new United Nations grant special authority to Britain, China, the United States, and the Soviet Union, the "Four Policemen" that had worked together to defeat fascism and which were supposedly united, as FDR said of Stalin at one point, in their desire "for a world of democracy and peace."[25] This claim, however, required an obfuscation of the true character of the Soviet regime that became impossible to sustain as the war drew to a close.

With the breakdown of the wartime alliance and the onset of the Cold War, the United States was forced again to abandon the dream of a truly global liberal order. This time, however, instead of withdrawing in disappointment and disgust, the nation set out to build what a 1950 strategic planning document described as a "successfully functioning political and economic system in the free world."[26] Although it would take some time fully to take shape, what emerged from this effort was a *partial* rather than an all-encompassing liberal international order; a sub-system of democratic states, organized and operating on liberal principles, that would eventually come to include the advanced democracies of Western Europe, Northeast Asia, and the Western Hemisphere. These nations were joined together by expanding flows of goods, capital, people, and information, by military alliances and other multilateral mechanisms for consultation and policy coordination, and by shared political values. The resulting loose coalition (often referred to with some lack of geographic precision as "the West") proved to be enormously successful in generating both wealth and power. Over a forty-year period of intense rivalry, its members were able to out-produce, out-innovate, and ultimately outlast their Communist competitors.

As the Cold War wound down, US officials sought once again to outline their preferred vision for the world. It should come as no surprise that they did so by describing a liberal international order using language and concepts virtually identical to those deployed by their forebears. "What is it we want to see?" asked newly elected President George H.W. Bush in the spring of 1989. "It is a growing community of democracies anchoring international peace and stability, and a dynamic free-market system generating prosperity and progress on a global scale."[27]

Despite the president's well-known aversion to "the vision thing," as he rallied the nation to liberate Kuwait from Saddam Hussein, Bush indulged in flights of Wilsonian rhetoric of a sort that had been largely absent from public discourse for most of the preceding half-century. What was at stake, he told a joint session of Congress in January 1991, was nothing less than "a new world order, where diverse nations are drawn together in common cause to achieve the universal aspirations of mankind – peace and security, freedom, and the rule of law." This supposed convergence of values, signified by the Soviet Union's willingness to vote in favor of intervention in the UN Security Council, meant that it might finally be possible to implement a working system of collective security: "[F]or the first time since World War II, the international community is united," Bush declared. "The leadership of the United Nations, once only a hoped-for ideal, is now confirming its founders' vision."[28] By the spring of 1992, a few months after the final collapse of the Soviet Union, even a hard-nosed pragmatist like Secretary of State James Baker could describe the administration's goals as being to create "a democratic peace" that would cover "not just 'half a world' but 'the whole world' instead."[29] A new, globe-spanning system would be built "on the twin pillars of political and economic freedom."[30]

Reflecting its deep, ideological roots, this image of a desired future was shared by Republicans and Democrats alike. Having replaced him as president, Bill Clinton essentially picked up where Bush had left off, recasting the same basic principles and assumptions into a new, formal grand strategic doctrine. In a 1993 speech entitled "From Containment to Enlargement," Clinton's first National Security Advisor, Anthony Lake, noted that the demise of the Soviet Union provided America with "unparalleled opportunities to lead." To the greatest extent possible, Lake argued, the United States should use its position of overwhelming strength to "promote democracy and market economics in the world." Thus, he concluded, " the successor to a doctrine of containment must be a strategy of enlargement – enlargement of the world's free community of market democracies."[31]

The case for enlargement was pragmatic as well as idealistic, but even the pragmatic arguments were based on long-standing liberal beliefs. "The addition of new democracies makes us more secure," Lake declared, "because democracies tend not to wage war on each other. . . . They are more trustworthy in diplomacy and do a better job of respecting the human rights of their people." As a result, "to the extent democracy and market economics hold sway in other nations, our own nation will be more secure, prosperous and influential, while the broader world will be more humane and peaceful."[32]

Material trends: democratization, marketization, globalization

Lake's bumper-sticker summary of America's new grand strategy never gained the same currency as George Kennan's notion of "containment," but it was apt nonetheless. As the post-Cold War era began, the United States set its sights on expanding the scope of what had been a partial, geographically constrained liberal order to include the entire world and, in particular, the swath of Eurasia that extended from Eastern Europe, across the newly independent republics of the former Soviet Union, to China. Here the aim was to "help democracy and market economics take root" where they had not already done so, and to "foster and consolidate" new liberal regimes when they did begin to blossom.[33]

In dealing with the nations that had arisen out of the wreckage of the Soviet empire in Eastern Europe, the United States and its allies used the promise of incorporation into Western political institutions and the global economy as a tool for encouraging liberal reforms. The states that eventually earned full membership in this way were, at the outset, weak, poor, and, for the most part, eager to change. More challenging and, in the long run, more important were Russia and, above all, China. Lacking sufficient leverage to compel their transformation, the democracies effectively inverted the strategy they had used to such good effect along the periphery of the former Soviet empire. Rather than hold out the possibility of inclusion as an inducement to liberalization, the United States and its allies worked instead to bring Russia and China as fully as possible into the existing order and, in particular, into the open global economy, in the hopes that doing so would help speed their domestic economic, political, and social transformation. Instead of change followed by inclusion, the formula was reversed to inclusion followed by change.

US and other Western policy-makers were highly confident that this approach would succeed. To a certain extent, this attitude reflected an "end of history" triumphalism, a belief that liberal democratic capitalism had finally won a two-hundred-year evolutionary struggle against other forms of political and economic organization and that its superiority over autocracy, fascism, and now Communism had been proven beyond a shadow of a doubt.[34] It seemed clear that, as George H.W. Bush put it, the movement towards markets and democracy had become "inexorable."[35]

This belief was not merely the product of wishful thinking, of course; there was ample evidence that seemed to back it up. The dramatic scenes in Berlin, the collapse of the Soviet Union, and the evident desire of people in many parts of its former empire to throw off their shackles and join the West all lent credence to the notion that liberalism had triumphed. Further to the east, China had already begun its march towards market-oriented economics. While Tiananmen represented a terrible setback, Americans, in particular, could take comfort from the fact that student demonstrators had quoted Thomas Jefferson, Tom Paine, and Woodrow Wilson and rallied around a papier-mâché "Goddess of Democracy" that resembled their own Statue of Liberty. It was easy for Western observers to believe that those reactionaries in the Communist Party leadership who still opposed liberalization were engaged in a futile effort to hold back the tide of history.

Philosophical speculation about world-historical tendencies aside, recent events appeared to be the product of some more concrete and observable long-term trends. By the early 1990s, the world was already almost two decades into what political scientist Samuel Huntington described in a widely read book as a "third wave" of democratization. As had happened between the early nineteenth and early twentieth centuries, and again from the mid-1940s to the early 1960s, since the mid-1970s the number of democratic states had increased sharply, growing from thirty in 1973 to fifty-nine in 1990.[36] Thus, even before the Soviet implosion, 45% of the countries in the world were ruled by democratic governments, the highest proportion since the 1920s. And the trend was clearly global: starting in Western Europe with Portugal and Spain in 1974–5, the democratic wave had traveled west to Central and Latin America, and south to parts of Africa, before propagating east, across Eurasia. Huntington was at pains to point out both that the causes of this phenomenon were varied and complex, and that past waves had been followed by periods of reaction (or "reverse waves").[37] Still, it is not difficult to understand why more casual observers, to say nothing of busy policy-makers, might have been drawn to conclude that the process unfolding before them was linear and irreversible.

Democratization was accompanied by a parallel trend towards what can best be described as "marketization": an increased emphasis on market mechanisms in national economic policy, as opposed to more statist, interventionist approaches to fostering growth and development. This tendency, too, had become evident well before the end of the Cold War. The so-called "market revolution" or "Reagan–Thatcher revolution" that began in Britain and the United States also reverberated across the global South.[38] During the 1980s, often under pressure from international financial institutions to which they owed large sums, many developing countries proceeded to abandon subsidies, state-owned enterprises, and high tariffs in favor of deregulated banks, reduced government spending, privatization of industry, and liberalized trade.[39] This package of policies embodied what came to be referred to as the "Washington Consensus": the agreed wisdom of international lending institutions, backed by the US and other Western governments, on the best way of promoting economic development.[40]

The evident success of the turn towards markets produced what historian Hal Brands has described as "a powerful sense of triumph" in Washington. Brands quotes a 1991 speech by Secretary of the Treasury Nicholas Brady that illustrates the point. Events in the developing world had proven that "freedom works," Brady declared. "Free markets work. These simple principles have moved nations; they have altered the course of history."[41] The collapse of Communism across the former Soviet empire and its evident retreat in China strengthened this sense of vindication while at the same time expanding the geographic and political space in which market principles could be applied to include virtually the entire planet.

The increasing integration of market-oriented national economies was the third and last trend that helped convince US decision-makers that the time to complete construction of a liberal international order was finally at hand. This phenomenon was the result of the convergence of mutually reinforcing developments in policy and technology that seemed by the 1990s to have acquired overwhelming momentum. As with marketization, these tendencies became visible first in the advanced industrial West before spreading to the South and finally to the East.

During the opening decades of the Cold War, driven by what political scientist Robert Gilpin has described as "the exigencies of survival" and with Washington leading the way, the members of the Western alliance created an integrated economic system based on "agreed-upon rules and close cooperation."[42] Working through the General Agreement on Tariffs and Trade (the precursor to the WTO), from the late 1940s through the late 1970s the United States and its democratic allies in Europe and East Asia negotiated successive rounds of multilateral tariff reduction agreements. At the same time, a series of post-war technological advances, most notably the invention of containerized shipping, were increasing the speed and cutting the cost of long-distance transportation. These simultaneous changes in technology and policy enabled a dramatic increase in trade among the advanced industrial democracies.[43] Falling communications costs (due to the expanding capacity of transoceanic cables and the development of communications satellites) and a relaxation of controls on capital markets made possible an accompanying expansion in international financial flows.[44] As the Cold War entered its final decade, the advanced economies were being knit together more closely than at any time in nearly a century, causing Harvard Business School professor Theodore Levitt to coin a new term in 1983 when he declared that "the globalization of markets is at hand."[45]

Starting in the mid-1980s, with the spread of the "Washington Consensus," portions of the developing world began to be swept up in the globalizing trend as dozens of countries in Africa, Latin America, and parts of Asia "moved aggressively to export, open their markets, privatize, and deregulate."[46] With the notable, but still partial, exception of China, the nations of the Communist bloc did not begin to follow suit until the collapse of the Soviet empire. This was a "world-historical watershed" after which "the rest of the Second World followed the Third" in attempting to implement market-oriented economic reforms.[47] Although the process was only starting to get underway, by the early 1990s the movement towards ever-closer economic integration appeared to have gained overwhelming momentum. For the first time since the eve of World War I, virtually the entire planet was being drawn together into a single global market.[48]

The second era of globalization was different from the first in a number of respects, one of which is particularly relevant to understanding the subsequent evolution of Western policy towards China. Rapid advances in microelectronics, computers, and fiber-optic cables that began in the 1970s reached critical mass in the late 1980s and early 1990s, triggering the so-called "ICT (information and communication technology) revolution." Among many other effects, the resulting, explosive growth in the volume and speed of data transmission, and the accompanying collapse in costs, created the conditions for an unprecedented shift in the structure of the global economy.

According to economist Richard Baldwin, the ICT revolution "meant that manufacturing stages that previously had to be done within walking distance could be dispersed internationally without colossal losses in efficiency or timeliness."[49] As Baldwin notes, "the international organization of production changed sometime between the mid-1980s and the mid-1990s," with the year 1990 serving as "a convenient bookmark."[50] Complex production processes could now be coordinated even after they had been broken into pieces and dispersed around the globe to places where the work could be done most cheaply. Large Western companies that mastered these techniques, relocating some of their activities to low-wage countries, were in a position to benefit greatly from the construction of "global value chains."[51] Provided that they had the necessary resources and adopted appropriate policies, so too were countries in the developing world. With its vast population and increasing openness to foreign investment, no country was better situated to benefit from these changes than China.

Interests and influence

As they entered the last decade of the twentieth century, American policy-makers believed that powerful historical tides were bearing their country, and the world, towards the safe harbor that their predecessors had long envisioned, but had never been able to reach. A truly global liberal democratic order was finally in sight. Some navigational adjustments would be required at times, to be sure, but the direction seemed set and the destination assured. A final factor that added ballast to this enterprise, helping to keep the ship of state on course, was the growing weight of commercial interests.

Unlike other participants in the network of multilateral trade agreements signed during the Cold War, China was not yet a full member in good standing of the US-led global trading system. The MFN status that it had been granted in 1980 meant that its exports were subject to the same low tariffs as those from most other US trading partners. But, in contrast to these countries, under the terms of the 1974 Jackson–Vanik amendment, China's privileges, like those of the Soviet Union and other Communist bloc countries, were subject to annual review and could be revoked if a president judged that the CCP regime was abusing the rights of its citizens.

Routine renewal of MFN status during the 1980s enabled increasing trade flows between the two countries.[52] Slowly at first, American companies also began to invest directly in China, often establishing joint ventures in which they provided the money and know-how, while a local partner supplied cheap labor and helped navigate a dense thicket of rules and regulations.[53] Despite the growing appeal of such arrangements, the enthusiasm of American business executives was constrained by their awareness of lingering political risk. If for some reason relations soured and Beijing lost its favored status, Chinese exports, including those made in American-owned factories, would suddenly face prohibitively high tariffs. Once-profitable investments could then become costly liabilities almost overnight.

The Tiananmen Square massacre and its aftermath brought these fears to the fore. But they also served to mobilize and solidify a powerful coalition of business groups that successfully fended off immediate threats to their interests and, in the process, helped to transform economic engagement into the central pillar of post-Cold War US China strategy. In response to the bloodshed in Beijing, the George H.W. Bush administration imposed limited sanctions and suspended the sale of arms and some sensitive dual-use technologies, but it resisted Congressional pressure either to revoke China's MFN status or to impose conditions for its renewal.[54] Having criticized his predecessor for being soft on "the butchers of Beijing," in May 1993 newly elected President Bill Clinton decided to take a different tack, renewing China's status but issuing an executive order demanding that it make "significant progress" on human rights if it wished to retain its trade privileges. One year later, however, despite Beijing's rejection of his demands, Clinton reversed course and restored China's status without condition or the threat of further review.

The most important cause of this consequential decision was the unprecedentedly intense and well-organized pressure brought to bear on Congress and the White House by substantial swaths of the American business community. Three aspects of this campaign deserve special note. First and perhaps most obvious is its sheer breadth and diversity. By one count, by the spring of 1994, "nearly 800 major companies and trade associations" were involved in what was described at the time as one of the "largest lobbying efforts ever" mounted by American business.[55] Among those taking part were corporate giants from across a range of sectors, including aerospace (Boeing, Hughes, Lockheed, and McDonnell Douglas), the automotive industry (Ford, Chrysler, and General Motors), energy (Exxon), electrical machinery (Westinghouse and General Electric), electronics (Motorola and Intel), and food processing (Coca-Cola, Pepsi, and McDonald's).[56] These firms were joined by major lobbying groups like the National Association of Manufacturers, as well as associations representing smaller industries and enterprises, including everything from wheat farmers and footwear retailers to the manufacturers of fertilizer. The views of the financial industry also received a sympathetic hearing inside the Clinton administration, thanks in part to the creation in 1993 of a new National Economic Council headed by former Goldman Sachs executive Robert Rubin.[57]

A second notable aspect of the effort to protect China's MFN status was its forward-looking, speculative quality. For many of those involved, support for delinking MFN status from human rights was driven less by the reality of present earnings than by the alluring promise of future profits. China was important and getting more so, but it was nowhere near the goldmine that many hoped it would someday become. Despite an upward trend during the 1980s, on the eve of Tiananmen the value of the United States' exports to China still accounted for just 1.6% of its total exports.[58] Meanwhile, by this point, the number of investment projects funded directly by US companies was only in the hundreds, accounting for just under 1% of total US foreign direct investment.[59]

While some of the industries and individual companies involved in pressuring the Clinton administration were already doing substantial business with (or in) China, many were not. The varying experiences of several large and influential corporations illustrate the point. According to a survey of references in the press and the Congressional record,

Boeing, AT&T, and General Motors were the three most vocal and visible players in the MFN campaign.[60] Of these, by the early 1990s, Boeing had already sold 200 commercial aircraft to China's still-antiquated airlines, amounting to fully one-sixth of its total overseas sales, with many more potential purchases in sight.[61] Meanwhile, despite having made the decision that China would be a critical "strategic manufacturing location," and a "key country" in its "globalization effort," AT&T's self-confessed "stumbles and missed opportunities" had left it with only a handful of small joint ventures dedicated to the manufacture of some pieces of network-switching equipment.[62] For its part, General Motors was eager to get into what promised to be both a booming market for car sales and a promising site for the manufacture of low-cost auto parts, but, with the exception of a recently signed joint venture agreement to build trucks, it had been absent from China since the Communists took power in 1949.[63]

While Tiananmen cast a temporary pall, subsequent events sharpened the appetites and restored the animal spirits of American business. After a period of disruption and retrenchment, Chinese leader Deng Xiaoping relaunched his program of "reform and opening up" with a highly publicized 1992 tour of the country's fast-developing southern provinces. A burst of renewed growth and an influx of foreign investment quickly followed. Between 1991 and 1993, China's economy expanded by 60%.[64] By 1993, its annual growth rate had risen to the astonishing figure of over 13%,[65] making it the fastest-growing economy on the planet and, according to a study released by the International Monetary Fund, the world's third largest, having surpassed Germany and closing in rapidly on Japan.[66] During this same period, foreign direct investment grew by 450%,[67] with Chinese companies signing over 83,000 contracts with foreign investors in 1993 alone.[68] Some of this money came from American corporations, but the even greater sums flowing in from Japan, Germany, and other sources meant that the US share of total foreign direct investment in China was starting to undergo a marked decline.[69] If the Clinton administration suspended China's MFN status, or even if it continued to threaten to do so, American companies feared that they would lose out on unprecedented opportunities, even if, in many cases, they had not yet begun fully to enjoy them. A letter to the president from a newly formed coalition of trade associations put the matter concisely:

"The persistent threat of MFN withdrawal does little more than create an unstable and excessively risky environment for US companies considering trade and investment in China, and leaves China's booming economy to our competitors."[70]

As James Mann explains, during the 1980s, Beijing had observed that former US government officials and politicians "often sought to make money from their China connections" once they left office.[71] The CCP was not shy about encouraging these "old friends" to weigh in on its behalf with their former colleagues, and the Chinese government also started to retain law and public relations firms in Washington for the same purpose.[72] What was truly distinctive about the fight over MFN status, however, was not Beijing's direct lobbying of US officials, but its broad, brazen, and systematic use of threats and inducements to shape the behavior of American companies, and through them the policies of the US government.

As early as 1990, a Chinese commercial counselor had written to American executives urging them to "display your impact" and "do some promotion work" with Congress, the White House, and the "news mediums [sic]." Exhortations were soon accompanied by action. Three years later, in the runup to yet another vote on MFN status renewal, Chinese trade delegations fanned out across the United States on a well-publicized, multi-city "shopping spree" that resulted in promises to purchase hundreds of millions of dollars' worth of cars, planes, and oil exploration equipment. At the same time, albeit more discreetly, US companies were being "regularly threatened with cancellation of orders or loss of future deals" if China lost its preferred trade status.[73]

By 1994, Beijing had honed its tactics to a fine edge, dispatching the "largest-ever trade and investment mission" and signing agreements worth a total of $11 billion with great fanfare, even as anonymous Chinese officials warned of unspecified "disastrous results" for American companies if MFN status was revoked.[74] At this point, writes David Lampton, "the essence of Beijing's strategy" was to convince the United States that it was "isolated internationally" and risked ceding "the 'big cake' of the Chinese market to its competitors" if it did not abandon attempts to link trade to human rights.[75] The tactics employed were hardly subtle. In one notable instance, at virtually the same moment as President Jiang Zemin was visiting Boeing's headquarters in Seattle and giving a speech in which he urged the removal of "negative factors and artificially imposed obstacles" to future business, a delegation of German executives was arriving in Beijing to ink an order for six aircraft from Airbus, Boeing's archrival.[76] The message was clear: if Boeing did not do enough to "display its impact" in Washington, China would take its business elsewhere.

According to a senior figure at one of China's leading think tanks, as the date for Clinton's decision approached, "[W]e began to realize that economic interests were deepening and started to think that the US wouldn't dare cancel MFN."[77] This judgment turned out to be correct, but the analyst's observation is incomplete and also rather coy. The mobilization of American business, and the political outcome that it helped to produce, were not simply the inevitable byproducts of an objective deepening in economic relations between the United States and China; they were the result also of a deliberate and highly orchestrated influence campaign by Beijing.

On May 26, 1994, President Clinton announced that he would not only renew China's MFN status but also, henceforth, "delink human rights" from the annual process of extension.[78] Despite appeals from human rights advocates, labor unions, and the representatives of older manufacturing industries already feeling the weight of import competition from China, Congress voted to uphold this decision. The impact was immediate. With the specter of suspension removed, at least for another year, and China's development back on track, trans-Pacific commerce was free to grow faster than ever before. Within weeks, companies like Caterpillar, Apple, Owens-Corning, and Kentucky Fried Chicken all announced plans for major new investments in China.[79]

Seizing an opportunity to win greater support from the business community, President Clinton had shrewdly reversed course. Henceforth, he argued, the United States should seek to change China not by threatening to constrict trade, but by expanding it. As trade and investment compounded during the 1990s, so too did the breadth and depth of enthusiasm for ever-expanding economic ties. Annual Congressional debates over MFN status renewal would continue until the end of the decade, but after 1994 the issue was never seriously in doubt. Finally in 2000, at the urging of the White House, and in response to another powerful lobbying campaign, Congress voted to establish "permanent normal trading relations" with Beijing, abandoning what had become an increasingly empty threat and clearing the way for China's entry into the WTO. The process of engagement had reached critical mass and was now self-sustaining, self-reinforcing, and, for all practical purposes, unstoppable.

2

Rationales and Expectations

By the time the Clinton administration "delinked" China's trading status from its human rights performance, the old, Cold War arguments for engagement had been discarded and a set of new ones had begun to emerge to take their place. The Soviet Union was gone, the world was unipolar, and the United States did not need help from China, or anyone else for that matter, to maintain a global power balance that tilted overwhelmingly in its favor. At the same time, Tiananmen made it impossible for American policy-makers, and the American people, to ignore the CCP regime's ugly, repressive face. Objections to closer relations with Beijing rooted in morality or ideology could no longer simply be brushed aside by asserting the primacy of *realpolitik*. What Henry Kissinger has described as the "ideological armistice" between the two sides had come to an abrupt end.[1]

Over the course of just over a decade, between Tiananmen in 1989 and China's accession to the WTO in 2001, US officials, political leaders, scholars, and policy analysts advanced three basic rationales for continuing and expanding connections of all kinds with China. First was the claim that, despite the end of the Cold War, the United States still needed Beijing's assistance in addressing an array of international challenges and in reinforcing a secure and stable global order. Second was the assertion that, in addition to being good for American business, deepening engagement would encourage an ineluctable, progressive process of economic reform that would help push China ever closer to a truly open, market-based system. Third, and in retrospect most controversial, was the argument that engagement in all its forms would ultimately serve to loosen the grip of the CCP, easing China down a path towards political liberalization.

Each of these rationales conveyed an expectation, or a prediction, about the future. Taken together, they pointed towards an obvious and appealing conclusion: if engagement was pursued with sufficient vigor and patience, China would eventually become a full member of a globe-spanning liberal international order. Engagement would have near-term benefits, to be sure, but it was also the means by which the ultimate aim of the grand strategy of enlargement was to be achieved.

The years examined in this chapter comprise a critical, formative period in the evolution of America's post-Cold War China strategy. By the start of the new century, the intellectual foundations for continued engagement were firmly in place and the broad trajectory of US policy had been set. It would take the better part of two decades for this approach, and the arguments that underpinned it, to begin to be called into question.

Geopolitics: from quasi-ally to "responsible stakeholder"

In itself, Tiananmen did nothing to alter the George H.W. Bush administration's assessment of the continued importance of a close strategic relationship with Beijing. While change was clearly afoot, in the summer of 1989 no one could foresee how quickly and decisively events in Eastern Europe and the Soviet Union were about to unfold. The Cold War might be thawing but, as far as Washington was concerned, it was still underway, and with it the great game of balance-of-power politics. At least for a time, the possibility of a "Sino-Soviet rapprochement" seemed still to be "in the air."[2] If the United States reacted too harshly, it might alienate and isolate Beijing, pushing it back into closer cooperation with the Soviet Union and lessening US leverage over Mikhail Gorbachev. Indulging in "an emotional response," Bush warned, "might throw China back into the hands of the Soviet Union."[3]

The administration's concerns on this score may have been misplaced, but they were clearly genuine. Justifying what critics would later charge was the unseemly haste with which he arranged a secret visit to Beijing soon after the killings in Tiananmen Square, National Security Advisor Brent Scowcroft wrote in his diary: "This has been a very delicate matter. . . . China is back on track a little with the Soviets, and they could indeed come back in much stronger if we move unilaterally and cut them off from the west." Resisting pressure for precipitous action would not be easy. As Bush put it privately in late June: "I'm sending signals to China that we want the relationship to stay intact, but it's hard when they're executing people."[4]

Even if China did not revert to an alignment with the Soviet Union, there was fear in some quarters that it might retreat into what Richard Nixon had described as a posture of "angry isolation," similar to the one it had adopted in the 1960s. Testifying before the Senate Foreign Relations Committee in 1990, Deputy Secretary of State Lawrence Eagleburger warned that if China was caught up in another of its "episodic convulsions," its energies might be directed outwards, threatening regional stability.[5] While there was no evidence at this point to suggest that Beijing still harbored Mao's revolutionary ambitions, Eagleburger nevertheless cautioned that an isolated China could "return to a 'spoiler role' in Asia, supporting subversive activities as it did in the 1950's and 1960's."[6]

James Mann notes that Eagleburger's testimony was a "landmark" that signaled a decisive shift in the mix of geopolitical rationales for continued engagement.[7] In addition to lingering risks from an earlier era, there were now an array of potential opportunities that the United States would forgo if it became estranged from Beijing. The dramatic events unfolding in Eastern Europe and the Soviet Union may have "altered the strategic scene," diminishing China's previous role as a counterweight to Soviet power and expansionism. Far from reducing its overall importance, however, Eagleburger insisted that these changes should instead transform the way in which US policy-makers viewed the PRC's international role. Beijing could play a critical and constructive part in resolving outstanding regional disputes, helping to preserve stability on the Korean peninsula, and "coping successfully with a number of transnational issues." Ever the tough-minded realists, Bush and his advisors were primarily concerned with the hard-power problem of restricting the spread of weapons of mass destruction (WMD), including missiles as well as chemical and nuclear weapons. But they also acknowledged the potential importance of other new types of challenges, such as dealing with the effects of environmental pollution.[8]

The case for diplomatic engagement and strategic cooperation with China underwent further subtle but significant evolution during Bill Clinton's two terms as president. Like his predecessor, Clinton placed particular emphasis on obtaining Beijing's assistance in controlling proliferation, both directly, by agreeing to restrict its own sale of missiles and control exports of materials that could be used in manufacturing chemical or nuclear weapons, and indirectly, by helping the United States to pressure North Korea to suspend its WMD programs.[9] In addition, over the course of the 1990s, the administration added more items to a rapidly lengthening catalogue of non-traditional security issues on which it hoped to work closely with China. By the end of the decade, this list included everything from "health challenges,"[10] "narcotics trafficking, alien smuggling, illegal immigration, counterfeiting and money laundering,"[11] to "humanitarian assistance . . . disaster relief . . . environmental protection and sustainable development,"[12] as well as "controlling the greenhouse gases that are causing climate change."[13]

Even as they made the case for closer cooperation on discrete issues, during his second term Clinton and his advisors began to place special emphasis on incorporating China into an assortment of international institutions and multilateral mechanisms. Included among these were the Comprehensive Test Ban Treaty, which Beijing signed in 1996 but did not ratify; the Chemical Weapons Convention, to which it acceded in 1997; the International Covenant on Civil and Political Rights, which it signed but did not ratify in 1998; the G-20, an organization established in 1999 to promote dialogue among the world's leading economies; and the WTO, which Beijing finally joined, with strong US support, in 2001. As the 1990s drew to a close, Clinton could point with satisfaction to the fact that, instead of standing "apart from and closed to the international community," China had joined a wide array of international organizations.[14]

Drawing China into a thickening web of global and regional institutions was both an end in itself and a means to a larger end. Assuming that it lived up to its obligations, Beijing's membership would help to resolve (or avoid) a range of potential economic, diplomatic, and security problems. Even more important in the long run, the very act of joining and participating in these institutions would, it was claimed, help to alter the calculations and behavior of Chinese policy-makers. As China benefited from its participation in an open international system, its leaders would recognize that they had an overwhelming interest in sustaining the prevailing order rather than seeking significantly to modify it, still less to overthrow it.

By the turn of the century, some serious and influential observers were prepared to argue that this transition was already far advanced.

China had long since shed its identity as the putative leader of world revolution, nor did it appear even to have serious, far-reaching revisionist aims. Instead it seemed well on the way to becoming a satisfied, status quo power.[15] In the minds of many analysts, the notion that the CCP regime might want more than merely to become a junior member in the existing, US-led order, or that its ambitions might expand as its power grew, seemed irrational, almost unthinkable. After all, as one leading scholar explained, the liberal system was "hard to overturn and easy to join" and provided ample benefits to all its members.[16] Especially with its entry into the WTO, there was arguably no country that had gained more from its membership in that system than China.

Engaging Beijing through institutions was expected to do more than merely change its calculations of material interest. As Under Secretary of State Peter Tarnoff explained in 1996, "encouraging China's integration into the world community" by incorporating it into multi-lateral institutions would have the effect of "fostering [its] adherence to internationally-recognized norms and standards of behavior."[17] Although Tarnoff did not say so in as many words, the norms and standards he had in mind were clearly those of the Western-built and US-led liberal international order: a commitment to free trade, respect for the rule of law, recognition of universal human rights, and so on. In time, it was assumed, Beijing would do more than simply adhere to these principles and practices in a superficial or opportunistic way. Rather, it would absorb and internalize them, becoming "socialized" into the rites and rituals of the existing system in much the same way as an individual might on join-ing a private club.[18] Institutional participation was thus an educational experience through which China would, in President Clinton's words, grow in "political maturity,"[19] eventually learning to become what his administration described in its last National Security Strategy statement as a "responsible member of the international community."[20]

In a widely read 2005 speech, Deputy Secretary of State Robert Zoellick took these arguments one step further. Having "joined the world" and taken its place as "a player at the table," China now had an obligation to move beyond mere membership and become "a *responsible stakeholder*" (emphasis in original) in the international system. Zoellick called on Beijing to help strengthen "the system that had enabled its success" by, among other things, doing more actually to resolve some of the many, much-discussed non-traditional security challenges, increasing transparency about its military programs, and following through on its new WTO commitments to cut subsidies and protect intellectual property.[21] Viewed from Beijing, Zoellick's formulation was a challenge and a stratagem for locking China more tightly into the existing order. As regards the American audience at which it was also directed, his speech was intended as both a display of toughness and a call for patience, ever-deeper engagement, and a willingness to accommodate Beijing's wishes, at least to some degree. After all, if the United States and the other Western nations wanted China to take more responsibility for helping to run the world, they would have to be willing to grant it a greater role in governing international institutions and a bigger say in shaping global norms. Assuming that China had, in fact, been properly socialized, and that its leaders were satisfied with the essential features of the existing order, there was no reason to expect that this would result in anything more than minor, marginal adjustments.

Economics: "markets over Mao"[22]

The economic rationale for engagement had two closely related parts. First and most obvious was the assertion that more trade with China was good, not only for particular firms and sectors, but also for the entire US economy, and for the nation as a whole. In addition to this fairly straightforward argument, policy-makers made the somewhat more complex case that deeper engagement would, in itself, serve to accelerate China's economic liberalization.

Claims about the potential importance of the Chinese market were deployed first by the George H.W. Bush administration as it defended its cautious post-Tiananmen policies from Congressional criticism. As White House spokesman Marlin Fitzwater pointed out in announcing the president's initial decision to continue to extend MFN status to China, by 1989 the country was already America's tenth largest trading partner.[23] Revoking its favored trade status would raise tariffs on imports from China as well as possibly provoking retaliatory restrictions on American products flowing in the other direction. The net effect, Fitzwater claimed, would be to "inflict severe costs on American business people, investors, and consumers." Jobs would be lost, businesses would fail, and a "multibillion-dollar surcharge" would be imposed on imported consumer goods.[24]

As China's reform and opening resumed, and growth took off, US officials preferred to frame the issue in more positive terms: expanding engagement would create vast opportunities for exporters and investors, even as it yielded lower prices for consumers. These basic claims were embellished and elaborated upon by President Clinton and his allies as they fought their own battles, first over MFN renewal, and then over granting China permanent normal trade relations (PNTR) status at the turn of the century in anticipation of its entry into the WTO. Thus, in announcing his decision to delink trade and human rights in 1994, Clinton noted that American exports to China were already worth more than $8 billion and supported at least 150,000 workers.[25] Making the president's case to Congress, Deputy Trade Representative Charlene Barshefsky predicted that increased exports to China would help to create "hundreds of thousands" more high-wage American jobs.[26]

For Clinton, whose informal slogan during the 1992 campaign had been "It's the economy, stupid," growth was the key to domestic political success, exports were the key to growth, and the China market was the key to expanding exports. It was a matter of straightforward logic and simple arithmetic. As the president explained in 1997, during his first five years in office trade had been responsible for more than one-third of US economic growth. Although they produced roughly 20% of the world's wealth, the American people made up only 4% of its population. If it wanted to continue "generating good jobs and higher incomes," the United States would have to find ways to sell more of what it produced to the other 96% of the people populating the planet. China, with the world's fastest-growing economy and a quarter of its population, was obviously the biggest potential source of growth in demand for US exports. Once fully integrated into the global economy, it would be a "magnet" for American goods and services.[27]

In 1999, the president could report that, as Barshefsky had foreseen, exports to China and Hong Kong supported nearly 400,000 American jobs.[28] Over the course of the decade, the value of US exports had more than tripled. Imports of goods from China, meanwhile, had grown by a factor of six, resulting in a trade deficit roughly eight times as large in 2000 as it had been in 1990 (see Figure 2.1).[29] Most professional

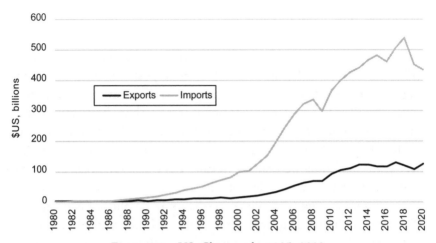

Figure 2.1 US–China trade, 1985–2020

Source: https://www.census.gov/foreign-trade/balance/c5700.html

economists did not regard this bilateral imbalance as a problem in itself, but it did reflect an underlying and increasingly obvious lack of reciprocity in the burgeoning trade relationship between the two countries. With its now routine annual renewals of MFN status, the United States had effectively opened its market to an influx of Chinese-made products. Meanwhile, for its part, Beijing continued to impose numerous restraints and restrictions on the ability of American and other foreign companies to sell, invest, and operate in China. Both sides might be benefiting, in short, but one seemed to be getting the better part of the deal. This perception presented a growing and potentially serious political problem.

The solution to the shortcomings of engagement, in Clinton's view, was yet more engagement. After over a decade of negotiations, by the end of the century China had pledged to the United States and other governments that it would take significant steps to open its domestic market in return for membership in the WTO. In order to complete the process and partake of these promised benefits, the United States now had to abandon whatever remaining leverage it might have from the threat of higher tariffs and grant China permanent status as a normal trading partner.

As presented to the American people, this was a deal without a downside, a "no-brainer," in the words of the lead US negotiator,[30] or, as the president put it, "the equivalent of a one-way street" in which the

United States gave up nothing in return for enormous potential gains.[31] Deploying another homey metaphor, Clinton told an Ohio business audience that China was making concessions in order to obtain "membership in the [WTO] club. What they give us are membership dues. That's the way you have to look at this."[32] "All we do is to agree to maintain the present access which China enjoys," Clinton explained, while China was required "to open its markets . . . to both our products and services in unprecedented new ways."[33] The proposed deal would "level the playing field,"[34] helping to reduce what the president acknowledged had become a "very large trade deficit"[35] by opening up China to "American products made on American soil, everything from corn to chemicals to computers."[36]

In a typical recitation of the good things to come, Treasury Secretary Lawrence Summers anticipated the lowering of tariff and non-tariff barriers on agricultural products and manufactured goods, as well as the elimination or reduction of barriers to American service providers in everything from banking and insurance to information technology and telecommunications.[37] According to Barshefsky, the Chinese government was also committed to do more to crack down on intellectual property theft, reduce "trade-distorting domestic subsidies," and "abolish requirements for technology transfer for US companies to export or invest in China."[38]

This last promise was especially important because it aimed to address what was already a growing concern about the full impact of globalization on American industry and American workers. As the president explained, China's accession to the WTO would make it easier for Washington to push back against requirements that American companies enter into mandatory joint ventures with Chinese counterparts, handing over vital intellectual property and helping to build up future competitors. Such measures were designed to "drain jobs and technology" away from the United States.[39] But with China in the WTO, "for the first time our companies will be able to sell and distribute products in China made by workers here in America without being forced to relocate manufacturing to China, sell through the Chinese government, or transfer valuable technology. . . . We'll be able to export products without exporting jobs."[40]

The second strand of the economic rationale for engagement extended beyond mere considerations of profit and loss. Deepening ties of trade and investment would improve the welfare of producers and consumers in China as well as the United States, but they would also have a beneficial impact on the long-term structure and performance of China's economy, pushing it ever closer to a fully functioning market system. This was expected to be so for a mix of political and economic reasons.

During the controversy over delinking MFN status in the early 1990s, and again during the debate over approving PNTR status at the end of the decade, advocates argued that action was necessary in order to strengthen the hand of those pushing for reform inside China. Thus, in the aftermath of Tiananmen, continuing to grant MFN status was justified in part as a way of bolstering support for a resumption of Deng Xiaoping's policies against the forces of reaction. As a Bush administration official explained: "The commercial opportunities created by MFN status give millions of Chinese workers and thousands of enterprises a stake in China's market-oriented reforms and opening to the West."[41] Similarly, one argument for supporting PNTR status was that it would reward and reinforce officials who had overcome stiff internal opposition to force through a series of measures necessary to qualify China for membership in the WTO. In addition to all of its other benefits, following through on America's side of the bargain would thus tilt the balance of political power in Beijing, strengthening "China's reforms and the reformers behind them."[42]

Encouraging China to engage more deeply in the global trading system would also have "important spillover effects," triggering a cascade of consequences that would lead inevitably to deeper reforms.[43] Over time, this would result less from a continuing exercise of political will by Party bureaucrats, and more from the irrefutable and presumably irresistible logic of the marketplace. As it reduced barriers to entry into its economy, China would strengthen the forces of market-based competition. As numerous scholars, business executives, and government officials explained during the PNTR debate, it was these forces that would drive the transformation of China's economy. First, and perhaps most important, enhanced competition from foreign companies would drive some inefficient state-owned enterprises (SOEs) out of business, thereby increasing the relative size and importance of the private sector. Whether public or private, firms exposed to international competition would have to downsize, reorganize, and adopt new technologies and management techniques if they wanted to survive.[44]

Despite their inefficiency, what President Clinton described as "state-owned dinosaurs" still gobbled up a disproportionate share of available investment. These enterprises were least likely to survive global competition and, as they became extinct, capital would be freed up to flow towards more dynamic private sector firms.[45] In addition to increasing the overall efficiency and productivity of the Chinese economy, a burgeoning private sector would produce growing pressure to define and protect property rights, including intellectual property rights, and to strengthen laws and procedures for adjudicating disputes.[46] Among other benefits, these changes would strengthen incentives for innovation by Chinese companies and ease the concerns of potential foreign investors.[47]

As the private sector flourished, and the state sector shrank, the reach and authority of the party-state would also dwindle. With the contraction of the SOEs, government would step back from controlling "vast areas of people's lives" and would no longer be, as President Clinton put it, "everyone's employer, landlord, shopkeeper, and nanny rolled into one."[48] As the state withered, the scope for individual choice, and the role of markets, would naturally tend to expand.

Like many other observers, China scholar Joseph Fewsmith anticipated that entry into the WTO would also lead to radical changes in the mechanisms of economic management. Massive and previously all-powerful planning bureaucracies would be eliminated or cut down to size. Government would move away from a direct role in setting prices and production targets, and towards the use of macro-economic instruments such as fiscal and monetary policy to regulate the overall level of national economic activity.[49] In place of state planning, wrote economist Nicholas Lardy, China would "rely more heavily on market forces to allocate resources."[50] In short, as the PRC became more fully integrated into the global trading system, both the structure and the functioning of its economy would come more closely to resemble those of the advanced industrial nations. While there might be some room for variation in the relationship between the public and private sectors, in the view of most Western economists (and many of their Western-trained Chinese counterparts), there was ultimately only one model, one market-driven path to prosperity.

Openness and competition would lead to change, which would create the need for yet more openness, which would produce even greater change – a virtuous spiral that would in due course have far-reaching consequences. According to National Security Advisor Sandy Berger, China's leaders understood that if they wanted to "make the next leap in development" as they opened themselves to the outside world, they would have to build "world-class industries and products that can compete in the global economy." But this would be possible only if China took steps to spur domestic innovation by lowering barriers to flows of data and ideas, as well as goods and capital. Entry into the WTO would thus, in itself, "obligate China to deepen its market reforms [and] increase the pace of change."[51]

Treasury Secretary Lawrence Summers described this self-sustaining process in similar terms: "As competition and integration proceed, China will need to become more market-based; more protective of personal and commercial freedoms, and more open to the flow of information and ideas." All of this would help boost productivity growth, increasing wages and creating more demand for imports of American products and services. It would also catalyze "broader changes" that would help "to promote core American interests and values."[52]

Politics: China's "short march" to democracy

Summers' concluding comment alludes to the third and final rationale for engagement: the claim, based on a family of interlocking assertions, that closer ties to the world's advanced industrial democracies would promote the eventual liberalization of China's own political system. These arguments were advanced with varying degrees of sophistication, emphasis, clarity, and candor by political leaders, middle-ranking government officials, business executives, and scholars in the years between Tiananmen and China's accession to the WTO.

Public discourse on this issue advanced through three phases. After initially making blunt claims about the links between trade and democracy, by the mid-1990s US officials had grown somewhat more guarded in their public pronouncements, generally preferring to stress the indirect role of deepening societal connections in strengthening civil society and creating the preconditions for political reform. While they took care to avoid explicit promises or specific predictions, by the end of the century the advocates of engagement had again become more open in expressing their optimism about the liberalizing effects of trade and investment.

In defending his decision not to levy harsher post-Tiananmen sanctions against Beijing, George H.W. Bush made the case that preserving economic and societal engagement would have a powerful and direct impact on the prospects for political liberalization. Bush was here expressing both the general "end of history" euphoria of the times, and his own sense, based on his experience as America's first unofficial ambassador to China during the 1970s, that he understood the country and where it was headed. As he told the Xinhua news agency shortly after his election: "[A]round the globe, I see increased respect for and interest in democratic values of openness, human dignity, pluralism, democracy, individual initiative, and entrepreneurship."[53] Moreover, contrary to skeptics who regarded China as "still the dictatorship it had always been," Bush "believed otherwise."[54] As he told a press conference the day after the mass killing of protestors in Tiananmen Square, "the forces of democracy" were now so powerful that they would be able to "overcome these unfortunate events." Popular pro-democracy sentiment had grown to the point where it would be impossible to "put the genie back in the bottle."[55]

The question was how to sustain what Bush described as an ongoing "process of democratization." The answer, in his view, was clearly not to sever the ties that had set that process in motion in the first place. It was trade, after all, that had triggered "this quest for more freedom." Once the "commercial incentive" has been unleashed, "the move to democracy becomes inexorable."[56] The connection between trade and freedom had more to do with the transmission of ideas than with the mere exchange of money and goods. As Bush told Yale University's graduating class of 1991:

[T]he most compelling reason to renew MFN and remain engaged in China is not economic, it's not strategic, but moral. It is right to export the ideas of freedom and democracy to China. It is right to encourage Chinese students to come to the United States and for talented American students to go to China. . . . If we pursue a policy that cultivates contacts with the Chinese people, promotes commerce to our benefit, we can help create a climate of

39

democratic change. No nation on Earth has discovered a way to import the world's goods and services while stopping foreign ideas at the border. Just as the democratic idea has transformed nations on every continent, so, too, change will inevitably come to China.[57]

Although Bush did not cite them, there were more academic, and more purely materialistic, arguments to be made in support of the idea that further economic engagement would promote rapid political liberalization. In his 1991 study of democracy's "third wave," Samuel Huntington had pointed out that, since the nineteenth century, there had always been a strong correlation between a nation's aggregate wealth and its form of government. Of the various factors contributing to this link, the most important appeared to be the fact that economic development generated an expanding and better-educated middle class. Possessed of the resources and the inclination to assert their rights and bring about change, it was these people who in almost every instance had taken the lead in pushing for liberalizing political reforms.[58]

With trade driving its growth, and growth creating a new middle class, there seemed every reason to expect that China would follow a similar path. Rooted in theory, these expectations nevertheless appeared to rest on a sound empirical footing. Based on the experiences of other countries, including those in East Asia like Taiwan and South Korea that had recently undergone similar transformations, RAND economist Henry Rowen calculated in 1996 that China would become a democracy when its national income reached a level of roughly $7,000 per person. Given its projected growth rate, Rowen anticipated that this transition would occur within two decades, most likely by 2015. China, he concluded, was on a "short march" to democracy.[59]

While few were prepared to endorse Rowen's prediction in all its bold specificity, belief in the direct, democratizing effects of growth was widespread during the 1990s. Justifying his support for extension of MFN status, Senator Bill Bradley explained in a 1994 op-ed that trade was "the real engine of democracy." The growth it enabled would lead to "the emergence of a class of prosperous Chinese" whose presence, in turn, would help to "fuel democratization."[60] Similarly, in 1997, one State Department official presented a Congressional committee with what was, in effect, a capsule summary of the prevailing conventional wisdom about the links between trade, growth, and democratization: "The recent history of Asia shows that over time, economic development leads to growth of an educated and aware middle class. . . . This in turn leads to democracy, and this is the path we want to encourage China to travel." Trade would help to accelerate this process, reinforcing "a positive evolution of China and its institutions."[61]

The interval between the conclusion of the 1994 debate over MFN status and the runup to the vote on PNTR status in 2000 marked a second phase in public discussion of the prospects for democratization. During this period, President Clinton and his advisors generally preferred to emphasize the more subtle, indirect effects on China's political evolution of enhanced societal (as opposed to purely economic) engagement. Beijing's refusal to give in to overt pressure in 1993–4 made clear that change would not come quickly or easily. Under the circumstances, loudly proclaiming that the true purpose of expanded trade was to help weaken the CCP's grip on power risked raising false hopes while at the same antagonizing the regime, potentially destabilizing a still-fragile relationship, and derailing the president's strategy of "comprehensive engagement."[62]

Even as he backed away from using the threat of trade sanctions as a lever, in 1994 Clinton announced what he described as a "new and vigorous American program to support those in China working to advance the cause of human rights and democracy." This effort would include increased broadcasts of news and information by Radio Free Asia, "increased support for nongovernmental organizations working for human rights," and a pledge to work with American business leaders to establish a "voluntary set of principles" to govern their activities in China. "We will have more contacts," the president declared. "The best path of advancing freedom in China is for the United States to intensify and broaden its engagement with that nation."[63]

Together with promoting trade, the aim of US policy, as explained by Assistant Secretary of State Wendy Sherman, was now to assist "those in China seeking to foster the growth of a civil society" and "to cultivate the synthesis of economic growth and civil society."[64] In using this term, administration officials were self-consciously invoking a concept that had gained prominence in Eastern Europe only a few years before. Here, during the 1970s and 1980s, various private associations and non-governmental organizations (NGOs) had emerged that enabled citizens to defend their interests, express their views, and apply pressure for change. Without posing a frontal challenge to ruling Communist regimes, these groups had nevertheless helped prepare the way for their eventual demise and for the largely peaceful transitions to democracy that followed.[65] The implication was obvious if also unspoken: with sufficient encouragement and support, China's still-nascent civil society could play a similar role in its political evolution.

The case for societal engagement and, more specifically, for assisting in the growth of civil society was also consistent with the evolving views of many academic China analysts. According to Andrew Nathan, one of the most respected figures in the field, in the aftermath of Tiananmen "many China specialists and democracy theorists – myself among them – expected the regime to fall to democratization's 'third wave.'"[66] Despite some initial disappointment, during the 1990s most scholars remained optimistic about the long-term prospects for change. This was due partly to the anticipated emergence of a reform-minded middle class, but also to a more general expectation about the cumulative effects of growth on society and politics. Huntington and other theorists noted that, as economies developed, they tended to become more "diverse, complex, and interrelated" and hence increasingly difficult for any centralized system to monitor and control. Growth also yielded up new sources of wealth and power in society independent of the state and capable of resisting its commands, thereby creating a "functional need to devolve decision making."[67] In sum, development created economies and societies whose growing complexity would eventually exceed the capacity of authoritarian regimes to control them.

Surveying the work of a number of his colleagues in 1998, Nathan concluded that they generally agreed about "the long-term inevitability of democracy," differing "more about timing than trajectory." Most believed that, thanks to its exceedingly rapid development, China was already facing near-term challenges and looming crises that its authoritarian political system would likely be unable to resolve. Ultimately, some form of democracy was therefore "the only effective way to respond to the demands and manage the problems of a complex, pluralistic society." Representative government would afford "all interests a chance to influence policy," generating "effective policy outcomes and political legitimacy" in the process.[68] How and exactly when this transformation would come about, and whether it could occur peacefully, remained uncertain.

By the end of the decade, some observers concluded that the CCP regime was clearly losing its "struggle to hold back a rising tide of self-organizing social and economic entities" and would have no choice but to liberalize and adapt.[69] While there were differences over what these developments signified, scholars pointed to the implementation of elections for some village officials and efforts to restructure China's legal system as indications that the Party recognized its predicament and, albeit slowly and reluctantly, was beginning to take steps towards meaningful reform.[70] Discreet support for such efforts, especially when provided by private US and other Western foundations and NGOs, seemed the best available means for moving the process along.

Testifying before Congress in 2001, Catharin Dalpino, a Deputy Assistant Secretary of State in the Bureau of Democracy, Human Rights, and Labor during the Clinton administration, spelled out the logic of this approach: "At this juncture in China's political development, it is more appropriate to support programs which build upon existing trends and which encourage political liberalization – defined as promoting open and responsive government, and greater voice for citizens in both public policy and civil affairs – but does [sic] not demand a specific level of democratization." As opposed to more direct pressure, "such an approach may, paradoxically, be the shorter and surer path towards encouraging eventual democratization in China."[71]

Bill Clinton was always at pains to insert caveats and avoid precise predictions when laying out the political rationale for engagement. "Unlike some," he told an audience in 1998, "I do not believe increased commercial dealings *alone* will inevitably lead to greater openness and freedom" (emphasis added).[72] After citing the good work of American NGOs in helping to set up private schools, "train journalists," educate lawyers, and "promote literacy for poor women," and noting "the emergence of political associations, consumer groups, tenant organizations, newspapers . . . and experiments in village democracy," the president nevertheless cautioned that "we don't assume for a moment that this kind of engagement *alone* can give rise to political reform in China" (emphasis added).[73] Still, while acknowledging that neither economic nor societal engagement in itself would be sufficient to force change, Clinton's carefully calibrated statements strongly suggested that the effects of the two combined could do exactly that.

During the third phase of the discussion of China's prospects for political reform, as the debate over PNTR approached its climax, the language of the president and his advisors grew increasingly hopeful, even exuberant. This was in part a matter of political salesmanship, a byproduct of the final push to win Congressional approval by claiming that China's entry into the WTO would open its society as well as its markets. But there is little cause to doubt that administration officials were sincere in their optimism. A new century was dawning, globalization and technology were transforming the world, American power and the power of the American example were at their peak, democracy was spreading. What reason was there for believing that China could continue to stand aloof from these world-historical trends?

The liberalizing effects of China's WTO accession on its economy were also expected to carry over into its politics. The retreat of the state and the expanded scope of the market meant that ordinary Chinese citizens would have greater control over where they lived, worked, and traveled. It seemed only reasonable to expect that the experience of these freedoms would also lead to demands for greater political liberty. By the same token, the legal reforms necessary to strengthen property rights and protect investors and entrepreneurs "against arbitrary government action" would also help to "reinforce the idea that individuals have rights" and "give added impetus to those trying to strengthen the Chinese legal system in a way that allows citizens to hold their government truly accountable."[74] Similarly, the requirement that the government publish its commercial laws and regulations so that they could be subject to international review would apply to China "the basic principle at the heart of the concept of the rule of law: that governments cannot behave arbitrarily at home or abroad." For all of these reasons, National Security Advisor Sandy Berger concluded with confidence that China's further integration into the global economy would help speed its transformation into "a more open society that upholds the rule of law."[75]

Some of the effects of increasing openness were expected to be even more direct. Among many other adjustments, joining the WTO would require Beijing to lift previous restrictions on access to its technology and telecommunications sectors. As Treasury Secretary Lawrence Summers observed, these changes were coming at precisely the moment when "the powerful revolution in information and communications technology is just beginning in China."[76] The country would soon be inundated with American-made computers, internet-switching equipment and software, and, even more important, an unstoppable flood of news and information from the outside world.

This was a subject on which Clinton was especially prone to wax lyrical. "In the new century, liberty will spread by cell phone and cable modem. . . . We know how much the Internet has changed America, and we are already an open society. Imagine how much it could change China." As for cracking down on the internet: "Good luck! That's sort of like trying to nail jello to the wall."[77] On a more serious note, the president made the classic liberal argument that "the more ideas and information spread, the more people will expect to think for themselves, express their opinions and participate. And the more that happens, the harder it will be for their government to stand in their way."[78] Given the explosive growth in access to cellphones, the internet, and satellite television, the implication was clear: positive political change was coming to China, and probably sooner rather than later.

Technological progress and political freedom were also believed to be linked in a final and somewhat less obvious way. In the new century, economic growth would be increasingly reliant on innovation, which would depend in turn on the free exchange of ideas and information. Political systems that enabled and encouraged such flows would be more dynamic, and, in the long run, wealthier and more powerful. On the other hand, as the outcome of the Cold War seemed to demonstrate, regimes that sought to stifle or control communications among their citizens, and between them and the outside world, would be at a decided disadvantage, destined to fall further and further behind. President Clinton summed this argument up succinctly: "Because wealth is generated by ideas today, China will be less likely to succeed if its people cannot exchange information freely."[79] "In the knowledge economy, economic innovation and political empowerment, whether anyone likes it or not, will inevitably go hand in hand." China would eventually have to face a choice between economic stagnation and political reform. Bringing it into the WTO would accelerate the process of change, compelling it "to confront that choice sooner" and making "the imperative for the right choice stronger."[80]

The thrust of all of these arguments was clear: engagement, societal and economic, would promote tendencies within China that would lead eventually to political liberalization. By the end of the century, belief in what James Mann has described as the "Soothing Scenario" had come to permeate the thinking of political elites on both sides of the partisan divide.[81] While there were differences over China policy, they were more a matter of semantics than substance. During the 2000 presidential campaign, George W. Bush criticized the Democrats for being too soft and unsteady in their handling of China and made a point of referring to the country as a "strategic competitor" of the United States. But he did not oppose the signature achievement of Clinton's China policy: his successful campaign to clear the way for its entry into the WTO. To the contrary, candidate Bush advocated expanded engagement in language virtually identical to his father's a decade earlier: "The case for trade is not just monetary but moral. Economic freedom creates habits of liberty. And habits of liberty create expectations of democracy. . . . Trade freely with China, and time is on our side."[82]

Conclusion

Soon after he became president, in May 2001, Bush gave a speech in which he said: "We trade with China because trade is good policy for our economy, because trade is good policy for democracy, and because trade is good policy for our national security."[83] Here in abbreviated form were all three of the rationales for engagement that had evolved over the course of the preceding decade. Beijing and Washington would work together to pursue their converging interests in addressing global challenges such as proliferation and climate change while China grew into its new role as an active supporter of the existing system of international rules and institutions. Expanding trade and investment would profit both sides, even as it accelerated China's ongoing transformation into a fully open, market-based economy. And, in the fullness of time, economic growth, the growing needs and demands of an increasingly complex society, and the cumulative effects of deepening societal engagement between China and the democratic world would help move it away from authoritarianism and towards political liberalization.

American officials would on occasion offer words of caution, reminding careful listeners that there were no guarantees and no precise timelines. But the overwhelming import of their message was unmistakable: engagement might make China richer and stronger, but it would also change the country in ways that rendered its newfound strength unthreatening to the security, prosperity, and values of the United States and its democratic allies.

3

Politics: "The Party Leads Everything"

In the wake of the Cold War, American and other Western leaders exaggerated the supposedly irresistible appeal of liberal democracy, overestimated the ease with which it would spread, and largely ignored the ways in which the openness of their own systems could be turned against them. Where they erred most grievously, however, was in their inability or unwillingness to grasp the essential features of the Chinese regime: the Communist Party's unwavering determination to maintain its unbreakable hold on power and its tireless creativity and brutal skill in doing so. As the next three chapters will demonstrate, these are the most important factors in explaining the course of China's domestic political and economic development over the last forty years, as well as the trajectory of its relations with the United States and the wider world.

From the start, the CCP leadership saw engagement as a trap set for them by the West, part of a clever strategy for transforming Chinese society, eroding the foundations of the Party's authority, and causing its eventual collapse and their own removal from power. In a sense, this was little more than a continuation of what Secretary of State John Foster Dulles had frankly described in 1953 as a policy of "peaceful evolution," a plan for liberating portions of the Communist bloc through the power of ideas and example rather than the force of arms.[1] This time around, however, instead of trying to seal their country off from the democratic, capitalist West, China's leaders were actively exposing it to outside influences.

Deng Xiaoping famously remarked that "opening the windows" in this way would inevitably let in "flies and insects" as well as fresh air.[2] Deng's apparent nonchalance belied his realization that some of the incoming "insects" carried a potentially deadly sting. Western ideas about freedom, democracy, and universal human rights exerted a powerful attractive force, but they were at odds with the tenets on which the CCP regime was based. Left to spread unchecked, they could bring about its rapid and untimely demise.

Further heightening the Chinese leadership's persistent fear of "bourgeois liberalization" was the fact that, following the Soviet collapse, they felt themselves to be isolated and encircled, ideologically as well as geopolitically. As they saw it, their country was the last bastion of socialism in an American-dominated international system that embodied, reinforced, and sought to promulgate liberal democratic values. Accepting Washington's seemingly warm welcome to join that system would expose Beijing to mounting pressure to abandon its principles and adopt the West's values as its own.

Keenly aware of their system's vulnerabilities, Deng Xiaoping and his successors developed and refined a counter-strategy designed to exploit the benefits of engagement with the West while neutralizing its potential perils. The purpose of this chapter is to analyze the Party's strategy for self-preservation and to trace its evolution over time. An obvious question hangs over this story: how is it, after nearly half a century of engagement, that China's political system has ended up disturbingly close to where it was when the process began? Why, instead of being transformed into a liberal democracy, has it once again become a one-man quasi-totalitarian dictatorship dependent on brutal repression and a militant ideology to sustain its rule?

Lenin's legacy

The PRC is a Leninist party-state, a system in which the party controls the state and the military, and the party, the state, and the military together control society. For its part, the party operates according to organizational principles, and deploys a set of distinctive practices first developed over one hundred years ago. Among the distinguishing features of Leninist systems, the most obvious is the degree to which they concentrate power, both within the party and in the party relative to society as a whole.

Although they supposedly operate according to the principle of "democratic centralism," in reality Leninist parties are top-down organizations in which "centralism" trumps "democracy" and decision-making power is consolidated at the very pinnacle of the system. Reflecting their origins in revolution, war, and civil war, Leninist parties place a premium on secrecy and military-style discipline; the most important decisions are made behind closed doors by a handful of leaders (and, not infrequently, by a single individual) and orders are to be followed with unfailing obedience by all party members.

The party claims the right to exercise complete and unchecked authority over every individual, organization, and group in society, including the armed forces, the police, and all the other organs of the state, the press, industry, educational institutions, and, if they are permitted to exist, churches and labor unions. Every form of art and cultural expression must also serve the party's purposes. Meaningful, organized political opposition is strictly forbidden and ruthlessly suppressed. If there are other political parties, they are puppets or "potted plants," whose sole purpose is to create the illusion of inclusiveness and representation.

Even as they seek to penetrate deeply into every corner of society, Leninist parties operate outside of, and stand above, the law; they use the legal system as another instrument of control but are not in any way constrained by it. Leninist regimes reserve for themselves the right to define crimes and to judge and punish as they see fit; their rule rests ultimately on "fear, intimidation, violence, and death."[3] Nor do they recognize the existence of any external standard of morality against which to judge their actions. In the words of Polish philosopher Leszek Kolakowski: "[E]verything which serves or injures the party's aims is morally good or bad respectively, and nothing else is morally good or bad."[4] All of this is justified by the claim that the party represents the forces of historical progress; it is in the "vanguard" of revolution and, once in power, it acts as a "dictatorship of the proletariat."

Leninist parties also purport to be in sole possession of a theoretical apparatus that gives them exclusive access to the truth; they proclaim "infallibility in doctrine" and parade themselves as "faultless scientists of human affairs."[5] Wielding this supposed monopoly on the truth is one among many ways in which Leninists use propaganda and what might today be called "information warfare" to achieve their objectives. The construction of convincing narratives is an indispensable tool for uniting and motivating supporters, dividing and demoralizing opponents, and justifying whatever policies the party may choose, or chose to abandon.

Skillfully blending persuasion and coercion, Leninist party-states are mighty engines for mobilizing and exercising power in all its forms.

Sociologist Franz Schurmann drew a distinction between "pure ideology," which he defined as "a set of ideas designed to give the individual a unified and conscious world view," and "practical ideology," which consists of "a set of ideas designed to give the individual rational instruments for action."[6] By this definition, Leninism is clearly a "practical ideology." In the words of historian Neil Harding, it is "an organizational code – a set of organizational precepts and mobilizing devices presided over by a centralized and disciplined political party."[7] These techniques and concepts were developed in a specific historical context and designed to fulfill a particular political purpose. Lenin's aim was to create a mechanism that could propel history along the path postulated by Marx: first by fomenting a proletarian revolution in a country where the working class was actually weak and underdeveloped, and then, having overthrown "bourgeois democracy," by guiding a process of economic modernization that would lead to socialism and finally to communism.

Lenin's practical innovations were intended to bring about the end goal of Marx's "pure ideology": the creation of heaven on earth; a classless, stateless society where private property had ceased to exist and in which each member gave "according to their ability" and received "according to their means." But there is no reason why similar methods could not be used to achieve very different aims, including the minimal goal of regime preservation. While it might continue to claim to be pursuing some lofty ambition, a Leninist party, once installed, could conceivably deploy the familiar techniques of control simply to crush opposition and keep itself in power. At some point, however, as its proclaimed goal and original justification for seizing power receded endlessly into the distance, it would become more difficult for the party to uphold its legitimacy and maintain its authority. The party-state would then need to work harder at shoring up the ideological foundations of its rule, either breathing new life into the old revolutionary dream or finding a fresh one to take its place.

The Party's evolving strategy for survival

The arc just described is essentially the one that the CCP has followed since the death of Chairman Mao in 1976. Over nearly half a century, it has been unwavering in its determination to retain an exclusive grip on domestic political power, but it has continually adjusted the mix of means – a changing blend of repression, cooptation, and ideological indoctrination – with which it has sought to achieve that end. The Party never feels secure but constantly monitors conditions, assesses its performance, and refines its methods, with the policies adopted by one leading group generally carried forward by the next. Although the dividing lines between them are not always clear-cut, it is possible to discern four phases in the CCP's ceaselessly evolving efforts to quell dissent, sustain popular support, and fend off challenges to its authority:

- When he took over from Mao, Deng Xiaoping inherited a society that was in shambles and a party ravaged by the internecine struggles of the Cultural Revolution. While he remained committed to "building socialism" and preserving the CCP's political monopoly, Deng sought to rely less on ideological appeals and coercion, counting instead on the benefits of economic growth to restore the Party's popularity in the eyes of the Chinese people.
- Deng and his successor, Jiang Zemin, held fast to this basic approach even after Tiananmen did further damage to the Party's reputation. While it continued to rely heavily on the prop of material progress, during the 1990s the party-state also expanded and refined its arsenal of repressive tools and began to increase the role played by popular nationalism in its program of ideological indoctrination.
- As the twentieth century drew to a close, Party leaders grew concerned that economic gains alone might no longer be sufficient to insure popular support and social stability. During the latter stages of Jiang's rule and the opening years of Hu Jintao's, the CCP began to experiment with new techniques of cooptation, including welcoming private entrepreneurs into its ranks, opening channels for public complaints, and attempting to address environmental pollution, corruption, and other quality-of-life issues. Anxious that the Party was losing its sense of purpose and its legitimacy, at Hu's direction CCP theorists also

52

engaged in an intensive but ultimately ineffectual effort to craft compelling new slogans and ideological formulations.

- As it became clear that enhanced cooptation had failed to reduce societal unrest, the regime resorted to yet more coercion and ratcheted up appeals to patriotic sentiment. The trend towards repression that began during the second half of Hu Jintao's reign has accelerated markedly under Xi Jinping. But Xi's most important and enduring innovation lies in the realm of ideology. With his elevation of the "China Dream" of achieving "the great rejuvenation of the Chinese nation," Xi has harnessed the Party's powerful Leninist machinery to an emotionally evocative nationalist goal. Under Xi, the Party has tightened its grip but, even more important, it has regained its *telos*, defining for itself a large and noble mission of indefinite duration that justifies its every action, reinforces its right to rule, and demands the enthusiastic support, and perhaps at some point the willing sacrifice, of every citizen.

Was democracy ever possible?

It is a tragic irony that the same events which caused Western policy-makers to focus expectantly on the prospects for political liberalization in China also effectively destroyed any chance that such changes would actually occur. During the decade that preceded the killings in Tiananmen Square, there was serious discussion about whether market-oriented economic reforms should be accompanied by far-reaching changes to the nation's political system. Support for this proposition was widespread among intellectuals and, while their appetite for experimentation was far more limited, political reform also had advocates within the Party, including for a time among some of those in its upper ranks.

After 1989, the scope for debate and the range of possible paths for China's development narrowed considerably. Many of the more prominent and vocal proponents of liberalizing reforms were silenced or driven into exile, while those insiders who had shown interest in even the milder variants of their ideas were removed from office and purged from the Party. Despite the three decades of engagement that followed, and notwithstanding persistent hopes in the West that there must be liberals or "soft-liners" waiting in the wings, no one with similar sympathies and seniority would emerge to take their place. While there would be periodic efforts to promote what has sometimes been described as "political reform," these always aimed to preserve and strengthen the Party's exclusive hold on power. Freely contested, multi-party elections, a free press, and strong legal protections for individual liberties were never on the cards. Looking back, it is difficult to escape the conclusion that any chance of China evolving gradually into a Western-style liberal democracy died at Tiananmen.

Not that the odds were very good to begin with. Deng Xiaoping was flexible in his interpretation of Marxism, and boldly experimental in pursuing what he labeled "socialism with Chinese characteristics." In this sense, his reputation as a reformer is well deserved. But his commitment to the core Leninist principles of party primacy and "democratic centralism" was unwavering. In order to revive and transform China's economy, Deng was eager to open up to the world and push ahead with market-oriented reforms, despite the profound skepticism of his more conservative senior colleagues. At the same time, he shared the hardliners' fears that growth, and an influx of foreign influences, would lead to "bourgeois liberalization," and, as historian Ezra Vogel explains, he was determined to counter "the broader appeal of Western ideals such as humanism, freedom, and democracy" that might be used "to challenge the ultimate authority of the Party."[8] To guard against these dangers, Deng made clear from the start that maintaining "the dictatorship of the proletariat" and preserving the "leadership of the Communist Party" were "cardinal principles," beyond challenge or debate.[9]

In order to overcome conservative resistance to his economic plans, Deng needed the support, and promoted the careers, of more liberally inclined officials like Hu Yaobang and Zhao Ziyang and, up to a certain point, he was willing to tolerate their exploration of possible adjustments in China's political arrangements to accompany the economic changes that were his primary focus.[10] But Deng's views on what was permissible in this regard were always narrow and strictly instrumental. The Cultural Revolution had seen the triumph of ideological fervor over expertise, damage to the apparatus of both the Party and the state, and a confusing commingling of administrative responsibilities between the two. Measures that reversed these trends, increasing efficiency and professionalism, reducing "bureaucratism," and clearing away obstacles to progress on economic reform, were acceptable and even desirable.

On the other hand, anything that even remotely threatened the Party's political monopoly was beyond the pale. After reviewing a series of proposed reforms in 1987, Deng reminded then-General Secretary Zhao Ziyang that "the main goal [of political reform] is to ensure the administrative branch can work efficiently; there cannot be too much interference. We cannot abandon our dictatorship. We must not accommodate the sentiments of democratization."[11] The reason for improving efficiency and strengthening governance, in turn, was to ensure the Party's grip on power. As Deng explained: "The purpose of reforming the system of the Party and state leadership is precisely to maintain and further strengthen Party leadership and discipline, not to weaken or relax them."[12]

Even more reform-minded officials like Hu and Zhao did not deviate from this "cardinal principle." Like Deng and the more conservative Party elders, their goal "was to revise and ultimately to strengthen the system, not to undermine it."[13] Within these shared constraints, Hu and later Zhao were willing to go further in contemplating the possible separation of party and state, the delegation of some decision-making powers to lower levels of the party-state system, greater efforts to inform the public about policy decisions, and some strengthening of the "socialist legal system."[14] They also protected and encouraged a wider circle of intellectuals who had even more radical ideas, in some cases going so far as to float proposals for limited government, representative democracy, multi-party elections, and a "fundamental reevaluation of the Leninist party-state."[15]

Whenever these dangerous ideas threatened to gain traction, however, and especially when they sparked public expressions of support or student demonstrations, Deng always sided with the hardliners. Between 1979 and 1989, he unleashed a series of five successive crackdowns and propaganda campaigns targeting "spiritual pollution" and "bourgeois liberalism."[16] When he concluded that his two top-ranking protégés and erstwhile allies had gone too far, Deng joined with the Party elders in purging them from power (Hu in 1987 and Zhao in 1989). And, when the moment of truth arrived and the Party faced its existential crisis, Deng did not hesitate to order the PLA into Tiananmen Square. Despite the image of him that had taken root in the West as an affable, elfin pragmatist, when it came to defending the Party's prerogatives, Deng was dogmatic, ruthless, and without remorse.

It is tempting to speculate about what might have happened if the crisis had been resolved peacefully or avoided altogether. Sometimes portrayed in retrospect as an ardent advocate of democracy, even Zhao Ziyang, the most reform-minded senior official, was still a good Leninist, at one point admonishing a group of liberal intellectuals: "[W]e can't carry out bourgeois liberalization, we can't have a two-party system, we can't have anarchy."[17] Had Zhao survived, the more modest measures he favored might have helped impose some constraints on the power of the Party, widening the scope for political debate, and perhaps moving China gradually down the path towards greater openness and deeper reform. As Minxin Pei explains, however, even in such a favorable scenario the combination of "the strong conservative forces within the CCP, Deng's own hostility to democracy . . . and the CCP's institutional interest in maintaining its power monopoly would have made a dramatic democratic breakthrough unlikely, if not impossible."[18] With the advocates of liberal political reforms silenced, their ideas discredited, and their opponents alarmed and empowered, the chances of such a breakthrough diminished from slim to all-but-none.

The lingering trauma of Tiananmen

The events that culminated in mass killings on the night of June 4, 1989, were a terrifying "near-death experience" for the CCP.[19] The ferocity of the Party's response reflects the magnitude of the perceived threat to its continued rule. Far from being an isolated incident, the protests in Beijing appeared to be part of a nationwide movement that was coordinated, broadly based, widely dispersed, and gaining in strength. In dozens of cities across the country, students and intellectuals demanding greater freedom were joined by workers and average citizens angry over petty corruption and the corrosive effects of inflation on their wages.

To make matters even worse, the Party leadership was convinced that, in keeping with its long-standing policies of infiltration and subversion, the United States was the hidden "black hand" behind the mounting unrest. As a June 1 report from the Ministry of State Security reminded the members of the Politburo, every US administration since the founding of the PRC had "pursued the same goal of peaceful evolution . . . aimed at over-throwing the Communist Party and sabotaging the socialist system. . . . The phraseology may vary, but the essence remains the same: to cultivate so-called democratic forces . . . and to stimulate and organize political opposition using catchwords like 'democracy,' 'liberty,' or 'human rights.'"[20] "The imperialists have never changed their original design," declared Vice Premier Yao Yilin. "They came to cooperate with us and express friendship not only for the purpose of making money, but also for the purpose of changing the nature of our country and remodeling our country to be a capitalist society."[21]

In justifying his decision to use force, Deng made plain that the CCP had faced a threat to its survival, the product of a diabolical confluence of internal and external forces. As he told a group of generals who had helped crush the protests, the demonstrators and their foreign friends had two immediate aims: "to overthrow the Communist Party . . . [and] to topple the socialist system." Their ultimate goal was nothing less than the establishment of "a bourgeois republic totally dependent on the West."[22]

Seriously shaken by Tiananmen, the Party's leaders were soon confronted by a seemingly ceaseless stream of troubling news from around the world. Throughout the fall of 1989, they watched in "shock and trepidation" as Communist party-state regimes across Eastern Europe fell to popular uprisings.[23] While most of these transitions were peaceful, in December Romanian dictator Nicolae Ceaușescu and his wife were hastily tried and executed before cameras by a military firing squad, an event that made an especially powerful impression on the CCP leadership.[24] The dissolution of the Soviet Communist Party and the subsequent fragmentation of the once-mighty Soviet Union at the end of 1991 further intensified the prevailing "siege mentality" in Beijing.[25] As David Shambaugh has shown, the Party would spend the next decade and more obsessively hashing over the developments and decisions that culminated in the Soviet collapse, hoping to extract insights that might help it to escape a similar fate.[26] The same events that appeared in the West as a harbinger of good things to come were seen in Beijing as a warning and an object lesson.

In the immediate aftermath of Tiananmen, the attitudes of CCP conservatives were characterized by "a deep sense of 'we told you so.'"[27]

As they had feared and warned, Deng's program of reform and opening up had destabilized China's economy and society, emboldened the proponents of political liberalization, and brought the Party, and the nation, to the brink of disaster. In their view, regime survival now depended on a reversal of economic reforms and an end to any discussion of possible political relaxation.

Deng shared his colleagues' concerns about instability and, as we have seen, he had no interest in deep political reform. As had been true from the start, however, he remained convinced that economic liberalization and the growth it generated were the keys to rebuilding the Party's popularity and preserving its primacy. "Why do the people support us?" Deng asked his senior colleagues in early 1990. "Because over the last ten years our economy has been developing." If reform was reversed and the economy stagnated, "this would be not only an economic problem but also a political one."[28] "Many nations in this world have fallen," Deng warned a subsequent meeting of Politburo members, "and the root cause has always been poor economic performance." Shoring up the Party's position would, he argued, require sustaining annual growth rates of over 5%. Such a feat could only be achieved by placing even greater reliance on market forces.[29] By 1992, despite having relinquished his formal titles, the aging patriarch had succeeded in outmaneuvering his opponents, jump-starting the reform process, and unleashing growth that, for the remainder of the decade, would reach average annual rates of roughly 10%, nearly double the target he had set.

The prospect of substantial, steady increases in the income of ordinary citizens was central to the CCP's post-Tiananmen program for restoring its battered prestige and fending off future threats. Indeed it was the key to what has sometimes been described as a tacit social contract in which the Chinese people gave their "grudging acceptance" of the Party's continued rule in return for the promise of a better life.[30] As always, however, the offer of carrots was accompanied by the threatened application of sticks or, more precisely, scalpels. Determined never to permit a recurrence of the sort of large-scale, nationwide protests it had just defused, the CCP set about to hone its capacity for selective, and preferably preemptive, repression. Once those deemed responsible for the June disturbances had been rounded up or driven into exile, the authorities shifted focus from mass arrests to strengthening informant networks and technical surveillance in order to identify, monitor, and intervene against individual "troublemakers."[31] Similar targeted tactics were also applied on a larger scale to "isolate and cauterize" local protests by farmers and laid-off workers, using cash or the promise of official investigations to mollify rank-and-file participants while arresting a select handful of leaders.[32]

Even as the regime's repressive weapons became more precise and refined, the organizational structures that supported them increased in size, cost, and bureaucratic importance.[33] The People's Armed Police, a separate paramilitary force created in 1983 to patrol borders and put down domestic unrest, grew by over 300,000 after Tiananmen to a force of 800,000. The manpower, authority, and budget of the Ministry of State Security were also expanded, enhancing its ability to spy on enemies, foreign and domestic, real or imagined.[34]

Events at home and abroad convinced the CCP leadership of the urgent need to harden the Party's Leninist core. If it was to survive, the Party would have to purge its ranks of corrupt or underperforming officials, recruiting new ones of higher quality, and doing more to instill in all of its members a renewed spirit of zeal. In 1990, Beijing reportedly took the unprecedented step of stripping all cadres of their Party membership, permitting them to "re-register" only after they had satisfied inquisitors of "their total devotion to Marxism and the party."[35] Over the course of the decade, the Party sought to improve the level of education of its rank and file by recruiting recent college graduates. It also worked to coopt the members of the emerging middle class, binding them to the regime by creating a new category of "reserve cadre" for ambitious young professionals who hoped that a visible token of loyalty would enhance their prospects for better jobs and higher salaries.[36]

Beyond the promise of material rewards for those who stayed in line, and the threat of punishment for those who disobeyed the CCP's dictates, the Party's strategists recognized that they needed to do more to shore up its ideological foundations. Following Mao's death, the CCP leadership had abandoned his attempts to position China as the leader of world Communism and jettisoned his concept of "continuous revolution" and the ceaseless cycle of self-destructive internal struggle to which it had led. Since the start of economic reforms, the Party also seemed to have backed away from many of the main tenets of Marxism. Instead of socializing the means of production and moving towards a classless society, China was de-collectivizing agriculture, expanding the role of markets, and encouraging entrepreneurship and the acquisition of private property.

Party theorists claimed that, despite appearances, such measures did not amount to an embrace of capitalism. To the contrary, it was only by first building what was formally labeled a "socialist market economy" that China could advance towards the ultimate aim of Communism.[37] For the time being, the nation would remain for an indefinite period in "the primary stage of socialism."[38] It did not take great discernment, or deep cynicism, to conclude that what Deng had described as "socialism with Chinese characteristics" now meant whatever the Party wanted it to mean.

Popular enthusiasm for ideological dogma and willingness to accept the Party's claims of infallibility had been waning since the end of the Cultural Revolution, if not before. Tiananmen threatened a catastrophic collapse of faith. Indeed, according to political scientist Joseph Fewsmith, the CCP's decision to use force against its own people, widely regarded as a tragic error if not a crime, "destroyed what little belief in Marxism-Leninism was left."[39]

Already worried about the corrosive effects of liberal ideas on Chinese youth, the Party's top leaders were painfully aware of this heightened danger. In his remarks to PLA generals on June 9, 1989, Deng averred that "our biggest mistake" in the preceding decade had been "in the field of . . . ideological and political education."[40] What was needed was not still more indoctrination of the sort inflicted on Party cadres in the mind-numbing and increasingly irrelevant intricacies of Marxism-Leninism-Mao Zedong Thought. To the contrary, the situation demanded something simpler, more visceral, and thus better suited to capture the minds and stir the hearts of the masses.

With these ends in view, starting in the early 1990s, the Party began to mount what would soon grow into a massive nationwide campaign of "patriotic education." Instead of class struggle within China itself, the central theme of the new narrative, injected into school textbooks and popular entertainment, and embodied in innumerable museums, monuments, and "memory sites," was the righteous struggle to resist foreign invaders. Rather than cast the Chinese people as victors in a glorious revolution, these materials presented them more as victims, citizens of a nation that had suffered greatly during the "century of humiliation" that began with the Opium Wars against Great Britain in the 1840s.[41] This new framing helped to highlight the Communist Party's role as the nation's savior, while keeping alive resentment of China's past and possible future antagonists, most notably Japan, but also the United States. By proceeding in this way, the Party sought to deflect residual popular anger away from itself towards "hostile foreign forces," and to build an additional prop to support its sagging legitimacy. While Western observers counted the days until, as Bill Clinton put it in 1992, China "went the way of communist regimes in eastern Europe and the former Soviet Union,"[42] the CCP was putting into place the pieces of what would prove to be a highly effective survival strategy.

"Consultative Leninism" and the search for a "Harmonious Society"

Over the course of the 1990s, CCP strategists developed a sophisticated appreciation for the potentially disruptive effects of modernization that mirrored the analysis of Western analysts while inverting their conclusions. Western theorists had predicted that development would create complexities, stresses, interests, and demands that would be difficult to manage in a top-down system. Their assessment, which, as we have seen, became an important part of the rationale for engagement, was that China would have no choice but to move towards some kind of deep, genuinely liberalizing political reforms. Rejecting this possibility out of hand, Chinese policy-makers, by contrast, looked for methods of alleviating or containing rising societal pressures, deflecting them in ways that strengthened the regime rather than weakening it.

As anticipated, a decade of rapid growth generated a staggering array of new challenges, including virtually unrestrained pollution and environmental degradation, illegal land seizures, and the expansion of an entire new class of itinerate laborers, workers from the countryside who held low-wage factory jobs in the cities but were denied the right to move there with their families. The gains from progress were unevenly distributed, creating both a growing middle class and widening gaps in wealth and incomes between urban and rural areas, as well as between coastal regions and the interior. Despite periodic, half-hearted efforts to bring it under control, corruption metastasized, with party-state officials at all levels, along with their families, using their access and influence to enrich themselves. Meanwhile, the downsizing of some SOEs resulted in increased unemployment and the disappearance of health, education, and retirement benefits for their former employees. One especially disturbing manifestation of the rising discontent to which these and other problems gave rise was a rapid multiplication in the number of so-called "mass incidents" (public protests involving 100 or more people), which grew from 8,700 in 1993 to 32,000 in 1999 to close to 40,000 in 2000.[43]

Despite the stresses that it produced, the resources and momentum generated by a decade of near-double-digit growth enabled the CCP to defer difficult decisions, effectively "kicking the can" of possible far-reaching reforms in governance "further down the road."[44] As the decade drew to a close, however, rising concern about where that road might be leading caused the Party to initiate what analyst Timothy Heath has described as a "deep and searching" process of introspection and attempted "self-renewal."[45] This process resulted in some significant adjustments in the CCP's strategy for maintaining domestic control that first became evident during the closing years of Jiang Zemin's rule and were even more readily apparent after Hu Jintao succeeded him as General Secretary in 2002.

The primary novelty of the new approach lay in its search for tools of cooptation that went beyond the promise of endlessly rising incomes. Rather than attempting simply to suppress societal demands, or continuing to rely on the diffuse, palliative effects of economic growth, the Party stepped up its efforts to alleviate some of these pressures at their source or, failing that, to channel them in directions that would strengthen, rather than weaken, its hold on power. As the twentieth century drew to a close, the CCP began to downplay its previous role as the vanguard of revolution and, in 2002, formally rebranded itself as a "governing party" whose highest aspiration was supposedly to address the practical needs of the Chinese people.[46]

Especially under Hu Jintao, the regime began to do more to visibly fulfill its promise to "serve the people," taking steps to address dissatisfaction over concrete problems like inadequate healthcare, education, and retirement pensions by boosting government spending on these public goods. Concerned by widening regional disparities and urban/rural gaps,

Hu also directed more investment to inland areas that had benefited less from the rapid growth of the preceding decade.[47] The party-state also permitted a variety of NGOs to flourish during the first decade of the 2000s, in the hope that these could address some of the growing needs of the population. In parallel with its own spending programs, the regime calculated that "by providing valuable social welfare goods and services," NGOs would help "reduce resentment toward the Party and its policies and therefore promote political stability."[48]

But what of the resentments caused by less tangible problems such as corruption and the arbitrary use of power? Here the CCP was willing for a time to discuss, experiment with, or at least tolerate a variety of mechanisms and techniques that provided outlets for popular frustration, and the appearance of consultation, while simultaneously generating information that the Party could use to track public attitudes, refine policy, and monitor the performance of lower-level officials. In addition to creating new or expanded channels through which citizens could report abuses or comment on proposed regulations, the regime discussed methods of increasing so-called "inner-Party democracy" (including possible expanded use of carefully controlled pseudo-elections in which citizens could choose lower-level officials from among a limited slate of pre-selected Party candidates), and took steps to back up its promises to strengthen the courts and make "rule by law" less capricious by improving the training of judges.[49] As internet traffic expanded, instead of reflexively cracking down, the Party at first explored ways of using its content to assess public attitudes, identify corrupt officials, and enhance the accountability of local governments.[50]

The intended purpose of all these initiatives was to perfect what Richard Baum has described as a system of "consultative Leninism."[51] Under this model, writes political scientist Steve Tsang, the Party would keep "its Leninist structure and organizational principles and [remain] totally dedicated to staying in power." But it would enhance its prospects for doing so in the long run by responding (or appearing to respond) more effectively to popular demands, thereby burnishing its image as "a benevolent and efficient one-party system" and preempting pressures for movement towards liberal democracy.[52] Upward flows of information would improve the party-state's capacity for top-down "social management."[53] According to Baum, the Party's goal was to "create more effective, responsive political institutions without relinquishing [its] Leninist monopoly of political power," increasing "popular *feedback* without encouraging political *pushback*" (emphasis in original).[54]

Together with the many obvious problems that followed in its train, a decade of rapid growth also created the potential for a deeper challenge to CCP rule. Those who benefited most from economic reform now comprised an emerging class of entrepreneurs and professionals with distinctive interests and substantial resources. CCP strategists were keenly aware that, just as Western observers had long hoped and predicted, the members of this new class could become influential advocates for democracy. To forestall this danger, the Party decided at the turn of the century to coopt them by bringing them into the CCP, formally opening its ranks to include not only the traditional categories of "workers, soldiers, and peasants," but also representatives of what were euphemistically described as "the most advanced forces of production" in society.[55] The Party now proclaimed itself the standard-bearer for these people, and for China's "advanced culture," as well as its "broad masses."[56]

Jiang Zemin's proudly proclaimed doctrine of "The Three Represents" may have helped to alleviate one pressing concern, but it heightened the ideological conundrum confronting his successor. If the CCP was now willing to embrace capitalists without evident embarrassment, in what sense could it still be said to be pursuing the dictates of Marx and Mao? With its latest rhetorical gyration, it seemed to have moved even closer to becoming "an ideologically 'hollowed-out' party," one that risked appearing to exist "solely to defend the privileges of insulated elites."[57]

Hu Jintao and his new leadership team recognized that the perceived absence of a sense of direction and higher purpose could encourage cynicism, demoralization, and self-serving behavior among the Party's members. Worse yet, it might weaken the Party's legitimacy in the eyes of the Chinese people. To counteract these dangers, at Hu's direction the CCP undertook a reexamination and a "systematic overhaul" of its ideology.[58]

Despite (or perhaps precisely *because of*) the fact that it involved thousands of hours of labor by untold numbers of theorists, propagandists, and other "thought workers," the results of this effort were, like Hu himself, technocratic and uninspiring. Primarily to provide internal guidance and direction, theoreticians concocted the concept of "Scientific

Development," using vaguely Marxist terminology to describe the task in which the CCP was now engaged. According to this formulation, the Party was working to resolve the "principal contradiction" between the still-underdeveloped means of production and the rising "material and non-material demands of the people."[59] In contrast to the initial stages of reform and opening up, however, the CCP was attempting to achieve these ends not only by promoting raw economic growth, but also by simultaneously addressing an array of social concerns, including pollution, public health, and unemployment.[60]

In order to ensure that its members were up to tackling these diverse and difficult problems, in 2004 the Central Committee issued an accompanying "Decision on the Enhancement of the Party's Governing Capacity." The leadership made clear that this was a deadly serious business and, given the nature of the challenges the Party now faced, a matter of "life and death" for the CCP and thus for the nation.[61] Drawing heavily on an analysis of the Soviet collapse, as well as an assessment of current problems, their goal, in the words of Politburo Standing Committee member Zeng Qinghong, was "to get all the Party's comrades . . . to wake up, think of danger in times of peace, heighten their sense of hardship . . . and earnestly strengthen the Party's ability to govern."[62] Lest anyone miss the point, Beijing ordered an accompanying eighteen-month "rectification campaign," involving intensive indoctrination and a grueling process of "criticism/self-criticism" that eventually included all 70.8 million Party members.[63]

Whatever emotions they might stir in the hearts of loyal CCP cadres, promises of more "Scientific Development" and enhanced "Governing Capacity" were hardly likely to capture the imaginations of ordinary people. For that purpose, continuing a trend that had begun in the mid-1990s, the Party leadership experimented with slogans rooted in China's pre-Communist Confucian culture. Jiang Zemin had invoked one such phrase when he described the regime's goal as being to transform China into a "comprehensively well-off" society by the early decades of the twenty-first century.[64] Hu Jintao followed suit when he vowed to build a "Harmonious Society," characterized by justice, equality, stability, and a wholesome balance between humankind and nature.

To this rather bland gruel, the Party continued to add a spicy dash of anti-foreign nationalism, occasionally altering the recipe and allowing the temperature to rise during diplomatic confrontations with the United States (in 1999 and again in 2001) and Japan (in 2005). The feelings evoked in this way could be powerful, so much so that at times they threatened to get out of control.[65] Still, the promise of a world in which past wrongs had been righted was negative, backward-looking, and inherently self-limiting; it was not a vision, in itself, sufficiently capacious and uplifting to sustain the indefinite support of the Chinese people, nor to bind them unbreakably to their Communist Party rulers. For that purpose, something broader and more ambitious would be required.

The demise of "soft authoritarianism"

The experiments and innovations of the late Jiang and early Hu periods were seen by many in the West as evidence that engagement was working and far-reaching changes were afoot. Growth had produced an expanding middle class that could not be expected to remain quiescent for much longer. As the Starbucks chain spread across China, *New York Times* columnist Nicholas Kristof assured his readers in 2004 that "no middle class is content with more choices of coffees than of candidates on the ballot."[66] In the less colorful language of Western social science, a "nonadaptive, brittle state" had proven itself incapable of coping with "an increasingly, organized, complex, and robust society," setting in motion a process that would lead to "accelerating political liberalization."[67] Even the Party leadership had supposedly become "increasingly aware that the efficiency of the state requires the use of elections and the courts to check state abuses."[68]

Unfortunately, far from being signs of a trend towards greater freedom, the developments that sparked these expressions of optimism were actually part of an effort to preserve the CCP's political monopoly by defusing societal pressures for much deeper, truly liberalizing reforms. Not only did they fail to do this, however, but as seen from Beijing they actually helped make matters worse.

As the century opened, the Party found itself confronted by a string of new crises and an intensification of troubling trends that combined to heighten its perennial anxieties and trigger its defensive reflexes. Rather than proceed any further towards what David Shambaugh has described as "soft authoritarianism,"[69] the regime began to revert to its Leninist

66

roots, ramping up repression and cutting back on attempts at cooptation. Reactive, tentative, and piecemeal under Hu Jintao, this crackdown was carried forward far more aggressively and with a clearer sense of urgency and strategic purpose by Xi Jinping.

In 2003–4, Hu and his newly installed colleagues watched with dismay as a series of peaceful, popular uprisings or "color revolutions" displaced authoritarian rulers in parts of the former Soviet Union. These events, writes Shambaugh, "had an effect on the CCP similar to that of the revolutions of 1989 . . . and the collapse of the Soviet Union in 1991," provoking a wave of "alarm, fear, even paranoia."[70] Four years later, the onset of the global financial crisis raised the specter of mass unemployment and possible social unrest in China itself. These concerns were heightened still further by the events of 2008, which saw demonstrations and violence in Tibet, public anger over the government's alleged mishandling of a devastating earthquake in Sichuan province, and the publication of Charter 08, a document signed by over 300 well-known Chinese dissidents and human rights activists that called for an end to Communist Party rule and the "rapid establishment of a free, democratic, and constitutional country."[71] This was followed in 2009 by the start of what would become an escalating cycle of protests and violent repression in the western, majority-Muslim province of Xinjiang. The decade closed with the arrival in 2010–11 of the "Arab Spring," another wave of popular unrest and regime change that soon engulfed much of North Africa and parts of the Middle East and "served as a mirror of Chinese leadership anxieties."[72]

Against the backdrop of these dramatic events, evidence continued to accumulate that the regime's efforts to boost its performance and improve "social management" were not having the desired effect. The number of "mass incidents" continued to grow, more than doubling from 40,000 at the turn of the century to 87,000 in 2005 (the last year in which the government released statistics), and doubling again to a reported 180,000 in 2010.[73] Labor disputes also became more common, with roughly 200,000 reported in 2001 and over a million in 2010.[74]

While they undoubtedly represented only the tip of a very large iceberg, statistics on "economic crime" revealed how high up in the system the rot of corruption had spread. Whereas in 1998 only 658 of every 10,000 cases filed involved mid- to upper-ranking party-state officials, by 2007 the ratio had risen to one in ten.[75] Incomplete and ineffective as they may have been, the CCP's efforts to crack down on corruption nevertheless tended to draw attention to just how serious the problem had become. This reality was highlighted in dramatic fashion in 2012 by the arrest of Bo Xilai, a powerful, popular, and ambitious Politburo member and the Party Secretary of Chongqing.[76] As the official announcement of this unprecedented development acknowledged, the revelation of malfeasance at the very pinnacle of the CCP hierarchy "badly undermined the reputation" of the Party and "significantly damaged" its cause.[77]

There were also worrisome signs that some of the Party's attempts at cooptation were having unintended consequences. Starting in around 2003, a growing number of lawyers began to respond to the regime's promises to strengthen "rule by law" by shifting their focus from "lucrative commercial cases to righting the wrongs of society through legal action."[78] This was followed by a rash of cases in which attorneys tried to use the courts to protect the rights of migrant workers, defend practitioners of various religious sects, and block seizures of rural land by powerful and well-connected developers.[79] In 2005, a group of activists established the Open Constitution Initiative, an NGO dedicated to investigating human rights abuses.[80] As the internet spread, Chinese citizens began to resort to it more frequently to call attention to instances of official corruption and incompetence.[81] Inspired by the Arab Spring, in 2011 a group of dissidents even tried to organize a "Jasmine Revolution" of their own, using the internet to call for demonstrations in cities across China.[82]

The regime's response to all of this was uneven, with shifts coming sooner in some areas than others. Across the span of a decade, however, each major crisis was followed by a further tightening of the screws. In the wake of the color revolutions, the CCP began to strengthen internet controls and media censorship and (allegedly in response to a personal warning to Hu from Vladimir Putin) to enhance scrutiny of foreign-funded NGOs.[83] The disturbances also encouraged the authorities to rethink their approach to legal reform, resulting in the start of what Carl Minzner describes as "China's turn against the law." In 2006, the CCP launched a "socialist rule of law campaign" that "stressed loyalty to the Communist Party and the need to avoid the pernicious influence of 'Western' rule-of-law theories" that emphasized the importance of an independent, apolitical judiciary.[84] According to Joseph Fewsmith, it was also at around this time that the CCP leadership lost their enthusiasm for proposals to enhance the role of lower-level members in selecting some local officials in favor of cosmetic procedural adjustments that effectively "took the democracy out of inner-party democracy."[85] While some officials, including Premier Wen Jiabao, continued to speak periodically about the need for political reform, Fewsmith concludes that changes that would have in any way loosened the control of the Party were "never on the agenda."[86]

The financial crisis and the outbreak of violence in Tibet and Xinjiang contributed to a recalibration of the Party's concept of "social management," with more emphasis placed on improving "public security work" than on the efficient delivery of services.[87] The priority attached to the former task was reflected in large annual increases in spending on domestic security that began in 2008.[88] The year also marked the start of a discernible increase in the Party's use of patriotic appeals to rally support and deflect popular frustrations. These efforts were focused first on the spectacle of the Beijing Olympic games and then, over the next several years, on a series of highly publicized territorial disputes with China's maritime neighbors.[89]

Increased resort to nationalism was accompanied by a campaign of intensified repression and a sharp, sustained rise in the number of political prisoners. Among the most well known of these was the writer Liu Xiaobo, one of the lead authors of Charter 08, who was tried, convicted, and sentenced to eleven years in prison for "inciting subversion of state power." The Party also began to harass so-called "rights defense lawyers," cracking down on civil society groups, and closing NGOs that advocated for human rights and political freedoms.[90]

Thanks in part to vigorous preemptive action by the party-state, instead of a similar blossoming of popular protests, the Arab Spring was followed by a "Chinese winter."[91] Together with more surveillance and further arrests, the regime demonstrated its determination and growing ability to monitor and control the internet, zeroing in on communications that used suspect words (like "jasmine") and deleting tens of millions of posts from popular websites.[92] Drawing on the lessons learned from its own experience, and from observing the failures of other authoritarian regimes, the CCP paid particular attention to ensuring that modern means of communication could not be used to mobilize and coordinate protests, whether locally or on a national scale.[93] In 2010–11, in a further reflection of the regime's mounting anxieties, spending on domestic security for the first time exceeded the budget for external defense.[94]

The totalitarian turn

By the time Xi Jinping assumed power at the end of 2012, many in the CCP elite believed that their party faced yet another existential crisis.[95] The challenges and societal pressures fueled by over twenty years of rapid development had increased in complexity and intensity. Yet, after what some now described as a "lost decade," Hu's administration had done little to deal with corruption, inequality, environmental degradation, or any of the myriad other issues it had promised to address.[96] Worse still, the experiments in enhanced cooptation undertaken during the Hu era appeared to have "favored social disarray and undermined the Party's position in society."[97] Finally, despite having acknowledged the need to do so, Hu's planners had failed to put forward a new model for sustaining economic progress. Slower growth now appeared to be part of what Xi Jinping would describe as "the new normal."[98] In a telling indication of the prevailing state of mind among the new leadership, as Xi took office a top deputy reportedly distributed copies of Alexis de Tocqueville's book on the causes of the French Revolution to his senior colleagues.[99]

Foreign analysts were fully aware of these concerns, but most seem to have believed that China's "looming crisis of authoritarianism" would lead either to "a new opportunity for democratic transition" or perhaps to some kind of catastrophic breakdown.[100] Either way, as Andrew Nathan reported on the eve of Xi's accession, the consensus among China watchers was "stronger than at any time since the 1989 Tiananmen crisis" that the resilience of the regime was "approaching its limits."[101]

Contrary to the way in which he is sometimes portrayed, Xi Jinping is not an aberration whose policies represent a radical departure from a prevailing trend towards moderation. Nor is he a revolutionary who has set about to transform the character of the Chinese system, or a renegade whose actions once in office defied the expectations of the Party elite. Xi can best be understood instead as *revivalist*; he is a product of the system who sees it as his mission to revitalize the Communist Party in order to ensure its continued primacy, and who was chosen by his colleagues to achieve that end.[102]

Xi inherited a dire situation in which most of the obvious alternative approaches to sustaining CCP rule seemed to be nearing exhaustion. Growth alone could no longer be relied upon to sustain popular support. Efforts at cooptation by non-material means had led to more rather than fewer problems and were now seen by some in the Party as signs of weakness. Attempts to breathe new life into tired official dogma had achieved what were at best lackluster results.

Faced with these conditions, Xi formulated a strategy that must have appeared to him and to most of his colleagues to be the best, and perhaps the only, one available. In most respects, Xi has tried to return the Party to its roots. First, he took immediate steps to reinvigorate the CCP's machinery, using a mix of fear and exhortation to galvanize its members, tightening its hold on China's government, society, and economy, and re-concentrating power within the Party at its center, in his own hands. Second, through a mix of means, both old-fashioned and modern, Xi has enhanced and expanded the Party's capacity for coercion, aiming not only to repress dissent when it rears its head but also to prevent it from ever arising. Last, and perhaps most important, Xi is attempting to reconstruct the ideological foundations of CCP rule, codifying, reaffirming, and putting his own stamp on the Party's formal, Marxist doctrine, while strengthening a powerful nationalist narrative that stretches backward into China's distant past and forward into its glorious future.

Whatever else he may be, Xi Jinping is an unwavering Leninist and a believer in the primacy of the Party. Accordingly, soon after taking office, he unleashed an anti-corruption campaign of unprecedented scope, duration, and ferocity. The purpose was not only to destroy or intimidate his potential rivals but also to improve the performance and, as important, the perceived moral standing of Party officials. Whereas Hu Jintao stressed enhancing efficiency and technical expertise, Xi has placed greater emphasis on cultivating virtue and building character, adapting terminology and techniques from the Mao era to inculcate "socialist values" in all members of the Party and insisting that they remain "down-to-earth, upright, and corruption-free."[103] To drive home and enforce these messages, in 2013 Xi launched a Mao-inspired "mass line campaign," complete with "criticism/self-criticism" sessions and new regulations governing everything from spending on entertainment to the requirements for promotion.[104] For Xi, these are matters of the utmost importance. As he explained at the start of this year-long campaign: "Winning or losing public support is an issue that concerns the [CCP's] survival or extinction."[105]

While strengthening the Party from within, Xi has sought to increase the depth of its penetration into, and control over, every other institution in Chinese society, starting with the state bureaucracy and the military. At his direction, the Party has also created or strengthened cells in all types of organizations, from foreign-owned businesses,[106] to charities, universities, and media outlets.[107] In 2017, Xi had one of his favorite slogans (also borrowed from Mao) inscribed in the CCP constitution: "Party, government, army, society, and education. East, West, South, North. The Party leads everything."[108]

As he tightens the Party's grip, Xi has taken steps to enhance his own authority within it. Towards this end, he has put himself at the head of all the most important "leading-small groups": top-level commit-tees responsible for overseeing and coordinating every aspect of national policy. Xi has further elevated his personal status by adopting the title of "core leader," a term first applied to Mao and Deng.[109] Beyond the confines of the Party apparatus, he has declared himself to be the Commander-in-Chief of the Armed Forces, a newly created position that implies a degree of direct, operational control over the military,[110] and he has modified China's constitution so that he can remain indefinitely as president, or head of state.[111] Xi's real power derives from his status as the Party's General Secretary, a position to which he is widely expected to be reappointed for a third term in the fall of 2022.[112]

Despite talk of "democratic centralism," Xi's maneuvers are fully con-sistent with the actual practice of Leninist political systems and with the concepts of hierarchy and command on which such systems are based. Nor are they at odds with the history and traditions of the CCP. It is true that Deng Xiaoping encouraged the adoption of certain practices that he hoped would avoid a repeat of Mao's disastrous one-man dictatorship. But, as the political scientist Joseph Torigian has argued, Deng himself exercised "an astounding level of authority" and rejected the idea of formal rules limiting the authority of top leaders.[113] The procedures followed by his hand-picked successors, including agreeing to serve only two five-year terms as General Secretary, adhering to a retirement age of sixty-eight, and avoiding the cultivation of a "cult of personality," reflected little more than weak, informal norms.[114] In brushing them aside, Xi is not overturning the system he inherited; rather he is attempting to snap it back to the principles on which it was originally designed and built. As Torigian notes of Xi's self-coronation as "core" leader, his actions represent "not a rejection of Deng's legacy but a return to it."[115]

No aspect of Xi Jinping's program for securing the perpetual primacy of the CCP has received more attention from foreign observers than its resort to brutal repression. Here too, however, the differences with his predecessors are matters of degree, not kind. The Party has always ruled with an iron fist, even if, at times, its leaders have sought to encase that fist in a velvet glove. What Xi has done is to shed any pretense of building a "kinder, gentler" form of authoritarianism, in which more effective cooptation might obviate the need for quite as much coercion. To the contrary, under Xi, the use of repression has been open, extensive, aggressive, and unapologetic, but also more systematic, sustained, and, in certain respects, more sophisticated than in the past.

Instead of trying to turn some of the manifestations of an emerging civil society to its own purposes, under Xi the party-state has sought to crush or uproot them before they can grow into a serious challenge. To foil the nefarious designs of the West and its domestic co-conspirators, the regime has imposed onerous new restrictions on NGOs, especially those engaged in human rights work or in receipt of funding from foreign sources.[116] This has been accompanied by the arrest, detention, and torture of hundreds of lawyers[117] and by new regulations that reiterate, codify, and further strengthen the Party's authority over the legal system.[118]

Ending the ambivalence of the Hu era regarding the role of the internet, Xi has overseen a drastic tightening of controls over flows of information into and within China.[119] In a closely related effort, the regime is investing vast resources in what could ultimately become a ubiquitous national surveillance network designed to monitor and track the movements, communications, and transactions of virtually every man, woman, and child in the country.[120] The Party's ultimate ambition is not only to punish those whose words or deeds have threatened "social stability" but also, through the development of algorithms and behavioral profiles, to identify people who might be prone to do so even before they have the chance to act.[121] This is a capacity of which the twentieth-century totalitarians could only dream.

Xi's repressive reign still relies on brute force as well as the clever application of high technology. Here again the goal is to forestall threats rather than merely responding to them. Whatever their actual offenses, the periodic arrests of wealthy businessmen or respected academics who show even vague hints of independence are meant to send a clear signal that no one is above the Party or beyond its reach.[122] The preemptive use of coercion is not always surgical or narrowly targeted. After eight years of sporadic violence and traditional, paramilitary "strike hard" campaigns, in around 2017 the CCP regime began to incarcerate large numbers of Uighurs in concentration camps spread across the western region of Xinjiang. The purpose of these facilities is supposedly to "re-educate" and "de-radicalize" their occupants, rendering them resistant to the appeals of Islamic fundamentalism. Those incarcerated need not have shown any sympathy for such ideas, and most have not been accused of committing any crime. It is their identity alone, and the possibility that they might someday act against the party-state, that renders them suspect and condemns them to harsh treatment.[123]

"Xi Jinping Thought," pseudo-Confucianism, and the birth of the "China Dream"

Xi Jinping may not be an intellectual but, more than any Chinese leader since Deng Xiaoping, and perhaps since Mao himself, he recognizes the importance of ideas in securing the Party's position and perpetuating its hold on power. Unless the CCP is seen to stand for something larger than itself, both by its members and by the Chinese people, its days will be numbered.

Of all the many challenges confronting the Party and the nation, none are more serious than those arising in the realm of ideas. In the words of "Document 9," a Party "Communiqué on the Current State of the Ideological Sphere" circulated soon after Xi took power in 2013, "Western constitutional democracy," "universal values," and "unrestrained economic liberalization" are foreign concepts intended to "weaken the theoretical foundations of the Party's leadership . . . [and] change China's basic economic system" (see Box 3.1).[124] Despite the growth in China's

BOX 3.1 **"Communiqué on the Current State of the Ideological Sphere"**

(Document 9)

April 2013

Seven "false ideological trends, positions, and activities":

1. "Promoting Western Constitutional Democracy" in an "attempt to undermine the current leadership and the socialism with Chinese characteristics system of governance."
2. "Promoting 'universal values' in an attempt to weaken the theoretical foundations of the Party's leadership."
3. "Promoting civil society in an attempt to dismantle the ruling party's social foundation."
4. "Promoting Neoliberalism" in an attempt "to change China's Basic Economic System."
5. "Promoting the West's idea of journalism" to challenge "China's principle that the media and publishing system should be subject to Party discipline."
6. "Promoting historical nihilism" in an attempt to "undermine the history of the CCP and of New China."
7. "Questioning Reform and Opening and the socialist nature of socialism with Chinese characteristics."

Four responses:

1. "Strengthen leadership in the ideological sphere."
2. "Guide our party members and leaders to distinguish between true and false theories."
3. "Unwavering adherence to the principle of the Party's control of media."
4. "Conscientiously strengthen management of the ideological battlefield."

Source: "Document 9: A ChinaFile Translation," November 8, 2013 wealth and power, and notwithstanding its superficially cordial and undeniably profitable relations with the West, "the contest between infiltration and anti-infiltration efforts in the ideological sphere is as severe as ever." So long as the Party holds fast to its principles, Western "anti-China forces" will continue to press for "urgent reform" and to "point the spearhead of . . . 'Color Revolutions'" at China. "In the face of these threats, we must not let down our guard or decrease our vigilance."[125]

To defend against all of these dangers, strengthening both the resolve of the Party rank and file and the loyalty of the masses, Xi has pieced together a three-layered ideational construct. In the middle tier, comprising the main body and the most highly developed portion of this structure, Xi has sought to refurbish and reinforce CCP doctrine, establishing himself as the ultimate arbiter of its content and demanding unquestioning acceptance from all Party members. Recognizing the limited appeal of arcane ideological slogans to ordinary people, however, Xi has gone further than his predecessors in trying to sink the regime's foundations deeper into the soil of China's culture and civilization, invoking select concepts from its history to justify the maintenance of one-party authoritarian rule. Finally, in his most important architectural innovation, Xi has sketched the outlines of a gleaming spire to be placed atop the entire edifice. Building towards the "China Dream" of the "great rejuvenation of the Chinese nation" is a goal meant to inspire and motivate members of the Party and the masses alike.

For Xi, nothing is more critical than maintaining the ideological commitment and esprit of the Party's cadres. In a closed-door speech to senior officials given in January 2013, the newly minted General Secretary returned to the questions that had haunted the CCP for over two decades: "Why did the Soviet Union disintegrate? Why did the Communist Party of the Soviet Union fall to pieces?" The answer: demoralization caused by ideological subversion, confusion, and loss of faith. Once the CPSU began to indulge in "historical nihilism," succumbing to pressure to question the performance of its past leaders and repudiate its own history, party organizations at all levels ceased to function, the party lost control of the military, and its members "scattered like a flock of frightened beasts. This is a lesson from the past!"[126]

To guard against the temptations of "revisionism," Xi has foreclosed the possibility of retrospective critiques of Party policy. In his new formulation, the history of the PRC can be divided into three periods: a "pre-reform era" from 1949 to 1976 during which the nation was founded and "stood up" under the leadership of Mao Zedong; a "reform era" from 1978 to 2012 during which it "grew rich" by fulfilling the vision of Deng Xiaoping; and a new era when it will "grow strong" under the direction of Xi Jinping.[127] The three eras are inseparable and the first two were necessary in order to reach the third. It would therefore be both pointless and dangerous to debate the wisdom of past decisions, as the Soviets did when they reexamined and ultimately renounced the legacy of Stalin. To do so would be to play into the hands of those "hostile forces both at home and abroad" who seek to "confuse the hearts of the people" in order to "incite them into overthrowing [the CCP]."[128]

Xi's declaration of a new era has the added benefit of elevating his own importance. In addition to controlling the levers of material power, he is now the CCP's premier ideologist, uniquely equipped to interpret novel historical conditions through the lens of Party doctrine, refining it as necessary in order to guide the nation unerringly towards its glorious future. By having "Xi Jinping Thought on Socialism with Chinese Characteristics for a New Era" incorporated into the constitution, Xi has put himself at a level of ideological authority equivalent to Mao's, thereby effectively precluding direct challenges to his ideas from other Party members.

As for its content, the most striking thing about "Xi Jinping Thought" is its vacuity: it is essentially a lengthy restatement of very familiar themes from the "reform era," spiced up with a few more recent refinements.[129] More revealing than the drab terminology of official doctrine is the sometimes fiery, even quasi-religious rhetoric that surrounds it. Xi has urged Party members to have "faith" in the "sublime ideals of Communism"; to be willing, like their forebears, to "shed their blood and lay down their lives" in moving towards "the ultimate goal of achieving communism." "Faith in Marxism" is "the political soul of the Communist Party member." At the core of that faith is a belief in the inexorable workings of "historical materialism" which guarantee that, in the end, Western capitalism will be defeated and socialism will triumph.[130] Not content merely to harangue, Xi has mandated that his "Thought" be taught at universities and drilled into the heads of cadres through the use of an app that they are "encouraged" to install on their smartphones. The point of all this appears to be less to convey a body of original and inspiring ideas than to enforce uniformity and compliance from Party members.[131]

For purposes of cementing the CCP's support among "the masses," Xi has made more frequent use of concepts and phrases from China's pre-Communist past. Whereas his predecessors occasionally deployed Confucian slogans to describe their goals and, implicitly, to bolster regime legitimacy, he has adopted a more systematic approach. With his approval, scholars and Party theorists have undertaken a reexamination of the works of pre-modern Chinese philosophers, selectively highlighting those writings that appear to buttress the ideal of rule by a wise and virtuous elite.[132] The Party's propaganda apparatus has also launched supporting nationwide campaigns, complete with posters and videos emphasizing "traditional Chinese values," such as filial piety, intermingled with "core socialist values" like "diligence" and "friendliness."[133]

This may be a cynical exercise but it is also a serious one. By invoking the wisdom of the ancients to justify China's current form of government, and by claiming (falsely) that the CCP has always been "a loyal standard-bearer and proponent of the excellent elements of traditional Chinese culture," Xi is attempting to shore up the regime's legitimacy by bolting it more firmly to the nation's past.[134] The assertion that there are distinctive Chinese values also serves as a counter to the "so-called universal values" of individual liberty and equal rights championed by the West. By emphasizing the importance of family loyalty, the Party clearly hopes to stir patriotic sentiments that will redound to its benefit. After all, as one slogan has it, "a nation is made of many families" but "there can be no family without a nation." Indeed, the notion that the entire nation comprises one big family is described in official propaganda as "a unique Chinese value" that can be traced back to Confucius.[135]

Since the start of the reform period, the CCP has struggled to define an overarching, shared goal that would justify its continued harsh rule while motivating and inspiring both its own members and the nation as a whole. The need has only become more obvious with the passage of time, as growth has slowed, societal pressures have continued to rise, and official doctrine has become more abstruse and more remote from the everyday experience of ordinary people. For better, and perhaps in the long run for worse, Xi Jinping appears to have found a solution to this problem in the form of the "China Dream" of the "great rejuvenation of the Chinese nation."

Xi certainly believes this to be the case. As he told an audience of Party propagandists in 2013, since these slogans were put forward they have "gained the sincere support of the broad cadres and masses." The China Dream is "the expression of an image . . . the masses can accept easily. It has established a struggle objective that inspires people's hearts and has made clear the beautiful prospects of the party and the country."[136] Whether or not it is correct, this assessment is revealing of the regime's intent.

At one level, the "China Dream" taps into widely shared, positive emotions of pride, both in the nation's recent achievements under the leadership of the Communist Party and in the long prior history of Chinese civilization. As Jacqueline Deal points out, it was Sun Yat-sen who first issued the call for "rejuvenation" at the turn of the twentieth century when China was reeling from a series of humiliating defeats and the Qing dynasty tottered on the brink of collapse.[137] By invoking this concept, the nation's current rulers link themselves more directly to their pre-Communist ancestors, placing them in a pantheon of patriotic heroes who have struggled for over a century to attain a shared objective.

The way in which the CCP leadership has framed the task of national rejuvenation also seems designed to provide additional motivation to the Party's rank and file, and to the people at large, above and beyond what is conveyed through the endless, rote repetition of official doctrine. Building "socialism with Chinese characteristics" is still vitally important, but in Xi's ideational scheme it has been subtly transposed into a means for achieving the larger, less abstract, and more emotionally evocative end of enhancing China's wealth, power, and status. Unlike the distant earthly paradise of Communism, rejuvenation is attainable within a measurable span of time; indeed, it is already close at hand. It was Jiang Zemin who first articulated the "two centenary goals" of building China into a "moderately prosperous society" by 2021 (the 100th anniversary of the CCP) and a fully developed "modern socialist country" by 2049 (the 100th anniversary of the PRC). Under Xi, these have become prominent, fast-approaching signposts on the road to rejuvenation. If they dedicate themselves fully to the task, many of those alive today can hope to see the China Dream fulfilled.

That dream has a darker side, less apparent to foreign audiences, that adds further to its mobilizing power. Xi's new formulations subsume the more negative, backward-looking nationalism that has been a staple of the Party's domestic propaganda since Tiananmen and transforms it into something much more potent and potentially aggressive. "Rejuvenation" and "renewal" have a moral valence that words like "growth" or "rise" do not. These terms imply not only reaching a target, but also restoring the proper order of things by regaining something that was lost or, in this case, stolen.[138] Xi's Dream thus looks backward to a glorious past when China was the richest, most advanced, and most powerful political entity on earth and forward to an imagined future when it will have displaced the United States and resumed its rightful place at the center of the world.

In the long sweep of history, the rise in the West's relative power and the century of humiliation that it enabled were merely an interruption, an unfortunate interlude during which China was overmatched and dominated. In order to fulfill their destiny, the Chinese people will have to struggle against many of the same "hostile foreign forces" that abused them in the past. But, under the leadership of the Communist Party, they will overcome all obstacles, rejecting the West's arrogant claims to be the guardian of universal human values, reasserting the material and moral superiority of their own civilization, and avenging the wrongs done to their ancestors. As William Callahan explains: "The optimism of the China dream . . . relies on the pessimism of the national humiliation nightmare. The China dream thus is not just a positive expression of national aspirations; at the same time, it is a negative soft power strategy that cultivates an anti-Western and an anti-Japanese form of Chinese identity."[139]

The China Dream has a final, troubling feature. In 2013, a Party publication exhorted cadres to "extensively promulgate that the future and destiny of every person is inseparably linked to the future and destiny of the country . . . that the China Dream is the dream of the nation, and is also the dream of every Chinese person." As Stein Ringen points out, these words are "not just a celebration of national greatness" but the hallmarks of an ideology in which "the person ceases to exist as an autonomous being and is subsumed in the nation." This claim of the organic unity of nation and person is, as Ringen notes, a core tenet of fascism. When such ideas last shaped the policies of great powers, "there was no limit to repression, no limit to aggression, no limit to evil, no limit to political murder, and no limit to sacrifice that was not for the good of the people."[140]

Conclusion

Nothing in history is inevitable, but some outcomes are certainly more probable than others. In light of the principles on which the CCP operates, the likelihood of its liberalizing – agreeing to share or accept limits on its power, still less to surrender it altogether – was always extremely low. For it to have done so would have required it to abandon its essence and to have taken steps that are virtually unprecedented in the history of Leninist political parties.[141] The ruling regimes in the Soviet Union and its former empire did not willingly stand down; they were swept aside in (mostly) peaceful popular revolutions. While it is understandable, especially in the immediate aftermath of these dramatic events, that some Western policy-makers might have believed that the CCP would soon follow a similar path, it should have come as no surprise that the Party's leaders were utterly determined to prevent this from happening.

As for the possibilities of incremental change driven from above, over the last thirty years those in China who advocated anything that might have resulted in movement towards genuine multi-party democracy never had the power to advance their ideas; some were jailed for their troubles. Meanwhile, despite the fact that they generated periodic discussion and occasional expressions of optimism in the West, proposals for "political reform" put forward by the CCP were always intended to reinforce its authority rather than in any way reduce it. The preservation of one-party authoritarian rule may not have been inevitable, but it was far more likely than any other outcome, and certainly than gradual liberalization of the sort envisioned by US and other Western policy-makers.

What about the shift towards something that has come increasingly to resemble a one-man totalitarian dictatorship? Was this an accident of history, the product of one man's guile and ruthless ambition? Or does it reflect the inner logic and natural tendencies of Leninist systems?

Here again, there are strong reasons to believe that the recent course of China's political evolution was, if not preordained, then at least overdetermined. While it may be comforting to blame the dictatorial impulses of Xi Jinping, the fact that his repressive policies built on those of his predecessor suggests that they represent the consensus response to a shared perception of danger among the CCP elite. Having tried and failed to implement an approach that would have loosened up in certain respects while retaining unchallengeable control, the Party reverted to the familiar tools of relentless indoctrination and ruthless repression.

Xi Jinping's concentration of power in his own hands no doubt reflects his personality and personal experiences. That said, it would appear that, at least to some degree, his colleagues shared the view that strengthening and preserving the system required a strong hand at the top. Certainly there was very little to prevent him from moving in this direction, no laws or alternative centers of power, only a few feeble norms passed down by Deng Xiaoping.

In fact, during their comparatively brief but often bloody history, Leninist systems have displayed strong centripetal tendencies, with all power flowing inwards from society to the Party, upwards to a small number of senior leaders and, within that group, into the hands of a single man. As the historian Graeme Gill has pointed out, this may be due to the fact that, despite its claims to scientific precision, Marxist-Leninist doctrine does not actually give clear, practical guidance on how to fulfill its objectives. If the doctrine is to retain its aura of infallibility, however, it cannot become a subject of debate and open disagreement among Party members. Such circumstances create "enormous pressures for the acknowledgement of one individual as the theoretician of the movement" who can "make the theory relevant to the practice by 'creatively developing' the corpus of doctrine in such a way that it [can be] brought to bear on contemporary problems." In time, that person tends to transition from the interpreter of doctrine to its source, accruing even more personal power into the bargain. For this reason, notwithstanding their "formally collective ethos," and their rejection, in theory, of the "great man" conception of history, Leninist systems can easily devolve into cults of personality.[142] This was something that Leon Trotsky recognized early on when he warned that Lenin's methods would lead to a process in which "the party organization is substituted for the party, the Central Committee is substituted for the party organization, and finally the 'dictator' is substituted for the Central Committee."[143] Xi Jinping may not be a tyrant on par with Stalin or Mao, at least not yet. But he is following in their footsteps along a well-trodden path.

4

Economics: "A Bird in a Cage"

For the better part of four decades, Western policy-makers believed that deepening engagement would help push China down a path towards economic as well as political liberalization; indeed, from the outset, they were probably more certain of the former outcome than the latter. After all, in contrast to the CCP's reluctance to countenance serious political change, China's leaders had declared themselves fervently committed to economic "reform and opening up." Based on their understanding of economic principles, and the experience of their own countries, most observers in the advanced industrial world assumed that such a process could end up in only one place. Once unleashed, market forces would take on an ever-expanding role, efficiently allocating scarce resources, propelling growth, driving the direction of development, and determining China's position in the global trading system. Ownership of the means of production would shift from primarily public to predominantly private hands and, while the state would not wither away entirely, its role in planning and managing the economy would be sharply circumscribed and diminished. Like the nations of the former Soviet empire, China was believed to be undergoing a progressive "transition" from Communism to a form of capitalism that, whatever its distinctive features, would end up closely resembling those found in the West.

Confidence in this assessment was bolstered at the turn of the century when China entered the WTO. This achievement had been premised on the CCP regime's promises that it would reduce barriers to trade and investment, thereby increasing the domestic economy's exposure to the forces of international competition and giving added impetus to market-oriented reforms. Movement towards ever-greater liberalization seemed to have such momentum behind it, and to be so obviously in China's best interests that, for a time, indications that this might not be happening were overlooked or explained away.

And yet, twenty years on, China's economic system looks very different than what most in the West expected it would become. Despite its solemn commitments, the CCP regime continues to find ways to help Chinese companies circumvent WTO rules, protecting them with non-tariff barriers, providing cheap land and other hidden subsidies, enabling intellectual property theft, and failing to enforce prohibitions on the forced extraction of technology from foreign partners. Although the private sector has grown in size and importance, SOEs continue to account for a significant fraction of economic activity and to dominate many key industries. Meanwhile, the party-state has enhanced its ability to oversee and control the activities of even nominally private companies, blurring the dividing line between "public" and "private." Government planners may no longer set most prices or parcel out all scarce materials, but they continue to control the allocation of land and capital, and they play an increasingly prominent role in trying to steer the nation's economy, including by launching ambitious and expensive programs to develop new technologies and promote entire industries.

As evidence of these developments has accumulated, Western observers have struggled to explain them. If the forces propelling liberalization were really so strong, and the advantages so great and so self-evident, why has China deviated from its presumed path towards ever-greater openness? Why has the process of reform slowed, "stalled," or gone into reverse?[1] Has the state truly "struck back," as economist Nicholas Lardy argues,[2] and if so, why and when did this begin to happen?

Various answers to these questions have been proposed, each with its own timeline. Perhaps the Trump-era trade war and the general worsening of US–China relations that accompanied it are largely to blame. Reaching somewhat further back, many analysts highlight the rise of Xi Jinping, with his alleged "leftist" leanings and statist inclinations, to explain the apparent turn in Beijing's economic strategy. Or perhaps the deviation began even earlier, following the turn of the century, when the SOEs and other interest groups that had to accept changes so China could enter the WTO began to reassert themselves and to exert a greater influence over policy.

Each of these explanations tries to fit events into a similar narrative in which an inexorable, linear process of liberalizing reform has occasionally been slowed or disrupted by retrograde forces. In retrospect, however, it is clear that such a process never really existed, at least not so far as Chinese policy-makers were concerned. While some may have been willing to go further than others, no one in the upper reaches of the party-state ever saw themselves as working towards the eventual construction of a Western-style, market-based, capitalist economy. To the contrary, this is an outcome that the Party was determined to prevent. The reasons should be obvious. Proceeding too far in this direction risked undermining the CCP's legitimacy by appearing to abandon its commitment to socialism. More concretely, by creating alternative centers of wealth and power, excessive economic liberalization could weaken the Party's capacity for societal control, clearing the way for China's "peaceful evolution" into a "bourgeois democracy."

In 1982, as economic experimentation was just beginning to get underway, Chen Yun, one of Deng Xiaoping's most influential senior colleagues, argued that the proper way to think about the role of the market was to see it as a bird in a cage. Market forces were dynamic, productive, and needed to be afforded a certain measure of freedom in order to produce their positive effects; but it was crucial that they also be controlled and harnessed to the purposes of the party-state. True to Chen's vision, over the past forty years, the Party has nurtured the market, allowing it to grow and periodically adjusting the dimensions of the cage in which it is contained. But it has never had any intention of letting the bird fly free.

"Mercantilist Leninism"[3]

The CCP's approach to economics is a byproduct of its overarching philosophy of politics. If it is to preserve its monopoly on power, the Party can never relinquish its role in guiding and controlling the national economy. Unlike their liberal democratic counterparts, China's rulers do not have any theoretical or moral commitment to freely functioning markets or private property and they reject the liberal notion that, to the greatest extent possible, politics should be kept separate from economics. As Chen Yun's comment suggests, while markets and private firms may be useful, their role can be expanded or circumscribed as needed to serve the purposes of policy. In the end, however, economics must always be subordinate to politics.

Like the mercantilists of seventeenth- and eighteenth-century Europe, China's rulers do not regard the aim of economic activity as being solely or even primarily to create wealth or promote prosperity for its own sake. Rather, the purpose of both domestic commerce and international trade is to generate power, enhancing the ability of those who wield it to shape the behavior of others and to resist the efforts of others to exert influence over them. The pursuit of wealth and the pursuit of power are thus inextricably linked: wealth provides the means with which to generate and exercise power, and power enables the further accumulation of wealth.

Seen in this light, economic exchange appears not simply as a mutually beneficial activity, as the liberal theorists of free trade and free markets present it, but rather as a domain of struggle, one of the most important dimensions in what must ultimately be a zero-sum game of power politics. This is because, while all nations, organizations, and individuals may be able to become richer at the same time, it is not possible for all of them to grow stronger simultaneously. Power is always relative, and in the long run what matters most is who is more powerful. Despite their rhetoric about "win-win cooperation," China's leaders believe that in any political system, international or domestic, there will always be winners and losers. And each system can have only one "hegemon," one player standing head and shoulders above all the rest. So, working with and through the organs of the state, the CCP pursues economic policies that are intended to maintain and enhance its own power in relation to all other actors in Chinese society, while increasing the power of the Chinese nation in relation to all others in the international system, and especially the present global hegemon: the United States.

This is a challenging task, to say the least. Domestic reform and economic engagement with the West have always been double-edged swords that carry danger as well as opportunity. Expanding the role of the market may help to raise incomes and enhance social stability, but it can also empower potential challengers to CCP rule. Increased trade has accelerated growth, fueling a buildup of China's military capabilities and strengthening its ability to use political influence operations, investment, and other tools of economic statecraft to achieve its strategic objectives. But deepening engagement in the global trading system can also expose the nation to external economic shocks and increase its vulnerability to sanctions, tariffs, export controls, embargos, and leverage attempts by its rivals.

The Party's evolving strategy for growth

Since Deng Xiaoping and Chen Yun, successive groups of CCP leaders have worked to maximize the beneficial impact of at least partial economic liberalization on the power of the Party and the nation while trying to minimize and control the risks. This is a balancing act, requiring ongoing adjustments and continual trade-offs between efficiency and security, and the result at any given moment is always a work in progress. Still, as with its overall strategy for maintaining political control, the Party's economic policies have progressed through four distinct stages:

- Faced with pressing internal and external threats, from the late 1970s to the late 1980s Deng Xiaoping and his colleagues permitted and then encouraged a series of what proved to be highly successful experiments in private ownership and "bottom-up," market-driven growth. During this period, the state retreated and elements of an entrepreneurial, private economy were allowed to emerge.
- Following Tiananmen, the CCP reasserted its role as the architect and engine of national economic development. Contrary to the perceptions and expectations of many Western observers, the 1990s were not marked by steady movement towards an open, market-based economy. Although the private sector expanded, SOEs remained prominent and the party-state implemented policies that directed capital towards investment in infrastructure, promoted the development of manufacturing industries, and encouraged an expansion in Chinese exports. This approach to propelling growth seemed to flag towards the end of the 1990s, but it was given new life after Beijing won admission to the WTO.
- By the time Hu Jintao assumed office in 2002, there was growing concern that, despite its evident success, the prevailing growth model was unsustainable. Most Western (and many Chinese) experts argued that, in order to maintain the nation's forward momentum, the party-state needed to relax its grip, placing ever-greater reliance on private

firms, individual consumers, and market forces. Although it paid lip-service to this approach, by the start of Hu's second five-year term the regime had begun to put into place an alternative model, one in which the party-state would play the leading role in funding and directing "indigenous" technological innovation, thereby reviving growth while at the same time consolidating and extending its control over the economy.

- As in the political domain, Xi Jinping has built on the policies initiated by his predecessor, directing massive additional investments to spur "indigenous innovation" and promote greater technological self-reliance. Under Xi, the party-state has tightened its grip on nominally private firms so as to better harness their dynamism to its purposes. Xi is also working to reduce China's dependence on (and vulnerability to) the advanced industrial democracies by increasing domestic consumption and cultivating markets in the developing world. Whether or not it succeeds in generating renewed growth, this approach cannot accurately be described as representing a dramatic reversal of some previously prevailing trend towards liberalization. Rather it is the latest in a series of attempts to balance the same economic, political, and strategic imperatives that have shaped the CCP's policies since the start of the reform period.

Deng crosses the river

The CCP regime's first moves towards greater reliance on market forces were driven by fear and even desperation. By the time of Mao's death, the nation had been riven by a decade of continual chaos and virtual civil war, leaving the economy in disarray. As many as a quarter of the population, over 200 million people, were unemployed, including millions of students, teachers, scientists, disgraced officials, and ordinary citizens who had been "sent down" to the countryside during the Cultural Revolution and were now eager to return to the cities and resume their lives.[4] On top of all this, China was beginning to feel the effects of its own baby boom, a period of extremely rapid growth in the overall size of its working-age population.[5] Failure to provide food, jobs, and adequate housing for all of these people risked sparking unrest and inflicting potentially fatal damage on the Party's already battered reputation.

Looking outwards, China's leaders recognized that in the race for wealth and power, their country was already lagging and risked falling even further behind. "We have lost a lot of time," Deng warned his colleagues in 1978.[6] If it was to stand up to superpower "hegemonism" and achieve reunification with Taiwan, among other foreign policy goals, the nation had no choice but to press ahead with the "Four Modernizations" (of agriculture, industry, science and technology, and defense). As Deng explained in 1980, modernization was "the essential condition for solving both our domestic and our external problems. . . . The role we play in international affairs is determined by the extent of our economic growth." As for the ultimate goal of demonstrating the superiority of socialism over capitalism, in the long run this would be revealed "first and foremost" by "the rate of economic growth." As a first step towards eventual supremacy, Deng advocated setting the goal of quadrupling the size of China's economy by the turn of the century.[7]

Offsetting these more troubling international trends was the fact that, at least for the moment, China was enjoying a marked warming in its relations with the United States and the other advanced industrial democracies. Indeed, for a brief period, Hua Guofeng, Mao's designated successor, hoped that an influx of Western aid and technology would be enough to jumpstart the economy without having to make any fundamental changes in China's Soviet-style system of central planning. The embarrassing collapse of Beijing's efforts to finance 120 "mega-projects," followed at the end of 1978 by Deng's displacement of Hua at the pinnacle of CCP power, ushered in a decade of intense theoretical debate and far-reaching experimentation.[8]

The central issue under discussion during this period was not whether China should abandon planning altogether in favor of a full market economy, but rather how to define the appropriate relationship between market and state.[9] With some in the Politburo (led by Deng) leaning more towards economic liberalization and others (led by Chen Yun) emphasizing the continuing need for balance and careful coordination, policy tended to fluctuate, with waves of rapid change followed by periods of at least partial retrenchment.

The initial steps in this process were "tentative and exploratory" and, at the outset, policy-makers lacked a clearly defined objective.[10] Despite this, over the course of the 1980s, the overall trend was towards far greater reliance on the market. Dissolving inefficient collectives and permitting farmers to profit from their labors led to sharp increases in productivity and output. Agricultural reform also freed up labor and capital for use in small businesses engaged for the most part in labor-intensive manufacturing. As farming flourished, thousands of so-called "township and village enterprises" (TVs) sprang up across the Chinese countryside. Hungry for foreign exchange and technology, Beijing also permitted the establishment of special economic zones (SEZs) in coastal cities. Here, albeit slowly at first, foreign firms began to invest in plants for the manufacture or final assembly of goods for export.[11]

Yasheng Huang has described the 1980s as China's "entrepreneurial decade," a period characterized by "a version of market-driven, small-scale, and welfare-improving capitalism."[12] Propelled by the unleashing of market forces in the rural sector, annual growth rates skyrocketed, reaching a peak of 15% in 1984 and averaging over 10% for the entire decade.[13] This was an era of "rags-to-riches capitalism" in which the story of China's success was "written by tens of millions of Chinese rural entrepreneurs" who had at last been freed to pursue their own self-interest.[14] For a brief period, the incomes of farmers and rural workers grew faster than those of city-dwellers. Millions of people were lifted out of poverty, not so much by wise and far-sighted policy, as Party propagandists would subsequently claim, but as a result of their own hard work and ingenuity.[15]

Notwithstanding their eventual economic consequences, the innovations of the 1980s were undertaken with considerable caution and a watchful eye on their potential political implications. As Barry Naughton points out, in its first moves towards liberalization the CCP leadership settled on measures that seemed to carry little risk of empowering potential opposition to the Party's rule. Farmers were desperately poor and there were "no powerful agricultural interest groups in the government" that might have gained strength from their improving conditions. Because the TVEs were "small, dispersed, and technologically backward," they were seen as unlikely to pose an immediate challenge to the big, urban-based SOEs. Finally, because they had "no standing to claim political rights or voice," foreign firms were "politically nonthreatening" and could be "penned up inside special zones" where their viability would depend on "special deals with the elite."[16]

Despite its care in "in crossing the river by feeling the stones," as Deng liked to put it, the Party's first steps triggered a rippling cascade of disruptive, destabilizing effects. As rural manufacturers increased in number and started to sell their products to urban consumers, and as small-scale private businesses began to spring up in the cities, many SOEs lost their accustomed monopolies and suffered an erosion in profits. That, in turn, constricted a major source of government revenue, weakening the ability of the party-state to provide public goods such as healthcare, education, and infrastructure and setting the stage for a severe fiscal crisis.[17] The emergence of a market sector created new opportunities for venal officials to enrich themselves, causing corruption to blossom and eroding public confidence in the Party.[18] Rapid growth and the lifting of many price controls also contributed to several bouts of inflation, including one that saw the inflation rate triple, peaking at over 16% in the months before Tiananmen.[19] Along with more abstract demands for freedom, complaints about corruption and fast-rising prices were what brought thousands of demonstrators onto the streets of Chinese cities in the spring of 1989. For all of its economic success, concludes one observer, the opening phase of the reform era "almost led to the fall of the Communist Party."[20]

Jiang engineers a miracle

Tiananmen and its aftermath resulted in a reshuffling of the Party's top leadership and a clarification of the hazards that they faced. CCP General Secretary and former Premier Zhao Ziyang and others who had advocated faster and more far-reaching economic liberalization were purged and their proposals largely, if not entirely, discredited. On the other side of the equation, by 1992 Deng Xiaoping had succeeded in maneuvering his fellow octogenarians into joining him in formal retirement, thereby removing the most obdurate opponents of change, narrowing the range of views in the Politburo, and enhancing the authority of Deng's handpicked heir, Jiang Zemin. Jiang was thus well positioned to formulate and push through a new policy synthesis, one that rebalanced the requirements for growth and control.

The events of the late 1980s provided vivid proof of what could happen if the CCP failed to maintain a sufficiently firm grip on the domestic economy. What came next – the imposition of sanctions by the advanced democracies and the abrupt end of the Cold War quasi-alliance with the United States – highlighted the risks of deepening economic engagement with the West. These developments served as a reminder of something Deng had understood from the start: for all its advantages, "reform and opening up" had significant and potentially perilous downsides.

Like his mentor, Jiang was convinced that the only way to mitigate these dangers was by continuing to move forward. Whatever the risks, rapid progress was essential for the survival of the Party, and the nation. Sustained high rates of growth were, if anything, even more critical to preserving social stability and ensuring continued CCP dominance than they had been before the crisis. As for external threats, America's suspicion and hostility might be muted for the moment but, for a mix of ideological and power-political reasons, the CCP leadership fully expected that they would become more intense with the passage of time. Building up all the elements of China's "comprehensive national power" (CNP) was therefore a matter of urgent necessity.[21] This would require expanding total economic output or gross domestic product (GDP), but also, more specifically, strengthening the nation's industrial base and enhancing its capacity for scientific advance and technological innovation.

Beijing's new, post-Tiananmen approach to economic governance embodied what appear at first glance to be contradictory impulses. On the one hand, the party-state continued to relax controls and to curtail its planning functions, allowing greater scope for market forces, permitting the private sector to prosper, and giving hope to those in the West who believed that China was back on track and headed towards full liberalization. At the same time, even as it retreated further from its previous position as sole owner of the means of production, the regime reinforced portions of the public sector and fashioned new policy instruments that kept it firmly in control of the nation's economic development. As Yasheng Huang explains, far from dwindling, during the 1990s "the power and reach of the state expanded even [as its] ownership role . . . declined."[22]

This bifurcation was reflected in Jiang Zemin's new, double-barreled strategy for sustaining growth. The larger element of this strategy was inward-facing, investment-driven, and dominated by SOEs. The other component was directed outwards, fueled by exports and foreign capital, and animated by private firms, albeit with the assistance, and under the watchful eye, of the party-state.

With Jiang at the helm, the CCP moved quickly to reassert control over the generation and allocation of capital within the Chinese economy. Starting in 1994, changes in tax policy reversed the erosion of revenues that had taken place during the previous decade and put an expanding flow of resources, comprising an increasing fraction of China's rapidly growing GDP, into the hands of the central authorities.[23] The state's monopolization of the banking sector also enabled it to implement a policy of financial repression. With nowhere else to invest, ordinary Chinese citizens had little choice but to put their savings into state banks, which paid them virtually no interest, while loaning their money at attractive low rates to businesses favored by officials.[24] Having used the tax and banking systems to extract resources, the party-state proceeded to steer them primarily into investment in infrastructure and construction, most of it in urban areas, and with virtually all of the work performed by SOEs.

Wasteful and inefficient, the SOEs nevertheless produced most of the nation's steel, aluminum, cement, and other basic materials, built out the transportation, telecommunications, and power generation networks needed to sustain further growth, and provided employment and, in many cases, healthcare, education, and other benefits to millions of workers and their families. By the turn of the century, SOEs were still responsible for three-quarters of all investment, two-thirds of total assets, and more than half of urban employment.[25] Broadly defined to include the state-owned banks, non-financial SOEs, and direct government expenditures, the state sector at this point accounted for fully 45% of GDP, with roughly half of that figure contributed by the non-financial SOEs.[26] In contrast to the bottom-up process of the 1980s, in which the motive force came primarily from rural entrepreneurs, this was a top-down, urban-focused, investment-heavy model of growth, propelled by large enterprises, all at the direction of a revitalized "technocratic state."[27]

During the 1990s, the CCP regime also actively promoted the development of an export sector made up mostly of private manufacturing companies, many of which received funding from overseas. Although the private sector played a greater part here, the role of the state was still decisive. New exchange regulations enabled foreign direct investment to grow from an amount equal to less than 1% of China's total output during the 1980s to a high of 6% in 1993–4 before declining to roughly 4% of a fast-rising GDP for the remainder of the decade.[28] Most of this money went to build factories and other facilities in coastal cities. To staff them, as well as filling positions in the public sector, the CCP put in place policies that helped to mobilize a vast army of cheap labor. By redirecting investment away from the countryside, the regime constricted opportunities for employment in TVEs or small private businesses, forcing workers into the cities, where they competed with one another for low-wage jobs.[29] Finally, starting in 1994 and continuing for over a decade, the government intervened to hold down the value of the yuan and, with it, the price of Chinese exports. The combination of foreign capital, cheap labor, and an undervalued currency helped drive the initial stage of China's emergence as a manufacturing powerhouse and a leading exporter of manufactured goods. Between 1992 and 2000, China's share of total world manufacturing output increased from 4% to roughly 8% (surpassing Germany), while its share of manufactured exports grew from 2.4% to 4.5%.[30] Net exports also became a significant contributor to overall growth, rising to 4.5% of GDP in 1997 and averaging around 2.7% for the period 1994–2000.[31]

China's increasing reliance on Western markets and capital meant that, at least in theory, it was becoming more susceptible to sanctions of the sort it had faced after Tiananmen. While they recognized the danger, it did not take long for the CCP leadership to conclude that these risks were manageable despite the more mixed and unstable character of their post-Cold War relationship with the United States. Recent experience had proven that, even in the face of blatant, brutal, and large-scale violations of human rights, neither the Americans nor their major allies had much appetite for a sustained campaign of economic pressure against China. In light of the outcome of the 1994 battle over MFN status, Beijing also had reason to feel confident that it could count on its friends in US industry and finance to oppose further leverage attempts by their government. More generally, the CCP regime assessed that the best way of avoiding future sanctions was by cultivating ever-closer ties with the United States, "talking up the economy" in its post-Tiananmen propaganda, encouraging more investment, holding out the promise of profits to American companies, and creating the perception, if not the reality, that the two countries had become equally dependent on one another for their future prosperity.[32]

Deepening economic engagement with the advanced democracies had other benefits that helped to offset its potential strategic hazards. Foreign companies seeking to establish production facilities in China often entered into joint ventures with local partners to whom, willingly or otherwise, they transferred technology, management techniques, and other forms of useful knowledge. In addition to being a source of capital, foreign investment was thus a vital part of China's state-directed efforts to close the technological gap with the West.

Zhu Rongji and the transition illusion

During his second five-year term, Jiang Zemin oversaw two related initiatives that further fueled what proved to be misplaced optimism about the direction of China's development. Following his elevation to the premiership at the end of 1997, Zhu Rongji implemented a major downsizing of the public sector, closing or selling off thousands of small, wasteful SOEs, restructuring the bureaucracies charged with managing them, and pushing millions of workers off the state's payroll. These measures aimed to cut costs, increase efficiency, and boost sagging growth rates but, contrary to the interpretation of many Western observers, they were not meant to be the next steps in "a long and yet-to-be accomplished journey" that would culminate eventually in China's transformation into a "fully-fledged market economy."[33]

Despite his reputation in the West as a "heroic"[34] or "brazen"[35] reformer, Zhu was, in fact, "an inveterate planner,"[36] "obsessed with the imperative of using the state's all-too-visible hand to guide market forces."[37] He was more willing than some to use those forces to impose discipline and improve efficiency. But, as journalist Richard McGregor has pointed out, Zhu and his more cautious colleagues were united in their desire to "consolidate and strengthen the power of the Party and the state, not let it wither away," and in their belief that the party-state "should maintain control of the commanding heights of the economy."[38]

The other half of Zhu's policy of "letting go the small" was a determination to "grasp the big," consolidating and providing various forms of government assistance to large SOEs in so-called "lifeline" and "pillar" industries such as electronics, steel, autos, aviation, and telecommunications. In many of these sectors, the government picked multiple "winners," pitting them against each other to sharpen their competitive reflexes. But Zhu's ultimate aim was to streamline and strengthen the state sector, building up a "national team" of over a hundred enterprises capable of fending off foreign competitors at home while beginning to carve out shares of the global market. This was reform of a sort, even if it was not what most Westerners had in mind when they used the word.

The need to prepare for intensifying international economic competition points to Zhu's second signature achievement: his negotiation of an agreement with the United States that made possible China's entry into the WTO. Despite fears that, in Jiang Zemin's words, "some countries" were trying to "take advantage" of globalization in order to "force their own values, economic regime, and social systems on other countries," by the second half of the 1990s the CCP leadership recognized that they had little choice but to partake more actively in the process.[39] Even the 1997 Asian financial crisis, which hit China less hard than other countries that had proceeded further down the path towards economic integration, failed to alter this basic assessment. If anything, the desire to boost trade and investment to help offset the aftereffects of the crisis reinforced Beijing's determination to join the WTO.[40] As Jiang explained in a 1998 speech, globalization was "an objective tendency . . . independent of man's will and cannot be avoided by any country."[41] Rather than stand aside and let the United States exploit prevailing trends to tip the balance of power further in its favor, the regime needed to turn them to its own ends.

Shedding inefficient firms while strengthening a core of SOEs in critical sectors was one part of this program. Joining the WTO was the other. The agreement that finally enabled Beijing's accession exposed some sectors of the Chinese economy to the bracing effects of international competition. But it also provided substantial immediate benefits, including assured access to Western markets and capital, in return for what were often little more than China's promises eventually to lift remaining tariff and non-tariff barriers to its own markets, better protect intellectual property, and cease subsidies, among other liberalizing measures.[42] Chinese officials may not have foreseen all of the ways in which it could be manipulated, but the agreement that they ultimately signed provided ample room for maneuver and left them well positioned to continue setting the terms of the country's economic engagement with the rest of the world.

The policies of the Jiang Zemin era did not represent the next stage in an ineluctable process of "transition," but rather a remodeling of the "cage" in which the market was permitted to function. While it was true that the cage had been enlarged in certain respects, its bars had also been strengthened. The regime took care to ensure that it remained firmly in charge, able to extract the benefits of rapid growth from an increasingly large and complex economy while containing the attendant domestic and international political risks.

Hu at the crossroads

China's entry into the WTO at the end of 2001 was greeted with applause and optimism in Western capitals, where it was widely seen as an inflection point in an accelerating and now irreversible process of domestic economic liberalization. In the words of one characteristic assessment, WTO membership would compel China "to comply with the principles and rules of the international trading system," give its "reform-oriented leadership" a lever that it could use "to complete the transition to a more market-oriented economy," and open up "enormous . . . commercial opportunities for foreign firms" while contributing to "the further transformation of the domestic economy."[43]

These conclusions reflected an understandable, if also a rather naïve, belief that Beijing intended to live up to the letter of the agreement it had just signed. But they were also rooted in a deeper misapprehension about the forces at play within the CCP regime. Even a presumed reformer like Zhu Rongji was no liberal, nor, as events would prove, was he backed by a high-level leadership faction determined to press ahead and complete China's "transition" to a full market economy. What one skeptical economist described at the time as the "attractive vision of China's economy rolling downhill towards a market outcome" was soon revealed to be an illusion.[44]

During their ten-year reign (2002–12), Hu Jintao and Wen Jiabao continued to reap the fruits of Jiang and Zhu's investment- and export-driven growth model, but they were also forced to confront its increasingly obvious limitations. In searching for an alternative, they considered but

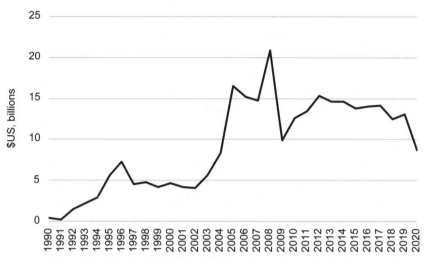

Figure 4.1 US foreign direct investment flows to China
Source: https://www.us-china-investment.org/fdi-data

ultimately rejected policies that would have placed more reliance on market forces in favor of those that further enhanced the power of the party-state.

The effects of Beijing's being granted permanent normal trade status by the United States and its subsequent accession to the WTO at the end of 2001 were abrupt and massive. With the removal of any lingering threat of Congressional sanction, China's desirability as a platform for the export of low-cost manufactured goods was assured.[45] Foreign direct investment from the United States and other countries, most of it in manufacturing, increased almost overnight, tripling during the first decade of the new millennium (see Figure 4.1).[46] Fueled by infusions of foreign capital and technology, China's share of world manufacturing output quadrupled over the same period, catapulting it past the United States into the position of the biggest producer of manufactured goods on the planet. Meanwhile, from the turn of the century until the onset of the global financial crisis in 2007–8, Chinese exports grew at 30% per year, quintupling in (dollar-denominated) value and making it the world's largest exporter, surpassing the United States.[47]

China's post-Tiananmen GDP growth had been impressive but it had also slowed steadily over the course of the 1990s, falling from a peak of

14% in 1992–3 to around 8% by the turn of the century. WTO accession helped supercharge the economy, propelling growth rates back up to a peak of 14% in 2007–8 (see Figure 4.2).[48] The relative importance of trade as a driver of overall national economic growth also increased markedly, with net exports increasing from around 2% of GDP at the turn of the century to over 8.5% on the eve of the financial crisis.[49] Capital investment also continued to expand, growing from 35% of GDP in 2000 to 40% in 2007 and then increasing by another 5 percentage points over the next two years.[50] As a global recession took hold and exports declined, the government unleashed a huge program of additional infrastructure investment to pick up the slack, stimulating demand, and preventing an even worse slowdown than the one that actually occurred.

The stunning success of the old model in the runup to the Great Recession concealed its shortcomings and limitations for a time but, even before the crisis hit, it was evident to many observers that, as Premier Wen put it in a 2007 speech, China's growth was "unstable, unbalanced . . . and unsustainable."[51] Among its other flaws, the existing "rough and quantity-based" approach to promoting development was exacerbating income inequality and defiling the natural environment at an extraordinary pace.[52] Demographic trends meant that the seemingly endless stream of young, low-wage workers would soon begin to slow. Although indications of an impending "demographic transition" to a rapidly aging society tended to be downplayed or dismissed by Chinese officials during the early 1990s, by the turn of the century the reality "could no longer be doubted."[53] Meanwhile, China's rapid growth was increasing its dependence on imported energy, natural resources, and food, potentially heightening its strategic vulnerability.[54]

Most worrisome of all, the old export and investment model was clearly nearing the limits of its ability to generate the jobs and income growth needed to maintain social stability and secure CCP rule. The investment share of GDP had now risen to unprecedented heights and, in contrast to the experience of the other major Asian industrial powers, it showed no indication of receding. Massive, state-directed investment was driving debt to previously unseen levels, increasing the risk of a future financial crisis.[55] Meanwhile, the allocation of resources to many redundant and unnecessary projects meant that the overall efficiency of investment spending was starting to drop. Especially in the wake of

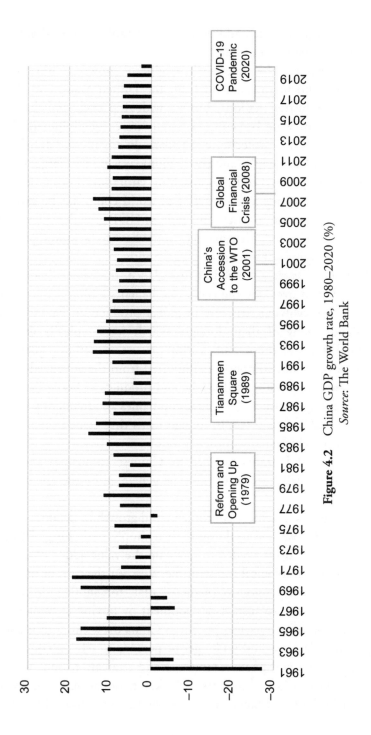

Figure 4.2 China GDP growth rate, 1980–2020 (%)
Source: The World Bank

the financial crisis, each additional unit of capital invested generated a smaller increment of output.[56]

As for exports, the other main engine of growth, China remained heavily dependent on demand from the United States and the other advanced industrial nations, but its widening trade imbalances with many of them were becoming a major source of diplomatic friction, raising the risk of a protectionist backlash. In any event, China's exports had expanded so rapidly, and their volume was now so large, that existing markets appeared to be approaching saturation. Future demand for Chinese-made goods in the developed world could not be expected to increase fast enough to sustain the rates of GDP growth achieved during the previous decade.[57] New markets would have to be found, presumably in the developing nations of the global South.

Impressive as they seemed at first glance, traditional trade statistics also tended to overstate the economic benefits China derived from its place in the evolving structure of global production. Factories on the mainland, many of them foreign-owned, were typically engaged in the final stages of the manufacturing process, assembling goods out of complex parts and components imported from the advanced industrial nations and then either selling the end products at home or exporting them to foreign markets.[58] Chinese companies also frequently had to pay royalties and licensing fees to foreign firms that owned the intellectual property on which many of these products were based.[59] As a result, the value added and profits retained by Chinese companies and workers were only a small fraction of the total generated by the sale of finished goods.[60]

If China was to achieve continued rapid growth in incomes and living standards, if it wanted to do more than simply settle for globalization's table scraps, its firms needed to move up the value-added chain by narrowing the technological gap with the West. At the turn of the century, one government economist predicted that, for another decade or so, "we can continue to sustain development by buying technology rather than developing it ourselves."[61] But as China drew closer to the technological frontier, it would no longer be possible to rely on companies (or countries) that had good commercial and strategic reasons to want to retain their existing advantages. As a key national planning document warned in 2006: "[E]xperience shows us that we cannot buy true core technologies in the key fields that affect the lifeblood of the national economy and national security."[62]

Chinese policy-makers were acutely aware of all these challenges and, from the start of Hu Jintao's administration, they sought to deal with them by advancing along two parallel tracks: on the one hand, by trying to readjust the mix of investment, consumption, and net exports in the nation's economy and, on the other, by embracing a form of high-tech industrial policy that called for government planners to boost growth by identifying and supporting the development of cutting-edge technologies and promoting what were described as "strategic emerging industries." The first of these pathways proved to be a dead end, not for lack of a compelling economic rationale, but because it would have required the regime to surrender a significant additional increment of its power to market forces and private economic actors. By contrast, the second approach had the decisive advantage of preserving and, indeed, enhancing the party-state's role in shaping national economic development.

In keeping with the advice of most Western experts, at the end of 2004 the CCP formally declared its intention to transform the nation's growth model, reducing dependence on investment and net exports and shifting to greater reliance on household consumption.[63] Yet, by the time Hu left office at the end of 2012, none of these variables had moved in the desired direction. Indeed, to the contrary, the investment share of GDP was larger, consumption was smaller, and, after rising rapidly, net exports had fallen back to roughly where they were in 2002.[64]

The financial crisis and its aftermath were partly to blame for this pattern but, in truth, the policy of "rebalancing" was dead on arrival. Economist John Lee points out that the necessary measures were widely understood and had been "continually proposed by . . . investment banks and [international] organizations."[65] Yet, in the end, the CCP was unwilling to run the risks associated with their implementation. To take the most obvious and important example: if the regime had been sufficiently committed to reducing excess investment, it could have cut subsidies, permitted market forces to determine interest rates, and freed the banks to make loans based strictly on expected financial returns. But this would have weakened one of its most powerful tools for boosting growth, likely killing off more SOEs, raising unemployment, and endangering plans to build national champions. Similarly, allowing market forces to determine the exchange rate would have caused the yuan to appreciate in value, increasing imports and cutting exports. This would have reduced trade imbalances, but relaxing controls on financial flows would also have risked triggering capital flight of the sort that had destabilized the economies and societies of China's neighbors during the Asian financial crisis.

Instead of letting go and trusting the market, the CCP chose yet again to reinforce its grip, prioritizing its own security over the single-minded pursuit of efficiency. While contemporary observers in the West were inclined to explain it away as a rearguard action, the product of "unorganized foot-dragging and resistance" by recalcitrant interest groups, in fact this outcome was the result of a series of deliberate strategic decisions by the regime's top leadership.[66] As Andrew Batson has demonstrated, the CCP's stubborn attachment to a state-controlled financial system, SOEs, and investment-driven growth was "neither a historical accident nor the unintended result of other factors, but an ongoing policy choice."[67]

"Indigenous innovation"

It is precisely for these reasons that the second formula for economic rejuvenation proved so appealing. Even before the hand-off from Jiang to Hu, a few astute observers like the economist Thomas Rawski had noted a trend towards "resurgent statism," a renewed inclination to concentrate resources and decision-making power in the hands of the party-state.[68] These tendencies grew even stronger and more visible once China had entered the WTO and after Hu and Wen assumed office in 2003. While hopeful foreign observers waited for "the 'penetrating power' of economic globalization and the increasing exogenous pressures for neoliberal economic reform" to work their effects, the party-state was taking steps to bolster its capacity for control.[69] Among other measures, the Hu–Wen team created two powerful new agencies: one responsible for overseeing the management of all SOEs and the other with enhanced authority to coordinate implementation of the Party's five-year plans.[70] With Premier Wen personally in the lead, the regime also began to lay the ground for a high-tech industrial policy that would eventually become the main engine and defining feature of the nation's new growth strategy.

As at every other major turning point, the Party's decision to push for "indigenous innovation" was the product of a mix of anxiety and ambition, a "fear of foreign domination" combined with the "desire to be a leader."[71] If it was to sustain forward progress, China could not continue for much longer to rely on ever-greater injections of capital and labor. Future growth would depend on improvements in efficiency and productivity, and these, in turn, would require major advances in technology. But here too the old ways would no longer suffice. Over two decades of relying on foreign technology had left the nation dependent on the West, lagging further behind in many areas, and confined to the lower links of global value chains. If it wanted to close the gap and move up the ladder, China needed to develop its own technologies, set its own standards, and control its own intellectual property. Commercial competition aside, foreign (and especially US) suppliers could not be relied upon to provide the technologies essential to the modernization of China's military. For all of these reasons, the need for indigenous innovation seemed "self-evident."[72]

In 2006, after three years of intensive debate, the regime unveiled its National Medium- and Long-Term Program for Science and Technology Development (MLP, 2006–20). Despite its anodyne title, the MLP was announced in language that put it on par with "reform and opening up" as one of the "two main drivers" of China's future growth.[73] Together with some general targets (including a 30% reduction in dependence on foreign technology by 2020), the MLP outlined a strategy for "leapfrogging in priority fields," gaining a march on foreign competitors not only through "original innovation" but also via the "assimilation and absorption of imported technology."[74] Although the document initially received scant attention in the West, this language did catch the eye of a few careful observers, such as China-based analyst James McGregor, who noted that it could be read as "a blueprint for technology theft on a scale the world has never seen before."[75] Several years later, an independent US commission would conclude that the MLP had indeed provided the "justification for greater theft of foreign-generated IP [intellectual property]," helping to create a problem that had grown to "unprecedented" dimensions.[76]

If the global financial crisis dealt a death blow to attempts at rebalancing, it imparted new energy and focus to the pursuit of indigenous innovation. Barry Naughton concludes that, among its other effects, the crisis boosted the confidence of Chinese policy-makers in the superiority of their own unique system of "vigorous, coordinated, top-down measures" over the American model of "complete marketization."[77] The need to stimulate the economy also freed up significant additional resources, some of which flowed into what became known as the Strategic Emerging Industries (SEI) program.

Announced in 2009, in the immediate aftermath of the crisis, the SEI program was a large and ambitious initiative that went well beyond the more traditional "megaprojects" funded under the MLP.[78] Instead of targeting specific end products, like passenger jets and nuclear reactors, planners identified seven broad industrial sectors (energy generation, energy-saving technologies, information technology, biology, high-end manufacturing equipment, new materials, and new-energy autos) that they regarded as critical to the nation's future economic development and to the international competitiveness of both state-owned and private companies.[79] Together with direct funding, the government unleashed a "veritable blizzard of new policies"[80] designed to encourage the development of targeted industries, including procurement regulations giving preference to domestic firms, standards requirements and other non-tariff barriers to keep out foreign rivals, and patent laws designed to protect Chinese companies accused in the West of violating intellectual property rights.[81] These measures were intended to help create favorable domestic conditions in which both public and private enterprises could become stronger and better prepared for international competition. The ultimate aim was nothing less than to catapult China into a position of leadership in the most important emerging industries of the twenty-first century, or, in the Party's preferred martial idiom, to "seize the commanding heights of the new technological revolution."[82]

By the end of Hu's second term, most of the elements of a new, technology-driven growth model had begun to come into view. Puzzled by the apparent lack of attention being paid to China's emerging industrial policies, two scholars concluded in 2013 that most Western observers were inclined to overlook or dismiss them because they did not conform to the prevailing "plan-to-market narrative that focuses on the purportedly universal, or convergent, macro-processes of marketization, economic liberalization, and privatization."[83] It would take several more years of increasingly aggressive and overtly mercantilist behavior by Beijing for this reassuring narrative to lose its persuasive power.

Xi recasts the cage

Given how things have turned out, it is ironic but unsurprising that Xi Jinping's accession to power should have been greeted with yet another wave of confident prognostications about the inevitability of economic liberalization.[84] After a decade of unsuccessful attempts at rebalancing, set back even further by the necessity of responding to the financial crisis, the limits of the old model seemed finally to have been reached. With growth slowing, debt soaring, and investment at an all-time high, surely there was no alternative to pressing ahead and finally making the transition to a more fully market-based economy? China's leaders did not entirely reject this assessment of the nation's problems but, as events would prove, they came to very different conclusions than most foreign analysts about how best to deal with them.

In certain respects, the view from Beijing was even darker than it appeared in Western capitals. Xi Jinping and his colleagues were well aware that if they failed to boost productivity, they risked falling into the dreaded "middle-income trap." As it exhausted some of its initial advantages, China, like most other countries that had relied on plentiful cheap labor, imported technology, and exports of low-end manufactured goods to fuel the early stages of their development, could find itself permanently consigned to slow growth and relatively low levels of per capita income.[85] The impending contraction of the nation's working-age population, a trend that became visible for the first time in 2012, raised fears that, without major increases in output per worker, China would "grow old before it could get rich."[86] For the PRC's new rulers, the possible implications of these trends for social stability and regime survival were, as always, top of mind.

Optimism in the West that Xi might finally be an agent for positive change ran strong, fueled by early perceptions of him as a "reformer" (and perhaps even a closet liberal), by various reports and proposals in circulation during his first year in office, and by the belief that, in the end, he had no choice but to proceed towards economic liberalization. Somewhat more concretely, at the end of 2013 the CCP unveiled a document outlining the new leadership's initial decisions on "Major Issues Concerning Comprehensively Deepening Reforms." Capping a detailed sixty-point action program was the promise that, henceforth, the role that market forces played in the allocation of national resources would be elevated from "basic" to "decisive."[87] But this bold and seemingly revolutionary proclamation was accompanied by another. Even as they pledged to elevate the role of the market, the Party's leaders also declared their determination to "unwaveringly consolidate and develop the publicly owned economy, persist in the dominant role of the public ownership system, give rein to the leading role of the state-owned economy, [and] incessantly strengthen the vitality, control and influence of the state-owned economy."[88]

To the extent that they noticed it at all, most Western analysts tended to dismiss this second statement as either tired, empty, and ultimately meaningless "CCP-speak," a nod to the interests of the SOEs, or, most likely, a symptom of the intellectual incoherence of the new regime's approach to economic policy. In fact, as a few observers noted at the time, and as has become more obvious since, the contradiction between the new regime's determination to elevate the role of market forces and its fealty to the state sector was more apparent than real. As journalist Peter Martin pointed out, "[P]ro-market reforms and moves to maintain a significant role for the state in the economy . . . are perfectly consistent in the eyes of the Xi administration."[89] China's new leader was prepared to make some significant adjustments in the relationship between the market and the party-state, albeit not the ones that advocates of liberalization had hoped for and predicted.

Instead of expanding the role of the market at the expense of the state, as conventional, linear conceptions of "reform" or "transition" envision, under Xi the CCP has sought to strengthen, and to increase its control over, *both* the private and the public sectors. On the one hand, as promised, the central authorities have worked "incessantly" to bolster the SOEs, not only by providing them with resources but also by attempting to make them more efficient through a mix of top-down direction and market discipline. State planners have reduced some of the nation's overinvestment in heavy industry by ordering the closure of excess capacity while at the same time brokering "mega-mergers" of SOEs that increase economies of scale and create bigger and presumably more competitive "national champions."[90] Policy-makers have also tried to add "market-like" incentives to improve the performance of SOEs by creating new funding mechanisms that reward managers for achieving good results.[91]

Notwithstanding the regime's preoccupation with the public sector, by some estimates the non-state segment of the economy now accounts for 60% of China's GDP, 70% of its innovation, 80% of urban employment, and 90% of new employment.[92] In an acknowledgement of these realities, under Xi Jinping the CCP has also looked for new ways to promote the fortunes of private firms and to guide them in directions that will allow the Party and the nation to benefit from their superior capacity for technological innovation. These mechanisms include investment funds that channel state capital to private companies in targeted sectors, an expansion of the role of CCP cells in the management of nominally private firms, and a program intended to increase private sector involvement in defense-related research and weapons development.[93] The Party has also not hesitated to crack the whip when necessary to bring the private sector to heel, including through the introduction of sweeping new regulatory measures to redirect the activities of China's biggest high-tech firms and periodic prosecutions of entrepreneurs perceived as oppositional, or overly independent.[94]

By blurring the dividing lines between the public and private spheres, the CCP is, in classic Leninist fashion, asserting its dominance over both. The result is a new synthesis, what Jude Blanchette has described as a "hybrid political market economy,"[95] in which the presumed distinctions between public and private, state and market no longer apply. Instead of one advancing while the other retreats, as a popular aphorism might suggest, both can, at least in theory, advance together. At Xi's direction, the party-state is attempting to organize a truly whole-of-nation effort, one that taps into both the public and the nominally private sectors, mobilizing all the resources of society in pursuit of the CCP's consistent, core strategic objectives: preserving its own rule while enhancing the power of the Chinese nation.

This is a program of breathtaking scope and the policies that support it are equally ambitious. To achieve its ends, the regime seeks nothing less than to transform China into the world's most innovative and technologically advanced nation, to restructure its domestic economy, and to reshape its commercial relations with the rest of the world.

Seizing the "commanding heights"

Xi Jinping has more than doubled down on Hu Jintao's technology pro-motion policies, making them the centerpiece of his economic strategy and effectively betting the nation's future, the Party's, and his own on their success. For him, science and technology are the key to meeting every challenge, the foundation on which "the country relies for its power, enterprises rely for success, and people rely for a better life."[96] In order to take "the commanding heights of science and technology," during his first years in office Xi rolled out three major initiatives in rapid succession.[97]

"Made in China 2025" (MIC 2025), unveiled in 2015, focused on helping both SOEs and, to a greater extent than had been true of previous plans, private firms to master productivity-enhancing "smart manufacturing technologies," including robots, advanced machine tools, new materials, and next-generation information systems. Thanks in part to the surprising candor with which it described its goals, this plan aroused understandable anxiety in the advanced industrial world. Chinese policy-makers clearly envisioned a strategy of import substitu-tion, using subsidies, local content requirements, and other protective measures to build up public and private enterprises, helping domestic manufacturers to squeeze out foreign competitors and claim numerically specified shares of the Chinese market before unleashing them to capture substantial portions of the global market as well (see Figure 4.3).[98]

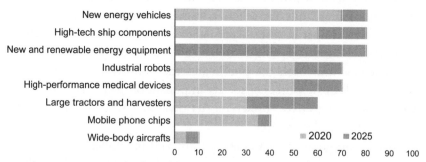

Figure 4.3   Made in China 2025: semi-official import substitution targets for
the domestic market share of Chinese products (%)
Source: Reproduced with permission from Mercator Institute for China Studies
(*https://merics.org/en/report/made-china-2025*)

The goals of the 2016 "Innovation-Driven Development Strategy" (IDDS) are even more far-reaching. This is a unified plan designed to integrate existing programs (including MIC 2025), so that the CCP can achieve its stated aim of transforming China into the world's leading "science and technology innovation power" by the year 2050.[99] Naughton argues that, in contrast to previous plans targeting a "grab bag of sectors," the IDDS is underpinned by a specific theory of economic development. Chinese planners believe that, thanks to the convergence of rapid advances in communications, data, and artificial intelligence, the world is in the initial stages of a new technological and industrial revolution. Like earlier disruptive transformations, this one has the potential to reshuffle the global hierarchy of wealth and power, providing China with a "once-in-a-lifetime opportunity to get in on the ground floor . . . and vault into the leading ranks of economic and technological powers."[100]

As befits the urgency and importance of its goals, under the rubric of "market-led, government-guided" development, this plan has unleashed an unprecedented flood of funds, flowing through various channels to both public and private enterprises.[101] "Cross holding" or mixed-ownership provisions encourage a "mutual fusion" of public and "social" or private capital, enabling SOEs to acquire shares in innovative private companies and vice versa.[102] Specialized "Industrial Guidance Funds" have also been established to raise money from public and private sources and to invest it in all types of enterprises working in sectors prioritized by the state. Naughton estimates that these funds have already been authorized to raise $1.6 trillion, a figure equal to over 10% of China's GDP, making this "the greatest single commitment of government resources to an industrial policy objective in history."[103] The IDDS has also reportedly helped to "turbocharge" China's existing programs for acquiring foreign technology, whether through the purchase of foreign companies, joint research projects, or via cyber- and more traditional forms of industrial espionage.[104]

Finally, in 2017 Xi's overall strategy was supplemented by a "Special Plan for Science and Technology Military–Civil Fusion Development." This document calls for an intensification and acceleration of ongoing attempts to knit together the various pieces of the national innovation system, public and private, military and commercial.[105] Joint research and development projects and more "two-way open sharing" of resources (including scientists and engineers) are intended to accelerate progress in all domains, enabling China to dominate the "new round of scientific and technological revolutions, industrial changes, and military revolutions."[106] Left unspoken is the possibility that, along with their other contributions, private Chinese companies and research institutions might be able to acquire militarily relevant "dual-use" technologies from unwitting foreign counterparts.[107]

The intensity of China's push to gain the "commanding heights" of high technology, and its evident willingness to use any means necessary in order to do so, have begun to provoke alarmed reactions from the United States and, increasingly, other advanced industrial nations. Rather than persuading it to back off, however, this response has served to justify an even more aggressive approach from Beijing. Under Donald Trump, the US government enhanced scrutiny of proposed investments by Chinese companies and state-sponsored "talent recruitment" programs, imposed restrictions on the export of certain critical technologies to China, and attempted to force changes in Beijing's predatory technology acquisition policies by levying tariffs.[108] The Biden administration has left most of these policies in place, and is working hard to persuade US allies to adopt similar measures.[109]

If the advanced industrial nations can coordinate their policies, Beijing's efforts to escape the risk of a technological "blockade" could well become a self-fulfilling prophecy. Because of China's continuing dependence on the West for high-end semiconductors and other "choke-point" technologies, the results could be damaging, at least in the short run. Rather than attempting to de-escalate, however, Xi Jinping has done the opposite, declaring his intention to achieve "self-reliance" in "core technologies" and promising to mobilize even more resources to achieve this goal.[110]

"Dual circulation"

Recent events have highlighted an additional cause for anxiety and given added impetus to the CCP's ongoing attempts to address it. China's reliance on the United States and the other advanced democracies as sources of demand for its exports remains high, although it has diminished since the turn of the century. In 2017, the United States and Europe each absorbed roughly 20% of China's exports, with Japan and South Korea together accounting for another 10%.[111]

This degree of dependence is concerning to Chinese strategists. Even before the sharp rise in tensions over trade, some analysts were warning that, as its own industries moved up the value-added chain, China's relations with the United States and other advanced economies would shift, as one put it in 2014, "from complementarity . . . to competitiveness."[112] The likely saturation of Western markets, and the possibility of rising protectionism, meant that China would need to secure other markets in order to sustain its own growth.

The recent tariff war with the United States, the possibility of growing trade friction with Europe, and the general disruption in global commerce caused by the COVID-19 pandemic have transformed concerns over the adequacy of demand into a high-priority issue, one that Xi is proposing to address with his so-called "dual-circulation" strategy. Although the details have yet to be worked out, this approach calls for significant adjustments in the structure of China's domestic economy (the "inner loop"), the pattern of its international trade (the "outer loop"), and the relationship between the two.

Returning to a goal that has proven elusive in the past, Chinese planners aim to increase the relative importance of domestic demand as a driver of future growth by boosting household consumption. This is the evolutionary path that most of today's advanced industrial nations followed once they reached a certain level of development; it makes sense from a purely economic perspective and, as we have seen, it is something that the regime has wanted to do for the better part of two decades. In the case of China, however, this will be a deliberate, state-directed process, the result, in Xi Jinping's words, of "a strategic choice to reshape my country's new advantages."[113]

Whereas in the past China sought to rebalance its economy in order to reduce overinvestment and ease diplomatic friction by cutting its trade surplus, today both its motives and its methods are the products of geopolitical calculation.[114] As Jude Blanchette and Andrew Polk point out, increasing reliance on domestic demand is part of a larger effort to "reduce external vulnerabilities" and shield China from "rising global uncertainty and an increasingly hostile external environment."[115] At the same time as it boosts demand, Beijing intends to increase the capacity of domestic producers to supply it, proceeding with plans for import substitution and using what Xi and others refer to as China's "ultra-large-scale market" to fuel the growth of emerging industries.[116]

Chinese planners are also focused, in Xi's words, on "maintain[ing] the safety of the supply chain,"[117] minimizing dependence on imports of energy and food, as well as technology, and, to the extent possible, developing an indigenous, top-to-bottom, "full-set industrial system" capable of manufacturing all the parts of many products.[118] At the same time, Beijing hopes to maintain its leverage over the advanced industrial countries, discouraging them from restructuring their own supply chains and reducing their dependence on China by preserving its position as a preferred platform for low-cost manufacturing. Once again, the motives are strategic rather than purely commercial. As Xi explained in 2020 to a high-level meeting of economic planners, "[W]e must tighten international production chains' dependence on China, forming a powerful countermeasure and deterrent capability against foreigners who would artificially cut off supply [to us]."[119]

As regards the "outer loop," China's leaders have no intention of completely turning their back on the West and will try to preserve access to its markets and technology for as long as possible. In the long run, however, they seek to shift a greater portion of the nation's trade towards countries over which they are confident they can exert a decisive political influence. In the near term, this will involve deepening relations with the more congenial of its advanced industrial neighbors.[120] More broadly, Beijing is trying to use the gravitational pull of its massive market to put itself at the center of a regional economic system, perhaps using trade agreements to build what one Shanghai-based academic has recently described as a "self-contained Asia-Pacific supply chain."[121] As another scholar explains, China's goal should be to "further replace the United States, Europe and Japan" as the major trading partner for all the countries in the region "so that East Asia gradually develops into an interdependent and relatively independent production chain." Because China will be much more important to its smaller partners than they are to it, Beijing can then "use this asymmetric dependence for political influence."[122] Some strategists speculate that the threat of economic marginalization would put intense pressure on Japan, forcing it to become more attentive to China's wishes and to distance itself from the United States.[123]

Looking further afield, Chinese planners have for some time stressed the economic potential of the developing countries along the main axes of its Belt and Road Initiative (BRI). Depending on which ones are included, these countries may already comprise close to two-thirds of the world's people and nearly one-third of its total GDP. Given the size of their collective population and their current low level of advancement, the developing nations of Southeast Asia, Africa, and the other parts of the global South could become a major driver of world economic growth in the coming decades.[124] In addition to gaining more secure access to natural resources, a prime purpose of BRI is to put China in the strongest possible position to exploit this potential.

As big as it undoubtedly is, BRI is only one piece of a larger strategy whose aim, in the words of journalist James Crabtree, appears to be nothing less than "the gradual creation of a new economic 'sinosphere,' in which global networks of trade and innovation that once focused on the industrialized West flow back and forth to China instead."[125] As for the United States, in 2017 Premier Li Keqiang reportedly told a group of visiting high-level American officials that its future role in the global economy "would merely be to provide China with raw materials, agricultural products, and energy to fuel its production of the world's cutting-edge industrial and consumer products."[126]

Conclusion

Most Western experts have been trained to think that the structure of the global economy is (or should be) shaped by the principle of comparative advantage and that large-scale changes in technology and industry come in waves of "creative destruction" too powerful for any single actor to control. In light of these beliefs, the idea that China under Xi Jinping is trying deliberately to steer progress, reshuffle the international pecking order of scientific and technological achievement, and restructure the global economy appears absurdly audacious, if not completely mad.

While there are many reasons to question whether these endeavors can succeed, there are none at all for doubting their seriousness. In the end, Xi's all-out push for technological self-sufficiency may turn out to have been premature, coming as it does while China still lags behind and remains dependent on the West in key areas such as high-end semiconductors. The CCP's aggressive technology acquisition campaign was designed to close critical gaps and speed China's progress, but it has also begun to stir a strong defensive counter-reaction. Meanwhile Beijing's plans to jump-start indigenous innovation with massive injections of capital will almost certainly be wasteful and could prove to be ineffective as well. Reducing imports while continuing to push Chinese exports will increase the likelihood of trade friction and tariff wars, and not only with the United States but with the other advanced industrial nations as well. The obstacles to development that many poorer nations face mean that it may take years for China's dream of cultivating new markets in the global South to come to fruition, if indeed they ever do. The leadership's long-declared goal of boosting domestic consumption will depend on increases in workers' wages that could undercut the competitiveness of China's exports. As economist Michael Pettis points out, "rebalancing" requires moving 10–15% of GDP to households and away from businesses, the wealthy, and the government. This would be a "massive shift of wealth – and with it, political power – to ordinary people."[127] Given its obsession with control, it remains to be seen whether the CCP is willing to take the risks that would inevitably accompany such a change.

Xi Jinping and his colleagues are presumably aware of all these difficulties, yet they seem certain that they can surmount or circumvent them. That confidence may well prove to be misplaced, but it is not entirely without foundation. In the four decades that have passed since the start of "reform and opening up," the CCP has managed to craft a series of strategies that have allowed it to sustain growth and to become the world's second largest economy without completing the transition to a fully market-based system and, most important, without permitting political power to slip from its grasp. In doing so, the Party has defied the expectations, and ignored much of the advice, of Western economists and policy-makers. Its leaders evidently believe they are succeeding. They see no reason to change direction now.

5

Strategy: "The Great Rejuvenation of the Chinese Nation"

When the Cold War ended, US policy-makers saw themselves as engaged in the grand strategic equivalent of a mopping-up operation. At a single stroke, the Soviet collapse had shattered the one possible source of challenge to America's superior material power while seemingly discrediting the only coherent alternative to its liberal ideology. All that remained for the United States and its democratic allies was to isolate and bring to heel a handful of weak, recalcitrant "backlash states" like North Korea, Iran, and Iraq, and to complete the process of "enlargement" by fully incorporating China, Russia, and the fragments of the former Soviet empire into the US-led, Western-dominated "liberal international order." This might take some time, but because the benefits of inclusion were so obvious and so substantial it was assumed that the process would be smooth and comparatively painless. After more than a decade of "reform and opening up," China, in particular, was already well on its way to becoming a member in good standing of the US-built system.

It is hardly surprising that this vision of peaceful integration, progressive incorporation, and eventual transformation should have been attractive to Western leaders. The fact that they believed it would be equally appealing to their Chinese counterparts, however, betrays a certain lack of strategic empathy, if not a complete failure of imagination. As seen from Beijing, the new, American-dominated order was profoundly threatening, both to China's prospects for becoming a world power in its own right and, more immediately, to the survival of its illiberal political system.

Despite these fears, Beijing's need for Western markets, capital, and technology required it to avoid anything that appeared to challenge the interests of its advanced industrial trading partners. This comparatively deferential posture was a product of circumstance and reflected China's relative weakness rather than the CCP regime's underlying preferences and long-term objectives. In fact, from the dawn of the post-Cold War era, China's leaders harbored a deep dissatisfaction with the status quo. For the most part, however, Beijing lacked the ability significantly to alter, still less to overthrow, the existing order. Things began to change after the turn of the century, most obviously in the aftermath of the 2008 global financial crisis and with ever-increasing clarity following the rise of Xi Jinping.

Since the start of the second decade of the twenty-first century, China has emerged not as a "responsible stakeholder," but as a revisionist state intent on reclaiming its place as the dominant player in eastern Eurasia and establishing itself as a truly global power with capabilities and influence equivalent, and eventually superior, to those of the United States. Albeit slowly and belatedly, American policy-makers have begun to acknowledge the full scope and severity of this challenge.

The changes in China's behavior that have now become impossible to ignore were not the result of a sudden inflation of previously modest ambitions, nor are they due primarily to the personalities of particular individuals. Rather they are the product of shifts in the collective judgment of the CCP elites about long-term trends in the relative power of China and the United States and in the broader structure and functioning of the international system. Put simply, as those assessments have grown more bullish, Beijing has abandoned the largely defensive stance it felt compelled to adopt in the immediate aftermath of the Cold War. Emboldened by what they see on balance as an increasingly favorable strategic situation, China's leaders are now trying to reshape the world in ways they hope will render it less threatening to the CCP and more conducive to the indefinite prolongation of its rule.

Beneath these generally optimistic judgments, however, runs an undercurrent of anxiety. As we have seen, the Party's leaders are acutely aware of their own domestic problems and are working hard to address them. CCP strategists have also long feared that, once aroused, the United States would put up a fierce fight to defend its position and its privileges. Although he is careful never to acknowledge weakness or doubt, Xi Jinping clearly worries that, if he fails to act decisively, a combination of nagging internal weaknesses and mounting external opposition could still greatly complicate and delay China's rise, even if he believes that, in the end, it cannot be prevented.

The roots of revisionism

Rising states tend to be revisionists and China is no exception. Throughout history, rapid growth in a nation's wealth and power has typically been accompanied by an expansion in the scope of its perceived interests and by efforts to exert greater influence on the outside world in order to advance and defend them.[1] In China's case, the drive to play a dominant role in its own region, and potentially on the wider world stage, also follows in part from its long and distinctive past. For many centuries prior to the intrusion of the West, China's rulers were accustomed to thinking of themselves as presiding over not only the most powerful empire in Asia, but also the most advanced and glorious civilization on earth. The desire to reclaim that exalted status is widely shared and deeply ingrained. As Orville Schell and John Delury point out:

> Like a set of genes that is firmly implanted on a genome and is then faithfully transmitted from generation to generation thereafter, DNA coding for this dream to see China restored to greatness and a position of respect has been reexpressing itself over and over since Confucian scholars . . . first began fretting over the Qing Dynasty's early nineteenth-century decline.[2]

But it is the character of the CCP regime and the content of its ideology that have played the greatest part in shaping the grand strategy of contemporary China, imparting to it an element of urgency and a sense of direction. Whatever their Western counterparts may profess to believe, China's rulers are convinced they are locked in a zero-sum struggle with the liberal democracies. In this view, the United States and its allies harbor a profound and irreducible hostility to the Communist Party, an enmity so deep that they reject its legitimacy and will not rest until they have brought it to its knees. From the founding of the PRC, the Americans have therefore sought to destabilize its society, stifle its economy, and weaken its government. Since the earliest days of the Cold War (with the exception of a relatively brief period of alignment against the Soviet Union), the United States has also taken the lead in trying to contain China, blocking its rise by encircling it with military bases and alliances. Since the collapse of the USSR, Washington is believed by Beijing to have turned its attention once again to trying to isolate and humiliate the CCP regime, discrediting it in the eyes of the world, and perhaps its own people, by proclaiming the universal applicability of rights and principles that are clearly incompatible with China's one-party authoritarian system.

These ideologically tinted perceptions of threat inform the way in which Beijing defines and pursues its objectives. As described in Chapter 3, since Tiananmen the CCP regime has relied more heavily on nationalism to bolster its legitimacy and mobilize popular support. A sense of external danger helps to stir those sentiments, directing them outwards at the "hostile foreign forces" that allegedly stand in China's way. An aggressive external policy and the resistance it provokes, up to and including friction and even potential confrontations with other states, have thus become integral parts of the Party's program for justifying its harsh rule and retaining domestic political power.

Beijing's efforts to restore China to a position of regional preponderance are driven in part by the Party's desire to burnish its nationalist credentials by claiming credit for righting historical wrongs and regaining past glory. More concretely, the regime seeks to break out of the encirclement imposed by the United States and its liberal democratic allies, undermine the credibility of US security guarantees, push back against the presence of American forces and bases, and ultimately demonstrate the inability of the democracies to stand up to the awesome power of CCP-ruled China. Bringing Hong Kong and eventually Taiwan back under the control of the mainland will also settle old scores while snuffing out systems that challenge the regime's claims that "so-called universal values" are actually Western creations ill suited to the needs of Chinese people.

The CCP's global ambitions have yet to come fully into view, but here too the ideological factor already looms large. Following in the footsteps of Mao and Deng Xiaoping, Xi Jinping has made clear that he intends to demonstrate the superiority of socialism over capitalism by building China into the wealthiest, strongest, and most advanced nation on earth. Gaining material superiority is not merely a matter of winning systemic bragging rights. Chinese strategic theorists believe that, in any international system, the prevailing norms, rules, and institutional structures reflect the interests of the most powerful state rather than any abstract philosophical principles. The portions of the "liberal international order" that the United States is still trying to use as a cudgel against its opponents are the lingering remnants of the hegemonic position it acquired at the end of the Cold War. Only when China has displaced the United States and established itself as the predominant power globally, or at least within an extended sphere of influence, will it finally be out from under America's overweening influence and free to dictate and enforce its own rules. In the meantime, Beijing is working hard to control, neutralize, or bypass institutions that Washington established and once dominated, and to subvert or supplant American-endorsed, liberal definitions of human rights and other potentially threatening concepts.

The ratcheting up of China's grand strategy has been propelled by a continuous process of assessment involving analysts, think tanks, government bureaucrats, and high-level Party officials. While its innermost portions are hidden behind a veil of secrecy, it is possible to draw certain inferences about the substance of this process, based on the official statements and observable shifts in policy that emerge from it, as well as glimpses into the wider discussion going on in public view around the periphery of the decision-making apparatus.

What all of this suggests is a collective effort to come to agreed and actionable conclusions about what is referred to in ancient Chinese writings as *shi*, a term sometimes interpreted as "the strategic configuration of forces" or "the propensity of things."[3] This illusive concept encompasses the material factors such as national economic output and military capabilities that Western analysts weigh as they attempt to measure the "balance of power" or "correlation of forces" between two opposing camps. But *shi* also refers to a much wider array of immaterial factors, including the psychological state, political conditions, and strategic inclinations of the competitors, as well as larger social, economic, and technological trends that are beyond the power of either side to control, but which may help determine the outcome of their rivalry. The troubling progression in China's behavior that has become so obvious in recent years reflects the considered judgment of its leaders that, despite growing resistance, occasional setbacks, and persistent challenges, "the propensity of things" is flowing increasingly in their favor.

The Party's evolving strategy for achieving regional preponderance and global power

Like their revolutionary forebears, Xi Jinping and his subordinates are troubled by fears of encirclement and containment and driven by a desire to reclaim what they see as China's rightful place in its region and the world. The CCP regime's nagging anxieties and long-term ambitions have been present since the founding of the PRC; what has changed dramatically in the past three decades is the nation's relative power. During this period, Beijing's shifting assessments of "the propensity of things" have caused its external strategy to advance through three phases:

- Believing their position to be comparatively weak, and fearful of isolation, for at least a decade after the end of the Cold War the nation's leaders continued to adhere closely to Deng Xiaoping's directive that China should "hide its capabilities and bide its time." Even as the CCP regime remained on the defensive and focused on economic development, it pursued a low-key but vigorous three-part strategy for avoiding encirclement and pushing back against containment. In addition to improving relations with most of its neighbors and cultivating closer ties with Washington despite several near-confrontations, Beijing began to invest in the capabilities it would need to counter US efforts to project military power into the Western Pacific.

- The first decade of the twenty-first century saw three events that caused CCP strategists to update and upgrade their assessments. Beijing's accession to the WTO, followed closely by the 9/11 terrorist attacks, was believed to have ushered in a twenty-year "period of opportunity" during which the Americans would be preoccupied and China would be free to increase its power and press ahead with its incremental strategy. The 2008 global financial crisis strengthened the conviction that the United States, and the West more generally, had entered into a period of accelerating relative decline. These events, taken together, led to the conclusion that China could now take a somewhat more forward-leaning posture, starting with the long-standing disputes with its maritime neighbors. Hu did not reject Deng's dictum, but he did modify it to emphasize that the time had come to "get some things done."

- The trend towards greater assertiveness that began during the closing years of Hu Jintao's second term accelerated sharply under Xi
Jinping. The Obama administration's "pivot" to Asia convinced CCP
strategists that, even as its power declined, the United States would
redouble its efforts to contain China. At the same time, the relatively
weak US follow-through in response to Beijing's growing activism
emboldened Xi to press ahead, openly challenging the status quo
and, as he put it, "striving for achievement" and seeking to fulfill the
"China Dream." China's increasing revisionism was focused at first
primarily on its extended periphery but, especially after the start of
Xi's second term in 2017, it became truly global in scope. This shift
appears to have reflected a judgment that the West had been further
weakened by mounting social and political turmoil, and that, in part
as a result, its response to China's rise would inevitably become even
more desperate and dangerous. The period of strategic opportunity
was now over and a new era of intense and open rivalry had begun.
These conclusions were reinforced after the start of 2020 by events
surrounding the outbreak of the COVID-19 pandemic.

"Hide and bide"

Attending to the "main task"

As the Cold War entered its final phase, China's leaders revised their
assessment of the strategic situation to reflect a growing sense of optimism about the future. After nearly two decades of tense and bitter
rivalry, Mikhail Gorbachev's "new thinking" on foreign policy led to
a thaw in Sino-Soviet relations. With the risk of conflict reduced and
economic relations with the West deepening, Beijing was free to concentrate even more of its energies on fostering reform and growth. In 1985,
Deng Xiaoping formalized these judgments by declaring that the two
"great issues" confronting the Party and the world were no longer "war
and revolution," as they had been under Chairman Mao, but "peace and
development."[4]

Together with a reduced risk of major war, the new era of peace and
development was expected to bring favorable shifts in the distribution
of world power. While the United States and the Soviet Union might

continue for a time to be the world's only superpowers, their margin of advantage would dwindle, thanks to the rapid growth of others, including China, but also Japan and the nations of Western Europe. The international system was thus evolving away from bipolarity and towards a more "democratic," or equally balanced, multipolar structure in which nations would compete for economic, scientific, and technological advantage rather than simple military superiority. "For the next several years," Deng's top foreign affairs advisor concluded in 1986, "strengthening Comprehensive National Power" would thus be China's "main task."[5]

The series of shocks that buffeted Beijing in rapid succession between June 1989 and December 1991 – Tiananmen, the crumbling of the Soviet empire in Eastern Europe, the stunning US victory over Iraq, and the dissolution of the Soviet Union – led to a darkening in official assessments and some significant adjustments in strategy. But these events did not alter Deng's conviction that "reform and opening up," and continuing engagement with the West, were essential to building China's wealth and power.

Deng was under no illusions about the dangers that lay ahead. With the Soviet Union in its death throes, he warned Party members that "everyone should be very clear that . . . all enemy attention will be concentrated on China."[6] Having seen off their Cold War nemesis, the Americans and their allies would pursue what CCP analysts and officials came to refer to as a "two-handed" or "dual-track" strategy towards the last remaining bastion of socialism.[7] "Engagement and containment" would be "used simultaneously, one openly and one secretly."[8] The United States would "take advantage of opening up," using trade, "ideological infiltration," and "financial assistance to hostile forces both inside and outside" of China to try to force it to "change the course of its ideology and make it incline towards the West."[9] At the same time, following the quick and decisive American defeat of Saddam Hussein's forces and the evaporation of the long-standing Soviet threat to Western Europe, the US military would, in the words of an advisor to Premier Li Peng, "move its forces eastward" in order to concentrate on "isolating" and "blockading" China.[10]

The combination of internal and external pressure was meant to disintegrate the authority and power of the CCP, "eventually rendering China innocuous" through democratization.[11] Once ideologically neutered, the nation would be free to take its place as a dutiful vassal in a US-run hegemonic system. For all their flowery talk of peace, prosperity, and freedom, this is what the Americans actually had in mind when they spoke of "enlargement" or the creation of a "new world order." Needless to say, this is not how things appeared on the other side of the Pacific. Supremely confident in the attractiveness of their model and the benevolence of their intentions, most US policy-makers were oblivious to the fear and loathing with which they had come to be regarded by their counterparts in Beijing.

Amidst these troubling portents, Chinese analysts and policy-makers were able to find some reasons for hope. The Soviet collapse was actually accelerating the "democratization" of international relations. Due in part to its extraordinary exertions during the Cold War, the United States now had an accumulation of unaddressed economic and social problems that would slow its future growth and hasten its relative decline.[12] Japan and Europe, meanwhile, were surging ahead and would soon emerge as major competitors to American industrial and technological dominance.[13] Rising friction over trade issues and the disappearance of the common threat that once bound them together meant that US alliances would soon begin to weaken. As Foreign Minister Qian Qichen told the UN in 1992, the world had now entered into "a new historical stage of development heading toward multipolarity."[14]

Surveying this scene, Deng Xiaoping concluded that, provided it could stay the course, time would be on China's side. "If we stand fast and make it through," he exhorted his colleagues, "our enterprise will develop quickly."[15] But this would require patience and a measure of self-restraint. Only by "keep[ing] a low profile and work[ing] hard for some years" could China hope to "become a big power," capable of exerting "more weight in international affairs."[16] This basic message of prudence and perseverance was conveyed in a memorandum circulated to top CCP officials in the spring of 1991. Faced with a daunting mix of domestic challenges and foreign threats, Deng advised that the Party take care to "observe . . . soberly, maintain our position, meet the challenge calmly, hide our capacities, bide our time, remain free of ambitions, and never claim leadership."[17]

Escaping encirclement

Deng's so-called "twenty-four-character directive" would continue to guide China's strategy for the better part of the next two decades. Despite its cautious tone, however, "hide and bide" was not a formula for passivity. Rather it provided the conceptual foundation for a three-pronged, indirect approach to advancing towards the nation's long-term strategic objectives.

Because trade and investment with the United States were essential to building China's wealth and power, the Party's first priority was to hold Washington close, resisting its pressure tactics while avoiding confrontation, giving time for economic ties to deepen and for the pro-engagement forces in American society to gain in strength.

Eager to escape the opprobrium and isolation it had experienced after Tiananmen, during the first half of the 1990s the Chinese government also initiated an omni-directional burst of diplomatic activity. To cement its position in eastern Eurasia and head off renewed US efforts at encirclement, Beijing moved quickly to improve relations with virtually all of its neighbors: recognizing South Korea and Singapore, two US friends with whom it had not previously had formal relations; resolving or tabling border disputes with Russia and India; establishing links to the new Central Asia republics on its western flank; and normalizing its troubled relationship with Vietnam.[18] In an attempt to "reassure regional neighbors [and] burnish its credentials as a constructive international citizen," Beijing also signed on to a number of multilateral arms control agreements that it had previously rejected, including the Nuclear Nonproliferation Treaty.[19]

Less widely publicized than the two diplomatic components of China's strategy but no less important were the shifts in military doctrine and spending priorities that began to take shape in the wake of the first Gulf War. To avoid suffering the same fate as Saddam's armies, which used equipment and tactics similar to their own, the PLA needed to find ways to offset or neutralize America's awe-inspiring ability to project military power. Before the dust had fully settled in Iraq, its planners had set to work on this task, initiating an exhaustive process of debate and analysis to extract the lessons of the recent conflict. This process would continue with increasing refinement throughout the decade, but its direction was clear from the outset. To counter America's strength and undermine its alliances, China needed to develop the means to locate, target, and destroy the forward-deployed forces, bases, and reconnaissance systems of the United States and its local allies, and to do so quickly, before they could blind and disarm China.[20]

As seen from Beijing, by the mid-1990s "hiding and biding" seemed in certain respects to be working tolerably well: normal trading relations had been restored, the economy was booming, and China was fully engaged in the "main task" of building its comprehensive national power. At the same time, however, there was little sign that the long-awaited era of multipolarity was finally at hand. To the contrary, while the United States had recovered smartly from the recession of the early 1990s and was experiencing an economic boom, Japan and, to a lesser extent, Europe remained mired in difficulties.[21] Although they continued to express faith that the world was moving towards what some now described as an intermediate system of "one superpower, many great powers," Chinese observers were coming to the conclusion that, as one put it, "the superpower is more super, and the many great powers are less great," than they had originally hoped.[22]

Reinforcing these developments in the global configuration of power was the fact that, far from crumbling, America's alliances were being renewed and refurbished to meet the challenges of the post-Cold War era. In Europe, NATO had begun a process of eastward expansion that would eventually incorporate large swaths of the former Soviet empire and which some Chinese analysts feared might someday extend all the way to their country's continental frontiers.[23] Meanwhile, to allay allied concerns about US staying power in East Asia, in 1995 the Clinton administration issued a report reaffirming its security commitments and promising to maintain a force of no fewer than 100,000 troops forward-deployed in the region.[24]

At least for the moment, "the propensity of things" seemed to be moving in favor of the United States. Always arrogant and overbearing, the Americans were behaving even more aggressively than usual, seizing the opportunity presented by their unmatched strength to "complete a global strategic layout" that would reshape the world in their own image.[25] In Iraq, Bosnia, and Kosovo, the United States organized multinational coalitions to wage war on what it claimed were brutal, authoritarian regimes. In the first two cases, as well as lesser interventions in Somalia and Haiti, Washington was able to win backing from the United Nations and, in every instance, it insisted that its actions were motivated in whole or in part by the desire to protect innocent civilians. Such claims were viewed cynically but also with concern in Beijing, where they were seen as setting a dangerous precedent that could someday be used to justify action against China. As Minister of Defense Chi Haotian warned his Politburo colleagues in 1999: "[I]ntervention in other countries' internal affairs on the [pretext] of . . . 'humanitarian intervention' . . . is becoming a habitual pattern" for the Americans and their democratic allies.[26]

America's "hegemonism" thus combined overwhelming force with what one scholar has described as the "manipulation of international regulations, rules, and norms" to "weaken and isolate its adversaries."[27] Both regionally and globally, the United States was proceeding with its openly declared plans to promote the spread of liberal democratic capitalism and to build an international system that was economically integrated and ideologically homogeneous. For as long as it refused to submit and continued to follow the path of "building socialism with Chinese characteristics," Beijing would be an outlier and a prime target of American pressure.

Two crises

China's commitment to its incremental, tripartite strategy for escaping American encirclement was challenged twice during the second half of the 1990s: once in 1996 when Washington dispatched two carrier battle groups to counter Beijing's attempt to sway Taiwan's elections by test-firing missiles into its coastal waters, and again in 1999, during the war in Kosovo, when US forces struck the Chinese embassy in Belgrade. In both cases, the CCP leadership ultimately chose to sidestep a direct confrontation with the United States, preserving the benefits of engagement while doubling down on the diplomatic and military elements of their countervailing strategy.

The 1995–6 crisis gave focus to Beijing's anxieties, convincing PLA planners both that they would have to face the United States in a future conflict over Taiwan, and that they were woefully ill prepared to do so.[28] The confrontation also spurred a shift in procurement priorities towards weapons that would be most useful in discouraging or delaying US intervention while quickly subduing Taiwanese resistance. Included among these were large numbers of short- and medium-range conventional ballistic missiles and more off-the-shelf, Russian-made surface vessels, submarines, torpedoes, and anti-ship cruise missiles capable of targeting US aircraft carriers. With Jiang Zemin reportedly insisting that no expense be spared, the political leadership also authorized accelerated development of entirely new types of high-tech weapons, most notably a long-range, land-based anti-ship ballistic missile.[29] Whatever their actual effectiveness, the mere existence of these so-called "assassin's mace" systems was meant to arouse fear and uncertainty in the mind of the enemy by threatening its most valued military assets.[30]

In tandem with its stepped-up preparations for a possible future war, Beijing began another diplomatic offensive aimed at forestalling US-led encirclement and enhancing its own freedom of maneuver. As always, maintaining at least the appearance of good relations with the United States was crucial. Swallowing any resentment he may have felt over American meddling in China's internal affairs, Jiang Zemin visited Washington in 1997 to sign a statement promising to work towards a "constructive strategic partnership" with the country that his military strategists had now identified as their most dangerous foe.[31] Seeking to reduce the possibility that it might find itself isolated in some future confrontation with the Americans, between 1996 and 2000 Beijing also entered into over a dozen new "partnerships" of various descriptions with other countries, including major US allies. In a significant step towards what would eventually become a de facto alliance, in 1996 China and Russia upgraded their relationship to a "strategic cooperative partnership" in which each side promised to support the other on territorial issues.[32]

These more traditional, bilateral diplomatic measures were accompanied in 1997 by the unveiling of Beijing's "New Security Concept." Couched in typically vague and vaporous language, this initiative actually conveyed a thinly veiled critique of the hub-and-spokes system of alliances between the United States and its democratic partners in East Asia and the kernel of an alternative concept for a new Sino-centric regional order. Both would be embellished and amplified in the years ahead.

Whereas it had previously been circumspect in its criticism of US security treaties, for a time following the Taiwan crisis, and the subsequent strengthening of defense ties between Tokyo and Washington, the Chinese government began to call for the abrogation of existing military alliances, which it now described as sources of "instability."[33] Denouncing the "Cold War mentality" of "some nations," which sought to divide the world along ideological lines and claimed to uphold universal values, Beijing argued that every country should be free to "choose its own social system, development strategy, and way of life." The nations of Asia should dissolve alliances with outside powers, renounce ideological blocs, and concentrate instead on strengthening economic ties among themselves, building "common prosperity, and resolving . . . differences through dialogue."[34]

As part of its new approach, Beijing began to participate more actively in selected regional multilateral institutions. Chinese strategists had previously viewed these as potential traps where they risked being isolated and outnumbered, but, as their own power grew, they came to recognize that, provided the Americans were excluded, such venues could be useful for reassuring neighbors and exerting influence over them. The CCP's "born-again"[35] conversion to multilateralism provided another means of pushing back against US influence without provoking a direct confrontation.[36] In the words of one Chinese scholar, Beijing's proposals for a new regional order were meant to "undermine the political and moral basis" of America's bilateral alliance system.[37] Showing a "kinder and gentler face" to its neighbors was also a way of easing their anxieties and delaying their resistance until, by virtue of its sheer size and central location, China could emerge once again as the dominant regional power.[38]

Because Chinese citizens died at the hands of American pilots, the May 1999 Belgrade embassy bombing posed a more visceral and direct affront to national dignity than the Taiwan crisis and an even tougher test of Beijing's commitment to its indirect and incremental strategy. For several months after the bombing, the Party debated whether "peace and development" were still the prevailing trends of the age, and thus, by implication, whether China should continue to "hide its capabilities and bide its time." The official answer in both cases was ultimately affirmative, albeit with some important caveats. Despite generally favorable long-term trends, "hegemonism and power politics" were clearly on the rise, as was "the trend toward military interventionism."[39] Needless to say, the Americans were responsible for these unfavorable tendencies.

Nevertheless, to avoid disrupting engagement and damaging growth, the Party leadership decided to limit their response to diplomatic protests. For the time being, China would continue to "struggle . . . but not break with" the United States.[40]

In order to forestall possible criticism that his response was insufficiently tough, at the Party's annual retreat in the summer of 1999 Jiang Zemin reportedly told his generals: "Go back and develop the capabilities to solve the Taiwan problem by force if peaceful methods fail."[41] The regime subsequently authorized a substantial additional increment in the PLA's budget for weapons procurement, on top of the double-digit increase that it was already slated to receive.[42]

The two near-confrontations with China, and the Taiwan crisis in particular, had an impact on US perceptions of Beijing's intentions, at least for a time and in some quarters.

On the eve of the 1996 crisis, the CIA's annual threat assessment report to Congress averred that "we still know very little about Beijing's . . . intentions." One year later, however, the report claimed that "Beijing's actions and statements show it is determined to assert itself as the paramount East Asian power." By 1998, CIA Director George Tenet described China's leaders as having "a clear goal; the transformation of their country into East Asia's major power and a leading economy on a par with the United States by the middle of the 21st Century."[43]

This moment of clarity did not last. Whether because such judgments were considered impolitic, or because of a reluctance to draw conclusions from the ambiguous available evidence, by the turn of the century Tenet was prepared to say only that China's leaders were trying to "propel the nation's economy into the modern world" in pursuit of "prestige, global economic clout and . . . new military strength."[44] According to Assistant Secretary of State for Intelligence and Research Stapleton Roy, "China's commitment to a multipolar world in which it would have major global influence" meant only that its interests would "occasionally lead to rivalry with the United States, sometimes in concert with Russia or France."[45]

In the wake of the Taiwan crisis, portions of the US military and intelligence communities began to devote more resources to tracking China's emerging military capabilities. At least in defense planning circles, their findings fueled anxieties that grew more intense with the passage of time. At the highest political level, however, officials remained intently focused on engagement and, above all, on securing China's entry into the WTO. As for Beijing's long-term intentions, these were widely regarded not as merely obscure and difficult to discern, but rather as unformed and therefore susceptible to shaping, for better or worse, by the actions of others. The implications seemed obvious: despite occasional friction, engagement would eventually pay dividends if pursued with sufficient vigor. Over reacting to indications of Chinese hostility, on the other hand, risked creating a self-fulfilling prophecy. A 1995 remark by Harvard professor and Assistant Secretary of Defense Joseph Nye encapsulated this oft-repeated bit of conventional wisdom: "[I]f you treat China as an enemy, China will become an enemy."[46]

"Get some things done"

The post-9/11 "period of strategic opportunity"

From start to finish, the 1990s had been punctuated by a series of international crises that the CCP saw as deeply threatening to its own security and advantageous to the United States. Starting in the first decade of the new century, this tendency was dramatically reversed. The long-term effects of the September 11, 2001 terrorist attacks, followed seven years later by the onset of the global financial crisis, were mixed and complex. In each case, however, Chinese strategists quickly concluded that the fortuitous arrival of these two "black swans" would have favorable implications for their rivalry with the United States. With the Americans distracted and their resources dissipated, the CCP leadership assessed that China would be freer to build its strength, closing the gap in comprehensive national power with the United States and advancing more rapidly, albeit still cautiously, towards its long-standing strategic objectives. At the turn of the twenty-first century, Party leaders fretted over the possible onset of unipolarity and pined for the arrival of multipolarity. Ten years later, they were beginning to entertain the thought of a bipolar world, one in which China and the United States stood head and shoulders above all the other powers.[47]

From Beijing's perspective, 9/11 was not an unmixed blessing. In the months that followed, the United States established bases in Central Asia, further enhanced defense cooperation with Japan and its other East Asian allies, improved relations with both India and China's traditional ally Pakistan, and confronted North Korea, a charter member of President George W. Bush's "axis of evil," over its nuclear weapons program. At first, the specter of renewed encirclement loomed large. As soon-to-be General Secretary Hu Jintao cautioned his colleagues in late 2001, the Americans were establishing "pressure points on us from the east, south, and west."[48]

On further reflection, Chinese strategists began to see that the emerging situation could have substantial benefits. As incoming Premier Wen Jiabao pointed out, it was true that America was determined to remain "the world's sole superpower" and the core of its policy towards China was still "engage and contain."[49] For the time being, however, Washington's energy and attention had been forcibly deflected from the Asia-Pacific towards South Asia and the Middle East, and away from preparations for a possible future war with what the Pentagon referred to as a "peer competitor" and towards the urgent necessities of counter-terrorism, counter-proliferation, and counter-insurgency. In the hierarchy of American strategic priorities, analysts noted that China had moved "from front burner to back burner,"[50] a change that "offered a new opportunity for improving . . . Sino-US relations."[51]

According to a former director of the Ministry of State Security's think tank, it was the juxtaposition of the 9/11 attacks with China's accession to the WTO that led Jiang Zemin to declare in 2002 that the nation had entered into a twenty-year "period of strategic opportunity."[52] Two decades of relative tranquility would enable Beijing to concentrate on building up its strength. Such an interval was more than welcome but, as an analyst at the Central Party School cautioned, it would not be "a long-term one, let alone a permanent one."[53] The Americans would eventually revert to their previous attitude of suspicion and hostility and the period of strategic opportunity would be followed by a period of rivalry more intense and dangerous than any that had come before. It was precisely for this reason that the Party and the nation needed to feel what one official described as "a sense of urgency," seizing the moment and working hard to acquire "a more favorable position in the increasingly fierce competition in terms of overall national strength."[54]

In theory, and for the most part in practice, Beijing remained cautious; the impulse to "hide and bide" was still strong. Despite this general inclination, some in the system were beginning to argue that China should adopt a "great power mentality" to match its improving circumstances.[55] Hu Jintao's initial 2003 slogan announcing China's "peaceful rise" was meant to square the strategic circle, highlighting the nation's growing wealth, power, and global outlook, while reassuring other countries about its intentions. Dismissed by some domestic critics for sounding overly aggressive and by others as savoring of timidity and weakness, this formulation quickly disappeared, to be replaced first by the more gently worded assertion that China sought nothing more than "peaceful *development*" (emphasis added), and then by the declaration that its ultimate goal was the creation of a "harmonious world."[56] Unveiled in 2005, the latter phrase was meant to suggest the existence of a tranquil Chinese alternative to the violent American "hegemonism" then on display in Iraq.[57] Subtly at first, China was indicating its dissatisfaction with at least some aspects of the status quo and signaling that it had its own ideas about how the world should be run.

Beijing's words implied an increasingly global perspective but, for the moment, its actions remained firmly centered on eastern Eurasia. As CCP strategists had anticipated, the 9/11 attacks deflected Washington's attention and upended its priorities, creating opportunities for Beijing. During its first months in office, the George W. Bush administration had formulated plans for heading off a potential Chinese challenge to the US position by maintaining an overwhelming margin of military advantage in the Asia-Pacific.[58] The wars in Afghanistan and Iraq upset this process and instead forced a large-scale reallocation of military and intelligence resources.

While the United States poured billions (ultimately trillions) into its "global war on terrorism," China's regionally focused buildup proceeded apace, with special emphasis given to acquiring the weapons needed to implement what Pentagon analysts now described as the PLA's "anti-access/area denial" (A2/AD) strategy.[59] Towards this end, following the signing of a twenty-year "Treaty of Friendship and Cooperation," China increased its purchases of Russian anti-ship missiles and launch platforms, including more ships, submarines, and aircraft. Expanded joint R&D programs, technology licensing agreements, and the expertise of several thousand Russian scientists and engineers working in Chinese labs and factories also helped Beijing to modernize its defense industries much more rapidly than would otherwise have been possible.[60]

Despite its post-9/11 preoccupations, the Bush administration did continue to work at maintaining a favorable balance of power in Asia, albeit primarily by diplomatic means. Ever-closer cooperation with Japan and a deepening strategic relationship with India were generally described in public as necessary to combat Islamist extremism and slow the spread of nuclear weapons. But these moves were also motivated in part by a desire to hedge against China's growing strength.

Still, CCP analysts were not wrong in their assessment that pressing new concerns would soften the attitudes of an administration that had come into office describing China as a "strategic competitor" and declaring its willingness to "do whatever it takes" to help defend Taiwan.[61] After 9/11, American officials were eager to win Beijing's support in dealing with what they sought to frame as the shared dangers of terrorism and proliferation. In the end, however, China's help amounted to very little. Hu Jintao was able to capitalize on the Bush administration's newfound obsessions at virtually no cost by extending what proved to be largely empty offers to cooperate in fighting extremism and by agreeing to host protracted and ultimately fruitless nuclear negotiations with North Korea.[62] Although there was no explicit quid pro quo, the United States reciprocated by taking what has been described as a "tougher and more Beijing-accommodating line toward Taiwan," at one point intervening sharply in the island's domestic politics to discourage what the CCP regime claimed were moves towards independence.[63]

Allegations of US unilateralism in the Middle East gave Beijing a fresh opportunity to burnish its multilateral credentials and to take the next steps towards building out the foundations for a new, post-American Asian regional order. To the west, China transformed the Shanghai Cooperation Organization, previously little more than a loose-limbed talking shop, into a functioning platform, headquartered in Beijing, and useful for coordinating counter-terror training, discussing development projects, and denouncing the United States. To the east, in 2002 Beijing sought to strengthen ties to the Association of Southeast Asian Nations (ASEAN), reassuring its mostly small and weak members that China would never use force to resolve outstanding territorial disputes by signing their Treaty of Amity and Cooperation. At the same time, in a move that foreshadowed what would soon become a dominant theme in its regional diplomacy, Beijing also sought to draw its Southeast Asian neighbors more closely into its economic orbit by proposing a China–ASEAN free trade area. Looking ahead, some Chinese analysts began to contemplate a future characterized, on the one hand, by "an intensification of internal divisions within the US Asia-Pacific alliance system"[64] and, on the other, by an overlapping network of regional institutions in which China would always be the strongest member. Overlaid on these would be what a professor at the Foreign Affairs University described in 2005 as a "China Economic Sphere" with "itself as the core."[65]

The global financial crisis and the shift towards greater assertiveness

Even before the onset of the global financial crisis, America's deepening difficulties in Iraq caused leading Chinese experts to conclude that the conflict had triggered an accelerated erosion in its position of global dominance. As one wrote in 2007, the war would impose "major long-term constraints on US resources, energy and attention," making it impossible for the United States to "effectively block the developing trend . . . in the balance of power . . . especially the rise of China."[66]

The unraveling of mammoth financial institutions and the near-collapse of the US and other Western economies in 2008 and 2009 reinforced these perceptions and helped transform them into official dogma. Chinese analysts expressed confidence that, coming on top of its recent foreign policy setbacks, the economic crisis would cause America's power to "inevitably shrivel" and accelerate "great changes" in the structure and functioning of the international system.[67] Along with its more tangible effects, the crisis also cast doubt on the supposed superiority of the Western model of political and economic development, bringing China what one scholar described as "rare historic opportunities" to "enhance its international status and improve its national image."[68]

Against this auspicious backdrop, Chinese analysts and policy-makers engaged in an unusually open debate over whether the time had finally come to dispense with Deng Xiaoping's strategic guidance in favor of a more openly assertive approach. Among those in agreement were a retired general from the PLA's Academy of Military Sciences who maintained that the nation needed to be willing to "show sword" in defending its interests, and a previously obscure colonel whose best-selling 2010 book *The China Dream* asserted that the nation should put caution aside and "sprint toward the goal of leading the world."[69] Arrayed against these exhortations were more familiar arguments for patience and restraint from a variety of academics, think tankers, and some senior officials, including State Councilor Dai Bingguo.[70]

The debate over "hide and bide" ultimately ended in a split decision, albeit one that in subtle but important ways favored the advocates of greater assertiveness. With characteristic caution, Hu Jintao eventually added two adverbs to a version of Deng's original directive, stating that, henceforth, China would "*continuously* keep a low profile and *proactively* get some things done" (emphasis added).[71] To those in the Chinese system attuned to fine adjustments in terminology and emphasis, the implications were clear: while no radical, across-the-board shifts were in the offing, under some circumstances China must now be prepared to seize the initiative.[72]

This more assertive attitude was manifest first in China's immediate neighborhood. Starting in 2009, the CCP regime began to make frequent use of threats and displays of force to back up its claims to the waters, resources, and land features of the East and South China Seas, or, as the Party preferred to put it, to "resolutely safeguard China's maritime rights and interests."[73] In a series of incidents involving Japan, the Philippines, Vietnam, and, indirectly, the United States, Beijing sought to demonstrate its resolve, impose its will, and extend its sphere of control. These limited confrontations also served a domestic purpose. At a time when, despite its gratification at the West's problems, the CCP was increasingly concerned about China's economic prospects and social stability, a measure of friction with foreign powers provided a convenient way to stir patriotic sentiment and shore up popular support.[74]

Beijing's bullying of its neighbors had another, presumably unintended, consequence. When it first came into office in 2009, the Obama administration had hoped not only to deepen engagement but also to broaden it, cooperating more closely with China in managing the global economy and enlisting its help in dealing with climate change, among other issues. These hopes were not abandoned but, as evidence of China's more aggressive attitude continued to accumulate, the administration felt compelled eventually to react to Beijing's actions, and to the anxiety they provoked among America's Asian allies. After a decade of war in Afghanistan and Iraq, in 2011 officials announced their intention to "rebalance" US foreign policy and "pivot" back to Asia.[75]

The CCP's response was revealing and indicative of what was to come. Rather than consider the possibility that Beijing's own actions might have been at least partly responsible for triggering a spiral of escalating tensions, Chinese analysts and officials placed the blame squarely on the United States. It was the Americans who were stirring up trouble by encouraging their local clients to resist China's rightful claims and challenge its sovereignty. Behind lofty talk of maritime rights and peaceful dispute resolution, Washington's true purpose was to reassert control over its allies while trying desperately to construct an "'all-under-heavens net' to contain China."[76]

Chinese assessments of "the propensity of things" had a similarly self-centered, even autistic, quality.[77] Hu Jintao's last year in office marked the halfway point in the twenty-year "period of strategic opportunity." Given the recent turn of events, it was natural to ask whether, in fact, the anticipated interval of tranquility was drawing to a premature close. The conclusion of discussion on this issue reaffirmed but also elaborated upon the Party's original prediction. The period of opportunity would continue, but its second decade would be different – more tense, more turbulent, and more fraught with risk – than the first.

The reason, simply put, was China's success, and the fear and jealousy that this aroused in others. In virtually every sphere, the nation could expect to encounter greater resistance precisely because of the speed and extent of its continued rise. This was natural, predictable, and, most important, unavoidable. It had nothing to do with what China *did* and everything to do with what it *was*. It therefore made little sense to worry about whether it might be possible to alleviate the problem (or make it worse) through the adoption or rejection of particular policies.

Chinese analysts sought to put the situation in broad historical perspective, noting that rapidly rising powers invariably encountered resistance from others in the international system. According to a Central Party School professor, the "outside world, especially the developed countries and neighboring countries," would feel a growing "sense of crisis, anxiety and urgency in dealing with the 'rise of China.'" As a result, their "mentality towards China" would "become more complex and sensitive" and "their misgivings and vigilance" and efforts at "prevention and containment" would all intensify.[78] China's leaders had to be "fully mentally prepared for this," but there was nothing they could do to avoid it.[79] Faced with mounting opposition, they had no choice but to press forward towards their goals.

"Strive for achievement"

Pushing for regional preponderance

By the time Xi Jinping assumed power, the various strands of the CCP's strategic assessment had tied themselves into the dangerous knot of a self-fulfilling prophecy. China's rise, increasing US-led resistance, an eventual end to the period of strategic opportunity, and a subsequent period of more intense struggle were all inevitable. Beijing needed to take advantage of the lingering aftereffects of America's latest setback, and what remained of the period of opportunity, to strengthen its position in anticipation of what was to come.

External circumstances dictated a more aggressive external posture; but such a stance was also integral to the other two main elements of Xi's grand strategy. An atmosphere of heightened international tensions made it easier for the new leader to mobilize the nationalist sentiments vital to sustaining the Party's legitimacy. Meanwhile, an escalating military competition and broader geopolitical rivalry with the United States served to justify tightening the regime's grip on the economy and the Chinese people.

From the start, Xi's entire program has been pitched forward and imbued with a sense of urgency. In contrast to his predecessor, who took several years before settling on a bland slogan, Xi announced his within days of assuming power. As discussed in Chapter 3, Xi's articulation of the "China Dream" also came with a specific timeline and two critical milestones: 2021, the CCP's centennial; and 2049, the 100th anniversary of the PRC. Xi promised that, by mid century the "great rejuvenation of the Chinese nation" would have been "inevitably . . . accomplished."[80]

With these deadlines looming, China's leaders could no longer afford to be patient. Accordingly, soon after taking office, Xi eased Deng

Xiaoping's "hide and bide" directive into final retirement, reportedly expunging the phrase from Party documents and internal deliberations.[81] Instead of Hu's careful "continuously keeping a low profile" while working to "get some things done," Xi told a Party conference in October 2013 that China was now "striving for achievement."[82]

By invoking the China Dream, Xi made plain that his country was not merely "rising," or becoming richer and stronger in material terms; it was also being "rejuvenated" and retaking its rightful place in the world.[83] At a minimum, rejuvenation would require restoring China to the central position it occupied in eastern Eurasia before the West's intrusions and the start of the "century of humiliation." Chinese officials have been reluctant to say so in as many words, presumably for fear of arousing anxiety in their neighbors, but the regional implications of Xi's slogan are obvious. As one prominent commentator explains, Xi's aim is "for China to take on a dominant role in the Asia and Western Pacific area. Over the long term, [China's] power and influence will . . . abolish US dominance in the region."[84] This will not be easy because, as Xi reminded an audience of PLA officers in early 2013: "The more our strength develops, the greater the resistance . . . and the more external risks we will face. This is an unavoidable challenge . . . an unavoidable threshold we must cross to achieve the great rejuvenation of the Chinese nation."[85]

The American pivot was thus unsurprising but, at least to date, it had also been underwhelming. Even several years after the financial crisis, Chinese analysts assessed that the United States remained weakened, its freedom of action limited by huge deficits and the need to deal with damage to its economy. Moreover, despite its declared intention to shift its focus to Asia, Washington was once again preoccupied with events in the Middle East. America's animosity was deep-seated and its intentions malign, but it had "not yet reached the level of comprehensive containment against China."[86] To the contrary, by the start of President Obama's second term his administration seemed eager to demonstrate its continuing commitment to engagement. Thus, shortly after his own reelection, the president took the unusual step of arranging an early "get acquainted" meeting with his newly elevated Chinese counterpart.[87] As seen from Beijing, there appeared to be a chance that an all-out US offensive could be delayed by dangling the prospect of enhanced cooperation and the promise of at least some superficial improvement in bilateral relations.

This is what Xi seems to have had in mind when he urged President Obama in 2012 and again in 2013 to join him in defining a "new type of great power relationship" between their two countries.[88] US officials were initially intrigued by this proposition, but what appeared at first glance to be little more than empty diplomatic happy talk turned out on closer inspection to contain a number of traps. Chinese interlocutors insisted that if the two sides wanted to avoid conflict and reap the fruits of "win-win cooperation," they had to accept one another as equals and promise to respect each other's "core interests." Because Beijing had defined these only vaguely, it was effectively asking the Americans to sign a blank check. More to the point, as the Chinese ambassador to the United States helpfully explained, while his country had never done anything to undermine "US core interests and concerns," Washington's behavior in this regard had been entirely "unsatisfactory." If there were concessions to be made, in short, it was the United States that would have to make them.[89]

If China's attempts to hold the Americans close were becoming increasingly *pro forma*, half-hearted, and even somewhat contemptuous, its efforts to chip away at the foundations of the US alliance system were growing more intense and overt than ever before. In addition to further accelerating China's military buildup, Xi elevated the priority of its ongoing maritime disputes, signaling a greater willingness to use force, if necessary, to advance the nation's claims. In his first published foreign policy speech in January 2013, he stiffened China's stance by declaring that he would "never bargain over our core national interests" and elevating "safeguarding rights" in the maritime domain to the same priority as "safeguarding stability."[90] This was followed by a series of escalatory steps intended to more forcefully assert China's claims, including the unilateral declaration in November 2013 of an Air Defense Identification Zone over the East China Sea, where Beijing was contesting Japan's control of the Senkaku Islands, and, one month later, the start of construction of a network of artificial islands in the South China Sea, where it was engaged in disputes over waters and maritime resources with Vietnam and the Philippines.[91]

By deploying military and paramilitary forces into contested areas, Beijing was testing American resolve, probing for potential seams in its alliances, and trying to raise questions about whether the United

States would really be willing to go to war over what senior administration official Jeff Bader described as "a bunch of rocks."[92] Washington's reluctance for over a year and a half to challenge China's expanding territorial claims by conducting regular freedom-of-navigation cruises through contested waters did nothing to dissuade Xi from pushing ahead.[93] And the Obama administration's mistaken belief that Beijing could be shamed into modifying its behavior by an unfavorable 2016 ruling from an international tribunal on the law of the sea reinforced perceptions of American weakness and cast serious doubt on the claim that China had been "socialized" by its participation in international institutions.[94] In the end, by successfully completing an unprecedented deep-water construction campaign, and then violating an explicit pledge not to militarize its new possessions, the CCP regime strengthened its own military position while making the United States appear, if not impotent, then at least incapable of stopping China from doing what it wanted in its own backyard.[95]

The centerpiece of Xi's push for regional preponderance was diplomatic and economic rather than military, and its focal point was not the United States, but rather the nations on China's continental and maritime periphery. Beginning in 2013, the CCP started to place greater emphasis on "peripheral diplomacy," eventually transposing the traditional ordering of its foreign policy priorities so that relations with China's neighbors ranked even higher in importance than its dealings with the great powers.[96]

This shift was based on an updated assessment of what officials described as the "new situation" created by the accelerated, post-financial crisis decline in America's power coupled with its increasingly hostile attitude.[97] Under the guise of "so-called 'strategic rebalancing,'" the United States had "revamped its old tricks" and was trying to defend its "'hegemonic superpower' status" by attempting "to trap China in . . . chaos," embroiling it in conflicts with its neighbors in the hopes of disrupting its "peaceful development and rise."[98] To ensure its continued success, Beijing needed to secure its periphery and build a buffer against US mischief-making. The vast expanses along its continental frontiers also created an opportunity for China to execute a pivot of its own. With the United States making "a strategic eastward shift," some influential commentators argued that China should "do the opposite," "stabilizing the east" by neutralizing US-backed provocations in the maritime domain while "marching westward" overland across Eurasia.[99]

Chinese analysts used various metaphors and figures of speech to convey the importance of a secure periphery, describing it as the "strategic support of China's rise"[100] and the "solid ground" beneath China's feet.[101] Above all, the periphery was a stepping stone, a "springboard" that would enable China to move "from a regional power to a world power."[102] Citing the historical experience of the United States, scholar Yan Xuetong concluded that "the rise of a great power is the process by which a country becomes a regional power first and then a global power."[103]

In order to secure its position as the preponderant regional power, China had to be strong and tough, but it also needed to learn to combine "both hard and soft," drawing its neighbors towards it even as it pushed back against the Americans and their disruptive schemes.[104] The primary source of attraction would be the enormous gravitational pull of China's now massive and still-expanding economy. China's neighbors should be encouraged to become "free riders"[105] on its development and to benefit from its "huge economic and financial strength."[106]

To further focus, amplify, and propagate China's economic force field, in the fall of 2013 Xi Jinping unveiled his so-called "One Belt One Road" (OBOR) initiative (later relabeled the Belt and Road Initiative or BRI).[107] Although the details of its eventual scope and precise dimensions were deliberately left vague, this was a hugely ambitious umbrella concept, encompassing hundreds and then thousands of actual and proposed infrastructure development projects, including railways, pipelines, ports, and telecommunications links. These were to extend over land across Central Asia to Europe and the Middle East, and by sea down through the South China Sea and the Indian Ocean to the Mediterranean and the shores of Africa (see Map 5.1). OBOR was meant to create ties of trade, investment, transport, and communication that would bind China more closely to its neighbors, eventually constructing a "peripheral economic circle with China at its center."[108]

As the American scholar Rush Doshi points out, none of this was entirely new.[109] Xi took ideas and programs that had been around for some time and welded them together into a supercharged vehicle designed to accelerate progress towards China's regional strategic

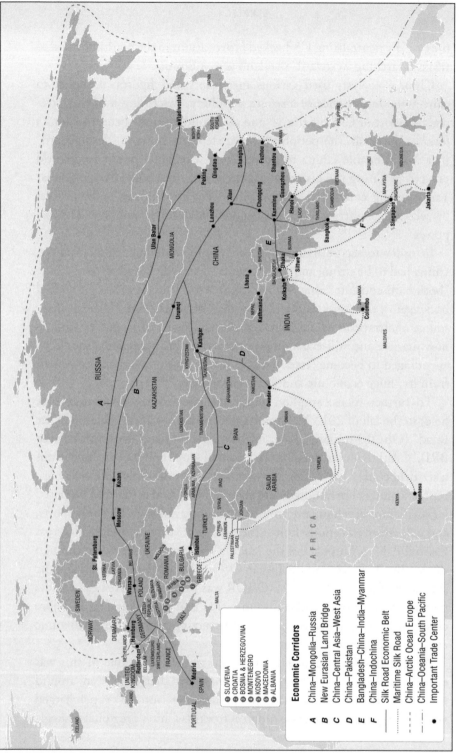

Map 5.1 The Belt and Road Initiative

Economic Corridors

- **A** China–Mongolia–Russia
- **B** New Eurasian Land Bridge
- **C** China–Central Asia–West Asia
- **D** China–Pakistan
- **E** Bangladesh–China–India–Myanmar
- **F** China–Indochina
  - Silk Road Economic Belt
  - Maritime Silk Road
  - China–Arctic Ocean Europe
  - China–Oceania–South Pacific
- ● Important Trade Center

① SLOVENIA
② CROATIA
③ BOSNIA & HERZEGOVINA
④ MONTENEGRO
⑤ KOSOVO
⑥ MACEDONIA
⑦ ALBANIA

objectives. Similarly, in defining those objectives, Xi repurposed and sharpened some older concepts, clarifying their meaning, at least to a degree. Hu Jintao had spoken of building a "community of common destiny" (CCD) that might someday unite mainland China with Taiwan. In 2013, Xi expanded the term to encompass China's entire periphery. Such a community would link China together politically as well as economically with other nations that respected one another's differences instead of insisting on the superiority of one set of values and institutions. The result would be a "non-aligned alliance" whose members would forgo "the old game of geopolitics" and live together like "an extended family coexisting harmoniously."[110]

As applied to eastern Eurasia, these parameters defined a regional system in which China would be the strongest member and from which the United States and most if not all of its democratic allies would be excluded. Any lingering doubts on this score were removed in May 2014 when Beijing unveiled its "New Asian Security Concept," a collection of ideas from the 1990s that had been rebranded and retooled into a weapon that was now used to launch a direct and sustained attack on the legitimacy of the US alliance system. Instead of being described merely as relics of the Cold War, America's alliances were portrayed bluntly as a source of instability and an obstacle to regional peace.[111] In place of the existing "Cold War . . . zero-sum" concepts and structures that divided Asia, Xi called for a new unified system to provide "common, comprehensive, cooperative and sustainable security" for the entire region. Outside powers would have little or no place in such a system because, Xi argued, "in the final analysis, it is for the people of Asia to run the affairs of Asia, solve the problems of Asia and uphold the security of Asia."[112]

Challenging America's global hegemony

Xi focused first on China's periphery, but from the outset he also had his eye on more distant horizons. For nearly a quarter-century the CCP leadership had felt compelled to live in a world they saw as dominated by America's overwhelming material power, regulated by rules and institutions that it had designed and still controlled, and shaped by the subversive influence of its supposedly universal ideals. As China's own power grew and, especially after the turn of the century, as its economic growth propelled it out into the world in search of resources and markets, this situation came to seem increasingly anomalous and uncomfortable.

Despite their growing dissatisfaction with the status quo, CCP strategists remained wary of doing anything that might be seen as posing a direct challenge to American global preeminence. Attitudes began to change somewhat after the global financial crisis, however, and by the time Hu Jintao left office Beijing was ready to declare its willingness to "play an active role" in reforming the international system so as to make it "more just and equitable."[113] But Chinese officials recoiled in horror when, in the wake of the crisis, some American commentators called for the two countries to form a "G-2" with special responsibility for global governance. The idea was a non-starter because, as one former high-ranking official revealingly explained: "When you mention leadership, you scare Chinese, because in [their] eyes . . . leadership equates [with] hegemony."[114]

As he ramped up China's efforts to reshape the periphery during his first years in office, Xi also took steps to prepare for a broader campaign of global revisionism. This involved first amplifying familiar criticisms of the existing international order as "unfair and unreasonable" and making the case that it was now inadequate and obsolete. Positioning themselves as the selfless defenders of the developing world, Chinese critics claimed that the post-Cold War order worked to preserve the privileged position of the West at the expense of the global South. Recent American efforts to spread "Western values" to other parts of the world for which they were ill suited had brought nothing but chaos and misery.[115] Faced with a growing "global disorder" for which they were largely responsible, US policy-makers were, as senior diplomat Fu Ying put it in a 2014 essay, "clearly struggling" and "betraying a sense of helplessness." The "world governance model" put in place by the United States at the end of the Cold War was "coming to an end" and a new historic period had begun, out of which a "new world order" would eventually emerge.[116]

The incoming CCP leadership team was initially circumspect about China's precise role in that process. Nevertheless, as Xi's first term drew to a close some authoritative figures were prepared to describe "the struggle over order" as the "core issue in China–US relations," one that "overcomes all others."[117] In remarks to a September 2016 Politburo study session on global governance reform, the General Secretary effectively endorsed this view, signaling an impending shift in policy. Summing up the Party's materialist theory of international norms and institutions, Xi noted that "the global governance structure depends on the international balance of power and reforms hinge on a change in the balance." Because the balance was shifting (meaning that US power was declining relative to China's), the old system was now susceptible to change. In CCP jargon, reform had become "the trend of the times." China needed to "take a chance and ride the wave," seizing the opportunity to challenge American leadership.[118]

Xi's exhortation reflected further adjustments in the Party's evolving assessment of "the propensity of things." As some Chinese analysts had anticipated, the US pivot to Asia had been constrained by budgetary pressures, as well as by unanticipated crises in the Middle East and Ukraine. Nevertheless, in its closing months, the Obama administration, increasingly disillusioned by the evident failure of its earlier approach, did try to take a tougher line with Beijing, stepping up freedom-of-navigation operations in the South China Sea, attempting to confront China over cyber-enabled intellectual property theft, and using strategic arguments to rally support for the proposed Trans-Pacific Partnership (TPP), a trade deal that Secretary of Defense Ash Carter described at one point as "as important to me as another aircraft carrier."[119] Chinese observers were quick to conclude that the old Washington Consensus in favor of engagement had finally broken down, giving rise to "growing calls . . . to contain and punish China."[120] Given the rhetoric of the two candidates in the 2016 presidential campaign, there seemed every reason to expect this trend to continue. The predicted end of the twenty-year period of strategic opportunity might still be a few years off, but the sand was slipping quickly through the hourglass.

Beijing was no doubt puzzled at first by Donald Trump's comportment and by the precise form and timing of some of his actions but, given its expectations about the long-term trajectory of US–China relations, the general direction of his policy initiatives could hardly have been surprising.[121] The Trump administration's formal designation of China as a "strategic competitor" in late 2017, its imposition of tariffs in 2018, and its harsh, ideologically tinged denunciations of the CCP regime following the 2020 outbreak of the COVID-19 pandemic were all seen as indications of America's mounting anxiety over its declining power and its increasingly desperate desire to check China's rise.[122] The fact that, despite their obvious differences, Joe Biden seemed inclined to continue many of his predecessor's policies towards China provided further confirmation of this assessment. As seen from Beijing, the combative turn in US policy was driven by deep historical forces rather than the preferences and peculiarities of any individual leader.

Starting in 2017, Party officials began to summarize their appreciation of the rapidly changing strategic situation by saying that the world was experiencing "great changes unseen in a century."[123] As Rush Doshi has shown, the proximate cause of this judgment appears to have been the United Kingdom's unexpected decisions to leave the European Union, followed a few months later by the even more surprising election of Donald Trump. Like many in the West, Chinese analysts saw these events as manifestations of a larger trend towards populism fueled by the lingering aftereffects of the global financial crisis. With their usual flair for generalizing about the West's alleged shortcomings, some Party theorists traced the roots of the recent upheavals even further back, presenting them as logical outgrowths of unconstrained American-style democratic capitalism.[124]

Trump's "America First" rhetoric, protectionist proclivities, resentment of traditional US allies, and hostility towards international institutions all seemed to presage a diminished American world role and an emerging deficit in global governance that China could exploit.[125] Rather than interpreting these developments as potentially temporary deviations from previously established policies, Chinese analysts were quick to fit them into their preferred narrative of inevitable, irreversible US retreat and wider Western decline. Subsequent events, especially the West's inadequate initial response to COVID and the deepening polarization of American domestic politics, including violent protests over the outcome of the 2020 presidential election, simply reaffirmed these judgments.[126.]

The "great changes unseen in a century" clearly referred to an impending, epoch-defining shift in the structure of the international system. While official statements continued to herald the return of multipolarity, some well-placed Chinese commentators were more blunt. Writing in 2017, one influential professor drew the conclusion that "the world structure is changing from one superpower, many great powers, to two superpowers, many great powers."[127] This was a bold departure from the usual practice of avoiding even vague suggestions of equivalence with the United States. Yet repeated invocations of a hundred-year timeline suggested that something even more remarkable was afoot. The world had already seen one transition from multipolarity to bipolarity (after World War II) and another from bipolarity to unipolarity (at the end of the Cold War). What it had not witnessed since the early decades of the twentieth century was the replacement of one global hegemon (Great Britain) by another (the United States). Noting that pandemics can have disruptive effects comparable to a world war, another prominent Chinese analyst concluded in 2020 that "the world after the pandemic will be much like the one after World War I when the British Empire was unwilling to relinquish leadership but the US was emerging." As had been true one hundred years earlier, "the old order is unsustainable while a new one is yet to come." This was "the essence of the changes unseen in a century."[128]

A grand strategy for a "new era"

Well schooled in Marxist theory, Xi Jinping had reason to feel confident that objective historical forces were driving the world in directions favorable to socialism, and thus to China. But, as a hard-headed Leninist, he could not be content simply to stand back and watch events unfold. To the contrary, as he repeated on innumerable occasions, the moment called for boldness and decisive action. It was in this spirit, at the end of 2017 and the start of his second five-year term, that Xi announced an open, if still largely indirect, attack on American global hegemony.

In his lengthy address to the 19th Party Congress, Xi made clear that his aim was nothing less than to match and eventually surpass the United States. Having "stood up," under Mao's leadership, and "grown rich," under Deng and his successors, China had entered a "new era" in which, with Xi at the helm, it would "become strong."[129] By the middle of the century, the nation would have established itself as "a global leader in terms of national strength and international influence."[130] Given that it already had the world's second largest economy, three more decades of steady growth would obviously propel it past the United States. By

2035, China would be "a global leader in innovation,"[131] and by 2050 its military would have been "fully transformed" into a "world-class" force "built to fight . . . and win wars."[132] Thanks to the success of its system, China's "cultural soft power and . . . international influence" would continue to increase.[133] The growth of all aspects of its comprehensive national power would propel China "closer to center stage"[134] in world affairs, enabling it to "take an active part in" (later amended to "an active part *in leading*") the reform of the global governance system.[135]

For over thirty years, the CCP had gone out of its way to avoid being seen as an ideological challenger to the West by denying the existence of a "China Model" potentially suitable for export. Now, in one of the most striking passages in his speech, Xi proclaimed that China had "blaz[ed] a new trail for other developing countries to achieve modernization." "Scientific socialism" offered "a new option for other countries . . . who want to speed up their development while preserving their independence."[136] Xi was here edging closer to saying in public what he had told his Central Committee colleagues secretly when he first took power back in 2013: not only did China have its own model, but that model was superior and would eventually triumph.[137] As intelligence analyst Daniel Tobin points out, "[T]his claim to have identified an alternative to the liberal democratic capitalist path to modernity is of immense significance."[138] The official Xinhua news agency summed up the message of Xi's three-and-a-half hour speech in a single sentence: "By 2050, two centuries after the Opium Wars . . . China is set to regain its might and re-ascend to the top of the world."[139]

Even in the absence of political turmoil in the West, Xi would probably have launched some variant of a global offensive during his second term. His eagerness to make progress towards the two centenary goals, his anticipation of stiffening US resistance, and the logic of his overall strategy of economic and political mobilization all pointed in the same direction. Still, the belief that the United States and its allies were weakened and distracted can only have encouraged his assertive impulses and may well have caused him to advance the schedule for some of his initiatives.

Instead of sticking with a sequential approach, in which it first concentrates on securing its dominance in eastern Eurasia before stepping out more forcefully on the global stage, Beijing is now attempting to do both simultaneously. Proceeding in this way risks further alarming the Americans and carries the obvious danger of overextension. But Chinese strategists may believe that an intensified global campaign can also help to constrict US freedom of action and deflect Washington from a single-minded focus on the Asia-Pacific.

The global dimension of Xi's strategy consists of three interlocking pieces.

First, China is attempting greatly to expand its presence and influence in the developing world and to establish itself as the leader of the global South. Especially since the start of his second term, Xi has made clear that the Belt and Road Initiative and the "community of common destiny," his two linked signature concepts, are meant to encompass not only eastern Eurasia, but large swaths of the developing world.[140] While all are welcome to join, both BRI and the CCD are clearly aimed at nations hungry for infrastructure and investment and sympathetic to Beijing's claims that the existing international system is dominated by wealthy, powerful, and arrogant Western nations seeking to impose their values on the rest of the world.

In the developing world, China seeks resources and raw materials, markets for its products, outlets for its SOEs, productive uses for its capital, low-cost manufacturing sites for its older industries, and vast new troves of data to feed its artificial intelligence algorithms. But Beijing is also taking advantage of expanding commercial relations and appeals to the idea of a "common destiny" to gain access to and influence over elites, both via the time-honored techniques of bribery and cooptation, and through more creative and forward-looking programs such as those designed to train the rising generation of bureaucrats, businessmen, military officers, and political leaders.

Despite the CCP's fervent denials that it seeks actively to spread its model, and the credulous acceptance of these claims by many Western observers, it is increasingly apparent that China is, in fact, more than willing to teach others how to monitor their populations, suppress dissent, and use state power to stimulate growth while retaining control of the private sector.[141] Success in these endeavors would benefit Beijing by rendering its clients more prosperous, more stable, and more likely to be supportive of its diplomacy and receptive to possible future requests for access to military facilities or other forms of strategic cooperation.

The second prong of Xi's global campaign involves a systematic effort to build on support from the developing world to "remake international order from the inside out" by coopting existing multinational institutions and redefining prevailing norms.[142] Beijing has become adept at exploiting the fact that most international organizations operate on the principle of "one nation, one vote" to gain greater sway in a variety of forums. By twisting arms, dangling inducements, and appealing to a shared sense of anti-Western solidarity, in recent years China has succeeded in installing its diplomats at the head of specialized UN bodies that set standards for international air travel, telecommunications, industrial development, and agriculture.[143] Once appointed, these officials act "to co-opt the institution and push narrow Chinese political objectives."[144] In this way, and through its ability to mobilize votes in the UN system more generally, China has been able to blunt criticism of its treatment of its Uighur minority, block Taiwan's participation in the World Health Organization, win UN endorsement of BRI, advance its conception of "internet sovereignty," and push technical standards designed to benefit Chinese companies.[145] Meanwhile, with the West fixated on its maneuvers at the UN and in Geneva, China is also building a set of alternative mechanisms (like the Asian Infrastructure Investment Bank) that circumvent existing institutions, advance its interests, and further enhance its influence in the developing world.[146]

Above the fray of day-to-day diplomacy, CCP strategists see themselves engaged in a "discursive struggle," a battle to push back against Western norms and narratives that is being fought in various international settings.[147] While Beijing likes to cast itself as the leading defender of the UN system, it now seeks to redefine some of the core principles on which that system was founded. Especially troubling from the CCP's perspective is the idea embodied in the 1948 Universal Declaration of Human Rights that there are certain inalienable rights and freedoms, including freedom of speech and assembly and the right to self-government. China has sought to undermine this conception of human rights by arguing that it is peculiar to the West and by putting forward its own definitions that prioritize the collective "right to development" over individual freedom. As Andrea Worden notes, these formulations are intended to be "attractive to the rest of the world, particularly to the developing and emerging countries in the 'global South.'"[148] Since 2017, Beijing has met with some success, pushing sympathetic resolutions through the UN Human Rights Council and, outside the UN system, organizing a "South–South Human Rights Forum" where representatives from an assortment of developing countries gather to dutifully endorse its views.[149]

For the Party, this fight over words is a deadly serious business. If supposedly universal principles are not, in fact, universally accepted, it becomes much harder for the West to use them to isolate and criticize China. Winning vocal support from others for its governing concepts can also help the CCP create "an international echo chamber" that will reinforce its messages to the Chinese people and render them less susceptible to subversive, liberal ideas.[150] Beijing's increasingly vociferous counter-critique of the supposedly failed West and its newfound willingness to present its own system as a model for others are also part of an effort to build a separate bloc of nations led by China and insulated from the West; they are the ideological glue that is meant to hold together a "community of common destiny." As Tanner Greer explains, Xi's vision for the future is of a world in which "democratization, free markets, and universal human rights would . . . be reduced to a parochial tradition peculiar to a smattering of outcast Western nations."[151]

Ideologically, economically, diplomatically, and perhaps eventually physically as well, Beijing seeks to isolate the West. This would not necessarily involve overthrowing and then creating a complete mirror image of the old US-dominated international order. At least for the moment, the goal appears to be to establish what Nadège Rolland has described as a "partial, loose, and malleable hegemony" over a large subsystem that would eventually encompass much of the global South.[152] If they can do this, Chinese strategists have reason to hope that they can finally free themselves from the threat of American commercial, military, and normative pressure. Commanding the world's biggest economy, dominating many international institutions, with a large portion of the planet's population behind them, and sitting astride critical sea lanes and terrestrial chokepoints, they may imagine that they will be well positioned to apply pressure of their own to the United States and its remaining democratic allies. An admirer of Mao Zedong, Xi Jinping may envision himself as implementing his hero's strategy for guerrilla warfare on a grand, global scale by using the developing world to outflank the West and "encircle the cities from the countryside."

As for the West itself, the third element of Xi's strategy requires the party-state to use all of the instruments at its disposal to delay a coordinated response to China's rise, dividing the democracies from one another to the extent possible and, above all, trying to drive wedges between the United States and its allies. While the proximate ends of this portion of Beijing's strategy remain unchanged from previous periods, the means with which they are being pursued have been greatly enhanced. Since Xi took power, China has been engaged in "a massive expansion of efforts to shape foreign public opinion in order to influence the decision-making of foreign governments and societies."[153] In addition to investing heavily in modern propaganda platforms to better "tell China's story," the Party has expanded its use of less visible, and in some cases covert, "united front" influence operations.[154] These aim to coopt foreign entrepreneurs, politicians, journalists, and academics, using them to try to shape the perceptions of their compatriots and the policies of their governments. Under Xi, these efforts have grown more extensive, more sophisticated, and more aggressive, so much so in fact that, in a number of cases, they have burst into public view, causing political controversy in the target countries and diplomatic tensions with Beijing.[155]

One of the most striking features of China's attempts to shape the behavior of the democracies, especially since 2017 and most dramatically since 2020, is the extent to which they have come to rely on coercive threats rather than purely positive inducements. Since the start of the reform period, Beijing has used the promise of access to its market to try to influence foreign companies and, through them, their governments. Under Xi, China has employed the threat of market *denial* more often, more openly, and against bigger and more powerful countries, including major advanced industrial allies of the United States such as South Korea, Germany and Australia. The clear purpose of these threats, and others like them, is to dissuade America's allies from joining it in taking actions that run counter to China's interests, to punish them for doing so, and to warn others of the rising cost of offending Beijing.[156] The CCP regime has also targeted large Western companies, attempting to silence foreign criticism of its human rights abuses by punishing those it accuses of meddling in its internal affairs.[157]

In a related initiative, reportedly at Xi's explicit direction that they show more "fighting spirit," since 2019 Chinese diplomats in democratic countries have adopted a remarkably harsh, bullying tone in their public statements.[158] These outbursts coincided with the onset of the COVID pandemic and may have been intended to rally popular support for the regime in the face of mounting foreign criticism of its handling of the disease. But "Wolf Warrior diplomacy" is also meant to intimidate democratic publics and governments, reminding them of the dangers of standing in the way of an increasingly powerful, and potentially vengeful, China. Beijing's ambassador to Sweden summed up the gangland mentality of his country's new approach to diplomacy best when he told an audience: "We treat our friends with fine wine, but for our enemies we have shotguns."[159]

Such statements may prove counterproductive in the long run, but they are unlikely to disappear even as the pandemic recedes. They are of a piece with the other elements of Xi's aggressive approach to achieving the CCP's regional and global goals and consistent with the view that, as China's power continues to grow, others will have no choice but to accede to its demands. After all, as Xi now regularly reminds his listeners, "the East is rising while the West is declining."[160]

Conclusion

The evolution of the CCP regime's external strategy has been driven forward by a mix of insecurity, ambition, and opportunism. Over the last three decades, US and other Western policy-makers have systematically underestimated the significance of each of these factors.

All the available evidence suggests that successive generations of CCP leaders have shared the same suspicion of, and animosity towards, the United States and its allies. Xi Jinping simply expresses more openly and bluntly what his post-Mao predecessors generally said behind closed doors or in more guarded language: no matter what they say or do, the democracies have always been the enemies of "new China"; they hate its socialist system, fear its growing power, and will do whatever they can to exploit, contain, and weaken it.

This is a classic case of projection: the CCP leadership assume that their democratic counterparts harbor the same ineradicable, ideologically rooted hostility towards them as they do towards the West. Indications of benign intent, such as the willingness of the democracies to open their societies and economies to assist China in its rise, are explained away as, at best, a result of greedy self-interest or, at worst, part of a nefarious long-term plan to undermine CCP rule. Meanwhile, the Party is quick to interpret every action of the United States and its allies as proof of hostile intent and justification for its own aggressive policies.

The CCP leadership's preoccupation with encirclement and subversion helps to explain why they saw the post-Cold War international order as threatening, went to great lengths to defend themselves against it, and then, as their own power grew, began to push back in an attempt to alter it. If they were aware of these perceptions, the original architects of engagement believed that they could be eased by reassurances and experience and would soften with the passage of time. Instead, the CCP's obsessions, and its desire for control, have grown stronger as China has become more powerful, but also more deeply integrated into, and exposed to, the rest of the world.

Even as they failed to appreciate the depth of the CCP regime's fears, Western strategists have been slow to recognize the extent of its ambitions. The two are linked, at least in part. As the CCP's assessment of the requirements for its own security have grown more expansive, so too has its determination to shape the policies and perceptions of others. Insecurity does not necessarily imply defensiveness. Indeed, to the contrary, when coupled with significant material power it is just as likely to act as a spur to aggression.

Over the last three decades, Western policy-makers have been compelled repeatedly to upgrade their assessments of Beijing's aims. The idea that China's leaders would want nothing more than to become a junior member of a US-dominated international system was always self-evidently dubious. By contrast, despite its inherent plausibility as an objective, American strategists were reluctant to acknowledge the fact that China was working to displace the United States as the preponderant power in East Asia.

As policy-makers focused more on the strategic intent behind Beijing's regional activities, they were slow to apprehend the scope of its emerging global ambitions. When CCP officials first began to express their discontent with the existing world order, many of their Western counterparts seem to have believed at first that all China wanted was a few more seats in various international organizations. Until very recently, the notion that Beijing was working actively to subvert, circumvent, or reshape existing institutions, and to redefine prevailing norms, would have been dismissed as conspiratorial and far-fetched.

Today, many Western observers still refuse to acknowledge the fact that China does, indeed, want to "spread its system," even if not in the same way or for the same reasons as it did under Chairman Mao. And the possibility that the CCP really means what it says about proving the superiority of socialism, and that it hopes ultimately to displace the United States as the world's predominant power, remains difficult for many to accept. The fact that China's current leaders have such grandiose ambitions does not mean that they will necessarily be able to achieve them. But understanding their thinking and acknowledging its seriousness is a necessary first step in devising a strategy to prevent them from doing so.

All of which leads to a final point: despite Beijing's self-assured claims of historical inevitability, since the turn of the century its behavior has been highly opportunistic. China's mounting aggression reflects its leaders' confidence in their growing capabilities, but also their assessment that the United States has been distracted and weakened by its own mistakes and misfortunes. This is true, up to a point. But in its eagerness to take advantage, Beijing appears to have misjudged "the propensity of things," or, more precisely, it has acted in ways that could cause it to change. By provoking the democracies and alerting them to the dangers of the policies they have been pursuing, China's leaders may have set in motion countervailing tendencies that will make it far more difficult for them to achieve their objectives and which could bring about precisely the results they have been working so hard to avoid.

6

Getting China Right

Contrary to the expectations of its architects and supporters, the policy of engagement did not induce the CCP regime to liberalize either politically or economically, nor did it result in China becoming a status quo power and a "responsible stakeholder" in the existing international order. Instead, over the course of the last three decades, Beijing has grown more repressive and militantly nationalistic at home, more aggressive and revisionist in its external behavior, and more committed to mercantilist, market-distorting economic practices.

Before turning to the question of how the United States and the other advanced industrial democracies should adjust their policies for dealing with China in light of these realities, this chapter will begin by addressing three final questions about the past: Is it, in fact, fair to say that engagement was a failure? To what extent can recent developments in China's behavior be attributed to the idiosyncratic decisions of a single leader, as opposed to the functioning of the CCP system as a whole? And, whatever the cause, why did it take so long for Western observers and policymakers to acknowledge what was happening and begin to respond?

The failure of engagement

Did engagement fail?

The increasingly repressive trend in China's domestic politics has triggered a wave of revisionism, especially, though not exclusively, in the United States: a reinterpretation or selective editing of the historical record that downplays the pervasive tone of optimism that persisted in many quarters well into the opening decades of the twenty-first century. Some analysts and former practitioners now go so far as to assert that encouraging China to become a liberal democracy was never "the goal or an achievable objective of US policy."[1] In the words of one leading scholar, it follows that "[e]ngagement can hardly be blamed for not achieving an outcome that it never took all that seriously or never expected to progress very far."[2] Political leaders may occasionally have used overly exuberant rhetoric to "shore up domestic support,"[3] but "for the most part, the US government's engagement strategy did not posit that systemic liberalization or democratization was inexorable or inevitable."[4]

These carefully worded assertions are misleading. Who was it, exactly, who never took liberalization "all that seriously"? As previous chapters have demonstrated at length and in detail, during the critical period extending from the early 1990s into the early 2000s high-ranking elected and appointed US officials, including presidents of both political parties, stated repeatedly that, among its other positive consequences, engagement would encourage China's eventual political liberalization. Such an outcome was presented as highly probable, even if it was not always described as being inevitable. While, especially during the mid-1990s, public figures sometimes tempered their statements with caveats or words of caution, these were more like fine print than bold warning labels, easily lost in a torrent of hopeful imagery, seemingly persuasive arguments, and uplifting language.

If leaders in democratic societies used these arguments in order to persuade others and to justify their preferred policies, then they were consequential, regardless of whether they were deployed cynically or in earnest. Yet, rhetorical flourishes notwithstanding, there is little reason to doubt that officials were sincere in their expressions of optimism. Far from being the unique preserve of canny politicians intent on lulling a gullible public, similar views were widely shared across broad swaths of the business, journalistic, and academic communities, including many specialists in the study of Chinese politics.

Political liberalization aside, advocates argue that engagement yielded many other valuable benefits, including cooperation on a variety of global issues, mutual economic gains, and Beijing's increasing acceptance of the existing international order. In the words of former Bush administration official Robert Zoellick: "Those who blithely assume that US cooperation with China didn't produce results in America's interests are flat wrong."[5] One recent attempt to "relitigate" the historical record notes that, starting in the 1990s, US policy-makers aimed "to prevent China from emerging as a security threat," to encourage it to shift towards "a more open, market economy," and, more specifically, to achieve a "consistent and concrete set of actionable goals," including "preventing WMD [weapons of mass destruction] proliferation in East and South Asia, preventing the nuclearization of the Korean Peninsula, cooperating on disease and environmental issues . . . [and] ensuring stability in the Taiwan Strait."[6]

Judged against these expectations, the record of the last three decades is unimpressive, to say the least. Engagement has obviously not prevented China from becoming a challenge to the security of the United States and its democratic allies, nor has it stopped nuclear weapons from spreading to the Korean Peninsula and South Asia. Far from helping to ensure peace, Beijing itself is today the major source of potential instability in the Taiwan Strait. Whatever China's past record of cooperation on public health issues, if it is not directly responsible for the COVID-19 outbreak, its initial handling of the pandemic helped unleash the worst global health crisis in over a century. Despite its professed commitment to green development, China, already the world's leading carbon emitter, has continued to build numerous coal-burning power plants both at home and abroad, and is now trying to win concessions from other nations in return for promises of future emissions reductions that it may very well be unable or unwilling to fulfill.[7]

Although decades of trade and investment with China did not result in its evolution into a fully open, market-based system, they did yield undeniable gains for many Western producers, consumers, and investors. To a far greater extent than most economists and policy-makers were at first willing to acknowledge, however, economic engagement also generated significant costs, including a loss of manufacturing jobs, productive capacity, and know-how, and the massive illicit extraction of intellectual property through theft or compulsory transfer.[8] As for the general claim that, via engagement, Washington succeeded in getting "Beijing to endorse, or at least not oppose, US goals across the globe,"[9] while this assessment may have appeared plausible during the 1990s or the early 2000s when China was still relatively weak, it is now badly out of date.

"There was no alternative"

A final argument advanced by the retrospective defenders of engagement is that, in the end, there was no alternative to it. This conclusion generally follows from a comparison between extremes, as if the only substitute for the policies actually pursued was an all-out, Cold War-style "neo-containment policy" designed to isolate China, stifle its growth, and prevent its rise.[10] If the United States had followed such a course, one scholar speculates that Beijing might have responded in ways that created a world "much more dystopian" than the one that exists today.[11]

Even if this retrospective assessment is correct, it is still possible that other, less drastic strategies might have produced more favorable outcomes. There are a number of points in the last thirty years, including in the aftermath of Tiananmen and during the runup to China's entry into the WTO, when the United States and the other advanced democracies could have modulated their approach to engagement, not cutting ties altogether but using their leverage more forcefully to try to compel Beijing to modify its domestic policies. The United States and its allies could also have taken steps to slow the growth of China's power and to impose constraints on its external behavior, for example by reacting sooner and more decisively to mounting evidence of China's massive intellectual property theft or to its increasing assertiveness in the aftermath of the global financial crisis.

Disagreements over how history might have unfolded if different decisions had been taken are ultimately impossible to resolve. Still, the claim that a full embrace of engagement was the only conceivable course, that any alternative to it would inevitably have produced even worse results, and therefore, by implication, that everything is for the best (or at least as good as it can possibly be) in this best of all possible worlds simply does not stand up to close scrutiny.[12]

Is Xi to blame?

Much recent commentary places responsibility for the unfavorable turn in Chinese foreign and domestic policy squarely on Xi Jinping's shoulders. Xi is widely perceived as having abandoned "hide and bide" and reversed China's supposed progress towards economic and political liberalization. Perhaps if he had not risen to power in 2012 the story of the past decade would have been dramatically different. And perhaps, once he goes, China will revert to a more moderate, accommodating approach to managing its own affairs and dealing with the outside world.

As we have seen, each of the main tendencies associated with Xi's reign – increased assertiveness, intensified repression, heightened nationalism, expanded reliance on high-tech industrial policy – was visible first under Hu Jintao. This is another way of saying that, in their broad outlines, Xi's policies are a product of the collective assessments of the CCP elite regarding the challenges and opportunities that the Party and the nation confront and the range of acceptable options for dealing with them.

Xi has continued to pursue the same goals as his predecessors. But that does not mean that his personality, strategic instincts, and leadership style have made no difference. To the contrary, unlike Hu Jintao, Xi is a bold, decisive, and risk-acceptant ruler. While he has not yanked the wheel and tried to change the direction in which China is moving, he has sought greatly to increase the speed at which it is traveling. Xi evidently hopes in this way to break through a daunting array of obstacles and barriers, both internal and external. This approach may yet succeed, but it could also result in a catastrophic crash.

Xi likely sees himself as the anti-Gorbachev, a man whose mistakes he has studied with great care. The last Soviet leader's attempts at reforms came too late and violated the top-down, centralizing, anti-democratic principles of Leninism, unleashing waves of political turmoil that wound up destroying the system (and the nation) they were meant to save. Xi intends to act preemptively to fend off a terminal crisis. And he is doing so by working along classic Leninist lines: strengthening the Party, tightening its grip on society, crushing dissent, and using propaganda to mobilize the masses.

Why did it take so long to acknowledge the failure of engagement?

The policy of engagement was not an obvious and self-evident mistake whose ultimate failure was predictable from the very start. Despite the lack of promising precedents, it was not entirely fanciful to have im- agined in the early 1990s that, with sufficient patience and the proper inducements, even a hardened Leninist regime could be lured and coaxed into liberalizing.

Engagement was a gamble rather than a blunder, but the odds were always extremely long. A more accurate appreciation of the character of the CCP regime might have instilled a greater sense of realism about the chances for success and a heightened sensitivity to early indications of failure. US and other Western policy-makers cannot fairly be faulted for placing their original bet. Where they erred was in doubling down on it repeatedly, and not hedging adequately against the possibility that the wager might not pay off, despite mounting evidence that this was, in fact, what was happening.

Once put in place, engagement was sustained by the convergence of several mutually reinforcing factors, all of which tended to grow stronger with the passage of time. The most consequential of these was undoubtedly the influence of business, the combined weight of the many companies, industry associations, and individuals who either benefited from trade and investment with China or hoped to do so. Business interests, in turn, were crucial in shaping the attitudes of political elites. In the United States, as the outcomes of the major trade policy battles of the 1990s made plain, the influence of the human rights groups, labor unions, and older industries wary of essentially unrestricted economic engagement was far outweighed by the combined clout of the agricultural producers, higher-tech industries, and financial sector firms that supported it. Aside from periodic expressions of concern and occasional performative gestures, most governors, mayors, and members of Congress had very little incentive to challenge existing policies and strong reasons to support them.

The views of professional politicians reflected and were reinforced by the climate of opinion in most democratic societies. Starting in the 1980s, engagement accumulated a widening circle of vocal supporters that grew to include business executives, economists, journalists, university administrators, academics, think tank analysts, and former government officials. These men and women were motivated by differing mixtures of material self-interest (including the prospect of investment, employment, access, and professional advancement), combined in many cases with a sincere belief that engagement would hasten desirable changes in China and improve the prospects for world peace.[13] The advocates of engagement were vigorous and sometimes vicious in its defense, often deploying what James Mann has described as "the lexicon of dismissal" to try to discredit critics and skeptics by labeling them as "anti-Chinese" or "China bashers" in the grips of a "Cold War mentality."[14]

Within the US government, engagement, like other major policies, acquired considerable bureaucratic momentum; once set in motion, it was sustained in part by inertia. While they were certainly aware of problems in the relationship, most diplomats and officials responsible for trade and finance were adherents of the conventional wisdom and supporters of the status quo. With the passage of time, widening pockets of dissent and concern emerged in parts of the intelligence community and the military. Well into the twenty-first century, however, even many national security professionals continued to mouth familiar bromides about the danger of "treating China as an enemy." In any event, major changes in policy could not come from the bottom up. Significant shifts in direction would have required intervention by top decision-makers convinced of the need for change and willing to invest the time, attention, and political capital necessary to bring it about.

One final factor must be taken into account, even though its impact is difficult to assess. For decades, starting in the early 1970s, the CCP worked tirelessly to shape the perceptions and behavior of Western political, business, government, and intellectual elites. The methods employed varied widely, from flattery and financial contributions to bribery and blackmail, but the basic goals remained constant: to persuade those targeted that engagement was working, that it served their individual interests as well as those of whatever companies, institutions, or governments they happened to represent, and that, in any event, there was no acceptable alternative. Still, for all of the resources that the CCP devoted to achieving these ends, it must be said that, until very recently, the regime was pushing on an open door. Like all of the best influence and deception operations, this one succeeded because it reinforced the preferences and predilections of those at whom it was directed.[15]

Like the proverbial person going bankrupt, support for engagement eroded gradually and then all (or, rather, not quite all) at once. While the process unfolded differently in other countries, in the case of the United States an accumulation of troubling evidence helped to peel back successive layers of a once-solid consensus. Already by the turn of the century,

China's military buildup was starting to raise serious doubts about its acceptance of the regional status quo. These concerns were amplified after 2008 by Beijing's increasingly assertive prosecution of disputes with its maritime neighbors, and again, after 2014, by Xi's island construction campaign. As for China's anticipated political liberalization: although some perceptive observers began to speculate about the sources of the CCP regime's "resilience" as early as the start of the Hu Jintao era, expectations of imminent, positive political change persisted for at least another decade, dissipating only after it became apparent that Xi Jinping was the antithesis of a liberal reformer.

Even before Xi took office, mounting frustration over China's state-enabled theft of intellectual property, limitations on access to its market, and systematic violation of both the letter and the spirit of its other WTO commitments had started to eat away at confidence that business as usual was really in the best interests of American (and Western) business. Especially following the 2015 publication of Beijing's "Made in China 2025" report, dawning recognition of the intent behind its high-tech industrial policies caused this process to quicken, both in the United States and in Europe. The fraying of the business coalition that had sustained engagement for so long helped change the tenor of the debate on China policy. By the closing years of Obama's second term, both Republicans and Democrats in Congress were urging the White House to take a tougher line with Beijing on a range of issues.

Regardless of who was in charge, by the second decade of the twenty-first century powerful trends were carrying China and the United States towards a more open and intense rivalry. Xi Jinping and Donald Trump helped accelerate these tendencies. Xi's ramped-up domestic repression and bluntly combative approach to international affairs served to dispel lingering doubts about the true character of the CCP regime and the nature of its intentions. Trump's willingness to say and do things that his predecessors had not, including imposing tariffs and otherwise constricting economic engagement, reinforced Beijing's long-held belief that the Americans were determined to hold China down. The fact that the ensuing trade war did not unleash a global catastrophe, as some Western experts had predicted, helped strengthen the case for taking a more confrontational approach to dealing with Chinese mercantilism.

Although there is little evidence that he knew or cared about the details, in addition to imposing tariffs Trump empowered people in the lower levels of his administration to implement tougher policies on a range of other issues, including controlling exports of some high-technology products, tightening restrictions on Chinese investments, calling attention to the CCP's political influence operations, and pressuring allies to block Chinese companies from building their next-generation telecommunications networks.[16] The combination of Trump's disdain for conventional wisdom and his combative impulses produced a sharper, more rapid shift in US policy than might otherwise have occurred, and accelerated the ongoing erosion of support for the old policy of engagement.

Despite Donald Trump's polarizing effect on virtually every other issue, Republicans and Democrats were able to agree on the need for a change in US China policy and, for the first time, ambitious figures in both parties began to compete to see who could stake out the tougher stance.[17] During the 2020 campaign, Joe Biden accused his opponent of failing to match tough talk with effective action[18] and, in his first address to Congress in 2021, the newly elected president made a point of urging bipartisan support for waging what he described as a "deadly earnest" contest with China.[19] In another indication of nascent convergence, at least during its opening months the Biden administration continued to pursue many of the policies it had inherited, leaving in place Trump's tariffs, export controls, and investment restrictions and even adding a few of its own.[20]

Unanticipated events also played a role in weakening support for engagement. Beijing's handling of the COVID-19 pandemic, including its unprecedented rhetorical and economic attacks on governments perceived as critical, and its refusal to cooperate in investigating the origins of the outbreak, contributed to a rapid hardening of attitudes in the United States and across the democratic world. Between 2019 and the summer of 2020, public opinion polls revealed a dramatic, double-digit increase in negative perceptions of China in both Europe and Asia (see Figure 6.1).[21]

Future historians may conclude that the pandemic dealt a mortal blow to engagement. The policy is far from dead, however, and many of its long-time supporters are working hard to revive its reputation and give

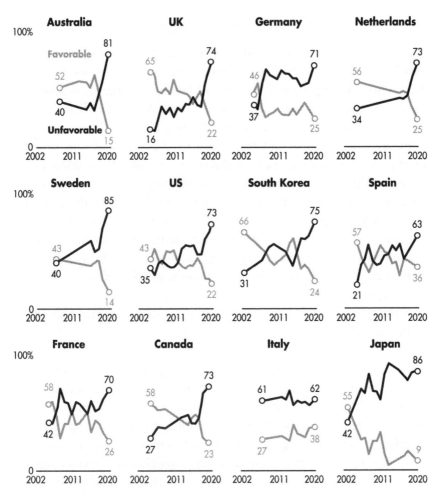

Figure 6.1 Public attitudes towards China, 2002–2020
Source: "Unfavorable Views of China Reach Historic Highs in Many Countries,"
Pew Research Center, Washington, DC, October 6, 2020

it new life. The COVID crisis helped shatter the old strategic consensus but, unlike previous galvanizing events, such as the Japanese attack on Pearl Harbor or the outbreak of the Korean War, it was not sufficient in itself to forge a new one. What a new strategy should look like, and whether the United States and its allies can agree on its details in the absence of a truly catastrophic setback, are the subjects to which we now turn.

The lexicon of strategic paralysis

Just as in the discussion of China's prospects for political liberalization that James Mann analyzed in his book *The China Fantasy*, so also in the debate over strategy there is an array of familiar "epithets, catch-words, phrases, and concepts that attempt to isolate the speaker before his or her ideas can be examined seriously."[22] Here too, while some messages originate with the CCP and are echoed by Western observers, in other cases traffic flows in the opposite direction, with the many finely tuned organs of the party-state picking up, amplifying, and retransmitting the opinions of foreigners that serve its purposes. Whatever their origins, these words and phrases tend to constrict thought, preemptively closing off contemplation of some options, and channeling discussion towards the conclusion that, in the end, any significant deviation from the policies of the past would be dangerous and doomed to fail. Call it the "lexicon of strategic paralysis."

Although the list is long, the following entries are among the most common and influential:

"New Cold War." Perhaps the most damning thing a Chinese official can say about a foreigner (and especially an American) is that they suffer from a "Cold War mentality."[23] This term implies an inclination to think in stark, zero-sum terms, to cultivate public attitudes of suspicion and hostility towards an imagined enemy, and to mobilize societal resources for a protracted economic, military, and ideological competition against a deceitful and determined opponent. Of course, these are precisely the attitudes and policies that China's leaders have adopted in their dealings with the West, and which they have sought to discourage it from reciprocating. The CCP regime knows that if the United States and its allies were ever truly to revert to a Cold War mentality, China could find itself faced with an awakened, focused, and unified opponent whose combined resources far outweigh its own.

Some Western analysts argue that, despite the recent downward spiral in relations, comparisons to the "old" Cold War are inaccurate due to the alleged absence of ideological rivalry between China and the democracies, and the undeniable existence of deep commercial linkages between them.[24] Mirroring the comments of their Chinese counterparts, others caution that adopting a "Cold War mentality" is a formula for overextension, miscalculation, and self-inflicted harm.[25] For many Americans, in particular, any reference to the Cold War immediately conjures up unhappy memories of McCarthyism and Vietnam.

Of course, no simple parallels can be drawn between past and present. However, on closer inspection some of the supposed differences between today's world and the Cold War era are less stark than they are made out to be, and others, while real, may not have the significance commonly ascribed to them. Despite what many commentators have claimed, it is evident that, from Beijing's perspective and increasingly from Washington's as well, there is indeed an ideological contest underway, albeit one that will take different forms and be waged in different ways than its predecessor. As for the supposedly soothing effects of economic interdependence, the last several years have served as a reminder that, instead of always promoting amity and cooperation, extensive commercial ties can also become a source of friction and a locus of geopolitical competition.

What is emerging today is an intense, global, economic, technological, military, diplomatic, and ideological rivalry between two superpowers, each of which is already trying to gather a coalition of clients and like-minded states around it. No doubt some pundit will eventually coin a pithy phrase with which to capture this reality. In the meantime, saying that it is not (or should not be) "another Cold War" will not wish it out of existence. And, while warnings against prosecuting this new form of rivalry with excessive zeal are no doubt appropriate, the democracies cannot allow fear of overreacting to become an excuse for continuing inaction.

"Containment." Chinese strategists have long harbored a deep, even obsessive, fear of containment. During the first two decades of the Cold War, this was hardly surprising, given that the express aim of US policy was precisely to contain China. Anxieties about containment and "encirclement" have, however, persisted down to the present. This mindset is due, in part, to geography: China now has fourteen contiguous neighbors, including several with which it has a history of animosity. The maritime domain also gives cause for concern. In order to reach the open ocean, Chinese ships must transit relatively narrow channels

susceptible to blockade by the naval and air forces of hostile offshore powers. As China's dependence on seaborne commerce has grown, so too has the significance of this potential vulnerability.[26] More generally, Beijing's current worries are also a manifestation of its desire to play a greater global role; a power that did not want to expand its presence and influence would be less concerned about being contained.

When Beijing's ambassador to the United States says, "I don't think anybody would be able to contain China," he is expressing a hope rather than a certainty.[27] Still, most Western commentators are inclined to agree that China's containment is impossible.[28] Unlike the Soviet Union, the PRC is arguably just too big and potentially powerful to be hemmed in militarily and too deeply enmeshed in global trade to be economically isolated. In part for these reasons, but also because they are not convinced that it poses an immediate threat to them, many other countries, and especially China's neighbors, may be unwilling to engage in an effort at containment, even if the United States tries to cajole them into doing so.[29]

The question of whether the democracies can or should try to restructure their economic relations with China will be taken up in the next section. As for the challenge of maintaining a traditional balance of "hard" power: the skeptics are correct to point to the sheer magnitude of the resources that Beijing already has at its disposal and the likelihood that these will grow in the years ahead. And they are right to highlight the difficulties that the United States and its partners will face in coordinating their efforts to counter China's power as it grows. But these observations define the parameters of a tough strategic problem rather than proving that it is unsolvable.

The assertion that China cannot be "contained" also mischaracterizes the nature of the challenge. The United States and its partners need not try to contain China in the way that they did the Soviet Union: by establishing a formal multilateral alliance, building up massive military forces to prevent it from crossing a clear territorial boundary, and resolutely opposing its every effort to project power and exert influence far from its borders. However, if they wish to ensure their own security, they are going to have to find ways to offset and neutralize China's growing ability to impose its will upon them, whether through coercive threats, direct attack, or by gaining control over key chokepoints or portions of the global commons.

This will not be easy, but there is no reason to conclude that it is impossible. Beijing's belligerence, and the unease that this has caused in capitals across Asia and around the world, have already helped ease some of the collective action problems that might otherwise doom any attempt to construct a countervailing coalition. China's resources are large but they are by no means infinite, especially when compared to the combined wealth of the countries that might come together to oppose it. If China's economic growth continues to slow while internal demands on state resources continue to rise, Beijing will have difficulty sustaining a military buildup as rapid as the one it has funded over the last thirty years. As for the actual conduct of military operations: as its strategists are keenly aware, China's geography complicates the task of projecting power beyond its coastal waters, and the difficulties will grow greater the further out into the world its forces seek to go. Meanwhile, China's heavy reliance on the sea for both imports and exports and its increasingly far-flung interests and investments create serious vulnerabilities that its opponents could exploit to strengthen deterrence or wage a future conflict. It may be true that China cannot be contained, but its power can certainly be counterbalanced.

"Decoupling." For all of the progress China has made, it remains heavily dependent on the West for markets, capital, and, above all, certain critical technologies. As the old consensus around engagement has broken down, Beijing has grown increasingly worried that the United States and the other advanced industrial democracies will take further steps to constrict its access to these resources. As part of its campaign to forestall or at least delay this eventuality, the CCP regime has sought to position itself as the defender of globalization and an opponent of "decoupling," which Xi Jinping described in a recent speech as working "against economic and market principles."[30]

Coming from a self-proclaimed Marxist, such statements are ironic, to say the least, but they are also deliberately misleading. What Xi has in mind when he speaks of globalization is a decidedly lopsided world in which other nations must leave themselves open to China, while China retains the right to restrict access to its own economy and society. Even as it decries talk of decoupling by others, Beijing now seeks actively, and more or less explicitly, to reduce its dependence on the economies of the democracies, especially in high-technology sectors, while trying to ensure that they remain dependent on it.

For their part, many Western analysts and business executives warn that decoupling from China "isn't just perilous – it's impossible."[31] The reasons given have mostly to do with cost. The structures of global production that have evolved since the 1990s are undoubtedly efficient, enabling companies from around the world to take advantage of China's massive and relatively low-cost manufacturing base to obtain parts or assemble finished products. Unraveling these supply chains and trying to relocate productive capacity to other countries could be enormously expensive and might take years to accomplish. The overall growth of the Chinese economy, and the emergence of a large population of middle-class consumers, have also created a vast market for goods and services. Many Western companies are eager, even desperate, to obtain, preserve, or widen their access to that market; some worry that decoupling from China could sound their "death knell."[32]

As with warnings against containment and a new Cold War, there is truth here, but also the danger of distortion. It is easy to generate staggering estimates for the cost of decoupling by comparing the situation that exists today to an imaginary one in which all ties of trade and investment have been cut or severely constricted, or in which it is assumed that only one advanced industrial country (usually the United States) would try to decouple from China while the others stepped in to fill its place.[33] Such extreme outcomes are not the only ones conceivable, of course, nor are they very likely, barring the outbreak of war or some other intense and prolonged crisis.

One difficulty with the use of the word "decoupling" is that it suggests an all-or-nothing proposition. In fact there are many possible equilibrium points between the status quo and complete, mutual economic closure. The real questions are (or ought to be): Which of these points would be most favorable to the security as well as the welfare of the advanced industrial democracies? What policies will be necessary in order to reach them? And who will bear the costs of adjustment?

"Regime change." The CCP leadership fret ceaselessly about the prospect of domestic instability and have never stopped warning Party members that "hostile foreign forces" are trying to foment unrest and promote

"peaceful evolution." To express such concerns too openly, however, would be to acknowledge that the regime might not, in fact, enjoy the unquestioning love and undivided loyalty of its citizens. Instead, when it feels under external pressure, the Party tries to wrap itself in the protective cloak of national pride. Any criticism of its policies becomes an attack on the Chinese people, who will, of course, resolutely reject attempts to "split" them from the CCP[34] and to "pitch them against one another."[35]

Precisely because it is such a sensitive subject, many analysts warn that democratic governments should avoid criticizing the CCP in ways that might appear to question its legitimacy. In this view, attempts to take the Party on directly, even if only with words, could easily backfire, causing patriotic citizens to rally around the red flag. Anything resembling an explicit policy of regime change would scuttle much-needed cooperation on the usual list of global challenges. If it made China's leaders feel that their backs were to the wall, such an approach might even increase the risk of war.[36]

History suggests that, no matter what Western leaders say and do, their CCP counterparts will remain convinced that the democracies are working day and night to bring them down. Beijing believes that rivalry with the West is inescapable and the stakes are existential. This is not an argument for reckless pugnacity, but rather a reminder of why attempts at reassurance are doomed to fail. By the same token, while China's leaders would certainly prefer it if they could dissuade Western countries from questioning the performance and the moral foundations of their regime, they will hardly be shocked by an intensification of such critiques. The CCP's obsessive insecurity is an obvious point of vulnerability, one that the democracies cannot erase without subordinating themselves to Beijing, and which they should not refrain from exploiting out of an exaggerated fear of provoking conflict.

Objectives

The United States and its partners have not yet come fully to grips with the difficulty of the strategic conundrum they now confront. As the preceding pages have made clear, the root cause of Beijing's objectionable and threatening behavior is the nature of China's Communist Party regime. With the failure of their efforts to promote "peaceful evolution," the democracies lack any obvious way to encourage liberalizing reforms and, not without reason, they have largely lost confidence in their ability to do so.

At the same time, however, there is little prospect of a stable and mutually satisfactory accommodation between CCP-ruled China and the West. This is not due to the predilections of a single, replaceable leader. The notion that removing Xi Jinping from the equation would somehow enable an easy return to a more constructive relationship is a pleasing illusion. To the extent that China refrained from challenging the West in the past it was because its rulers assessed their position to be relatively weak. The combination of the CCP's Leninist, zero-sum view of politics, the scope of its long-standing ambitions, the depth of its animus towards the West, and, now, its confidence in China's growing power mean that, at least for the foreseeable future, true "peaceful coexistence" is unlikely. In the end, there is little overlap between what China's rulers really want and what Washington and its allies can, or should be willing to, give.

What this suggests is that, in the first instance, the goals of a new strategy must be defensive. Having tried and failed to transform China by drawing it into an inclusive and globe-spanning liberal international order, the democracies must once again band together to strengthen and protect the core of what American planners described in 1950 as a "successfully functioning political and economic system in the free world."[37] In practical terms, this will require pursuing the four main lines of effort described in more detail below: the United States and its partners must mobilize their societies for a protracted rivalry with China and harden them against CCP influence operations; partially disengage their economies from China's while strengthening ties among themselves; intensify military preparations and diplomatic measures to deter coercion or aggression; and actively challenge Beijing's ideological narratives, both in the developing world and, to the extent possible, inside China itself.

A purely defensive strategy might have been adequate to check the revisionist ambitions of a relatively weak rival, but it will no longer suffice against an opponent as powerful and aggressive as China has become. Instead of simply responding to the CCP regime's initiatives or trying to match its strengths, the democracies must therefore identify and exploit some of its critical weaknesses and vulnerabilities. The offensive elements of a new strategy should be designed to impose costs on Beijing, to slow the growth in its power and influence, and to force it to redirect some of its resources towards defending itself rather than expanding its sphere of control or preparing to attack or coerce others. At a minimum, if they wish to hold their own, the democracies can no longer afford policies that enable China to grow stronger more quickly than it would otherwise be able to do.

Lenin advised his disciples to "probe with bayonets. If you encounter mush, proceed. If you encounter steel, withdraw." China's current leaders have yet to fully encounter steel. As they do, a period of intensified competition will ensue, perhaps followed eventually by an interval of stalemate. This will be, at best, a dynamic and potentially unstable equilibrium of the sort that prevailed during the middle stages of the US–Soviet Cold War, rather than any kind of mutually agreed, permanent settlement.

In the longer run, by blocking the thrust of Beijing's aggression and forcing it to confront the full costs and contradictions of its policies, both foreign and domestic, the democracies should seek to compel the CCP leadership to alter their assessment of "the propensity of things" and to moderate their approach and modify their direction. If it comes, change will take time. Over the last two decades, the Party's strategists have become increasingly confident that they have the wind at their backs and, as always, its leaders claim to believe that ultimate victory is inevitable. Still, as was true of the former Soviet Union, an accumulation of failures and frustrations, the exhaustion of the Party's preferred policies, growing dissatisfaction among both elites and the "masses," and the rise of a new generation of leaders could at least set the stage for experimentation with alternative approaches.

A final point: as they push back against CCP-ruled China, the democracies should try to avoid measures that might delay or foreclose the possibility of more fundamental changes in the character of the nation's political system. To the contrary, even as they acknowledge that China's future is not theirs to decide, the United States and its allies should continue to articulate the hope that liberal reforms will someday be possible and to try to create conditions that may make them more likely. What is at stake is not only the well-being of the Chinese people, as important as that may be. For as long as it continues to be ruled by a Leninist regime, a powerful China will pose a threat to free nations and democratic principles.

Objections

Some critics will object that the strategy described here makes cooperation impossible, increases the risk of war, spurs nationalism, and empowers CCP "hardliners." Others may also argue either that a new strategy is unnecessary because China is weaker than it seems, or that it is too late to implement one because China has grown so strong. None of these claims is persuasive.

- Provided there is a genuine convergence of interests, there is no reason why the democracies cannot reach agreements with China on discrete issues, including climate change. But democratic leaders need to disabuse themselves, and their publics, of the notion that cooperation in one area will lead to broader understandings, still less to an eventual commonality of visions and values.
- Rather than increasing the risk of war, a firmer and steadier approach to dealing with China can actually help to reduce it. Despite their sometimes overheated rhetoric, the current CCP leadership have shown no inclination to lash out blindly or to enter into confrontations that they have reason to fear they might lose or that could spin out of control. That said, as competition intensifies, Beijing may try deliberately to manufacture crises and "war scares" in hopes of intimidating its opponents and weakening their will to resist. For this reason, mechanisms that can help to prevent accidents and enable emergency communications would be desirable. Unless current trends are reversed, however, the greatest risk of miscalculation is likely to arise from an underestimation by China's leaders of the capabilities and resolve of the democracies.
- Faced with greater external opposition, the CCP will use yet more nationalist rhetoric and attacks on "hostile foreign forces" to sustain popular support. These are familiar tactics, deployed even when the United States and its partners were bending over backwards to be obliging to Beijing. At some point, they may begin to lose their persuasive power. In any event, all that the democracies can do is to convey as clearly as possible that their less accommodating stance is a direct response to the CCP leadership's own misguided policies.
- Concerns about empowering CCP "hardliners" are also misplaced.

The notion that there were doves nestling quietly in the Party's ranks was always dubious, and there is certainly no evidence that any currently exist. Sustained opposition to Beijing's current course is more likely eventually to force change than further fruitless attempts at accommodation. The policies of the dominant hawks must be defeated and their ideas discredited before any doves can be expected to emerge.

- While it is possible that the rigidities and distortions of China's economic system will eventually be its undoing, this will not happen quickly. It will certainly take longer, and might not happen at all, if Beijing continues to enjoy anything like its current levels of access to the resources of the true market economies. Simply standing back and waiting for the CCP's current policies to fail would not be a prudent strategy; continuing to help the regime to sustain its momentum without having to undertake fundamental reforms would be even worse.
- After decades of hiding its capabilities, Beijing is now doing what it can to exaggerate them. The CCP's triumphalism is meant to encourage the belief that resistance is futile. Although the hour is late and the danger real, there is no reason at this point to conclude that China has grown too powerful to oppose. As Figure 6.2 makes clear, the combined

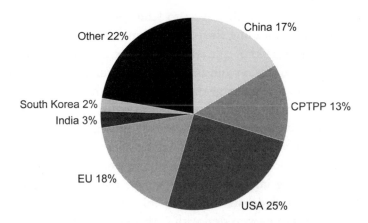

Figure 6.2   Shares of global GDP, 2020
Note: The Comprehensive and Progressive Agreement for Trans-Pacific Partnership (CPTPP) includes Australia, Brunei, Canada, Chile, Japan, Malaysia, Mexico, New Zealand, Peru, Singapore, and Vietnam. Calculated in current USD with GDP in 2020, with the exception of Japan's GDP from 2019.
Source: The World Bank

resources of the United States and its advanced industrial partners amount to over half of global GDP, far outweighing Beijing's share of 17%.[38] If the democracies fail to defend themselves, it will be because, as was true in the inter-war years, they lacked "those elements of persistence and conviction" necessary to preserve their own security.[39]

Mobilization

Without popular backing, democratic governments cannot hope to generate the resources and implement the policies they will need to engage in protracted, costly, and potentially dangerous rivalries with powerful and determined illiberal opponents. The point is no less important for being obvious: in a democracy, political mobilization is the essential precondition for strategic success and, at times, for survival. Here democratic leaders often find themselves confronted by a paradox: because of the many diverse interests and divergent demands that characterize their societies, mobilizing public support to address an external threat is generally difficult in the absence of a severe crisis or catastrophic setback. Yet one of the primary goals of sound strategy must be precisely to forestall such disasters.

Squaring this circle with respect to China will not be easy. Decades of soothing and misleading rhetoric, combined more recently with dire warnings about the risks of cold wars, trade wars, and even hot wars, have left a residue of confusion and uncertainty regarding the true nature of the CCP regime, the challenge that it poses, and the possible dangers of confronting it. In the United States, but to a degree in other countries as well, it may be especially difficult to rally support at a moment when economic progress has been disrupted by a once-in-a-century public health crisis, political and social divisions run unusually deep, and the viability of existing institutions, and perhaps even of democracy itself, are topics of serious debate. Given all this, it is hardly surprising that most discussions of how to deal with China begin, and many end, with the recommendation that the United States, in particular, must first "put its house in order." As with other tropes they find useful, this is one that Chinese officials are only too happy to repeat.[40]

For the democracies, attending to their numerous and now all-too-visible shortcomings and sources of potential weakness is a necessary but insufficient condition for competing successfully against China. Instead of having the luxury of tackling these tasks in sequence, both will have to be addressed simultaneously. As daunting as these conditions may appear, they are not unique. In the 1970s and early 1980s, as they started to face up to the implications of the Soviet Union's ongoing military buildup and its increasing adventurism in the Third World, US policy-makers were also dealing with oil price shocks, high inflation, slower growth, and the lingering aftereffects of political assassinations, racial unrest, a presidential impeachment, and a painful defeat in Vietnam. Then as now, it is no coincidence that illiberal powers chose to become more belligerent at a moment when the democracies appeared to be hobbled and preoccupied. Today as in the past, however, the belated recognition of a gathering threat can serve to galvanize democratic societies, helping to overcome partisan divisions, and giving them an added impetus to address some of the stubborn societal problems that tempted aggression in the first place.

Democratic leaders seeking to build popular support for competition with China need to navigate two distinct challenges: achieving what social psychologists refer to as "othering" without indulging in dangerous and damaging excess, and preserving the openness of public deliberation and debate while limiting the extent to which these can be manipulated by the CCP.

Public officials must begin by acknowledging and explaining the failure of past policies and conveying as accurately as possible the extent and urgency of the dangers their nations confront. The purpose should not be to cast blame but to build consensus. Above all, political leaders and opinion-makers have a responsibility to be precise about the root cause of the problem, the identity of the "other" against whom their societies must now rally in self-defense.

As political scientists Jeff Colgan and Robert Keohane point out, "othering" is crucial to the formation of both individual and national identities because "a clear sense of who is not on your team makes you feel closer to those who are." Colgan and Keohane argue that strengthening feelings of solidarity and national identity among Americans, in particular, "will require othering authoritarian and illiberal countries." For this purpose, the authors urge leaders to stress that "although the United States may have an interest in cooperating with undemocratic countries, it identifies only with liberal democracies and reserves its closest relationships for them."[41] Other democratic governments should follow the same advice. After decades of trying to assume away or blur over the distinctions, it is past time to highlight the vast gulf in values and practices that separates liberal and illiberal regimes. The corollary is clear: whatever their differences and disagreements, the democracies have far more in common with one another than they do with their authoritarian rivals.

As regards China, the process of "othering" must be focused very precisely on the CCP. The United States and its democratic partners have no quarrel with the Chinese people, still less with people of Chinese origin who are living in, or may be citizens of, other countries. Nor can the true source of their difficulties be found in the words or deeds of China's present government or the personality of its leader. The opposition between China and the democracies is systemic; it springs from the fundamental character of the CCP regime, the illiberal principles on which it operates, and the repressive and aggressive policies that flow directly from them.

Ugly talk of the sort in which Donald Trump indulged when he insisted on referring to COVID-19 as "the China virus" risks arousing xenophobic, racist passions and provoking unfounded suspicion and even violence against people based on their perceived ethnicity. This is abhorrent and dangerous in itself, but it is also corrosive of the very social cohesion that the United States and other democracies ought to be trying to cultivate. At the same time, leveling accusations of racism against responsible critics of Beijing is unfair, makes reasoned discussion impossible, and tends to reinforce the CCP's claims that it alone speaks for the Chinese people and that anyone who opposes it is a "brazen . . . China-hater."[42]

One of the great advantages of liberal societies is their openness to debate and disagreement over important issues. As they mobilize to compete more effectively against China, the democracies must take care to preserve this source of strength, but they must also do more to defend their deliberative processes from foreign interference and influence operations. These will intensify as Beijing tries to prevent a coordinated response to its increasingly menacing behavior. The challenge for the democracies will be to protect legitimate expressions of divergent opinion while constricting the CCP's ability to interfere in debates over critical questions of national policy.

In some cases, new laws may be required, as in Australia, which in 2018 barred non-citizens from contributing to its political campaigns, or in the United States, where Chinese state media organizations are now required to register as agents of a foreign government. For the most part, however, greater openness and transparency are preferable to more rules and government oversight. The democracies should strive to reduce the effectiveness of CCP "United Front" tactics by increasing the public's knowledge about how they work. The Party typically uses seemingly unofficial organizations and nominally private individuals to gain access to often-unsuspecting institutions and influential people in target countries in hopes of shaping their views. More readily available information about the links between these intermediaries and the organs of the party-state would raise awareness and reduce the risks of manipulation. Their counterparts in democratic societies must understand that, in today's China, no think tank, foundation, university, or company is truly independent; all must ultimately answer to the CCP. Even if they are not restricted by law from doing so, former politicians, government officials, and private institutions in democratic countries should face public scrutiny and possible reputational consequences if they accept funds or agree to affiliations with entities acting on behalf of the party-state.

Partial disengagement[43]

Thirty years of engagement have fueled China's growth, accelerated its technological development, and given it extraordinary access to, and increasing leverage over, the societies and economies of nations its leaders now regard with open hostility and no small measure of disdain. If they are to preserve the autonomy of their political systems, promote the welfare of their citizens, and protect the physical security of their nations, the democracies must radically restructure their economic relations with China. Nothing is more important and nothing will be more difficult.

The place to begin is for the advanced industrial democracies to acknowledge that China is a different kind of economic actor and that they can no longer afford to treat it as if it were not. It should now be clear beyond any doubt that Beijing has no intention of abandoning its market-distorting trade, technology, and industrial policies. The CCP regime will continue for as long as it can to subsidize its industries, restrict access to its domestic market, and enable the theft or forced transfer of foreign technology. The potentially harmful impact of all this on the welfare of other countries has been magnified by the massive size of the Chinese economy. Unless and until they can find a way to compel Beijing to abandon its predatory practices, the democracies now have no choice but to defend themselves. If China will not reciprocate their openness, the advanced industrial nations must close their economies, at least in part, to China.

But the difficulties run deeper than the particulars of Beijing's trade and industrial policies. The mercantilist mentality of China's rulers causes them to approach commercial relations as a domain of political struggle. In this view, the object of trade is not to improve the lot of China's people, or to achieve mutual gains along with its partners, but to enhance the nation's power relative to other nations. Given the nature of Beijing's ambitions, its economic policies thus pose a threat to the security of the democracies as well as to their future prosperity. The problem is not just the manner in which the CCP regime seeks to generate wealth, but the uses to which that wealth will be put.

Trying to incorporate a mercantilist-Leninist system into an open global economic order, treating it like an aspiring liberal state in the hopes that it would become one, has produced an array of vulnerabilities that the democracies have only recently begun to address. The fact that even nominally private Chinese corporations must ultimately do the bidding of the party-state means that it would be imprudent to treat them the same as if they were headquartered in a true market economy. To defend themselves against surveillance or sabotage, the United States and its allies must prohibit Chinese companies from building portions of their information technology networks, power grids, and other sensitive infrastructure. Democratic governments also need to do more to protect the personal data of their citizens from falling into the hands of entities beholden to the CCP. The practice of allowing Chinese SOEs to acquire and manage ports in democratic countries should be curtailed and, where possible, these facilities should be put back in the hands of trusted operators. And Chinese companies should not be permitted to raise capital in Western financial markets without first submitting to careful scrutiny of their accounting procedures and links to the party-state.

The past openness of the democracies enabled China to develop its scientific and technical capabilities more rapidly than would otherwise have been feasible. If its political and economic systems had evolved differently, this might not have been a problem. As things stand, however, it is essential for both commercial and military reasons that the United States and its partners restrict China's access to technology in order to retain an edge in at least some key areas. It is now generally agreed that the US government, in particular, should do more to foster innovation by investing in education and basic research, adopting immigration policies that attract men and women of talent from around the world, making it easier for the public and private sectors to work together, and engaging in collaborative research and development with like-minded countries.[44] Less widely acknowledged and more controversial is the proposition that, if they are to stay ahead, the advanced democracies must also cooperate in reducing the pace at which ideas and technologies first developed in their national R&D systems diffuse to China. Such measures will not prevent China from advancing, but they will slow it down in some areas and require it to bear more of the cost of the innovations from which it benefits.

In part, this will be a matter of strengthening defenses against scientific and industrial espionage, tightening enforcement of laws against intellectual property theft, and punishing Chinese firms for violating rules against forced technology transfer by imposing tariffs on their exports and restricting their ability to raise money in Western capital markets. Here again, however, the democracies can no longer afford to treat China as if it were just another normal trading partner, albeit one with some bad habits that it can be coaxed into abandoning. Even when they are not clearly in violation of previously existing national laws and international rules, potential transactions between Chinese companies and their Western counterparts must be subject to greater government scrutiny and special restrictions. In recent years, many of the advanced industrial nations have moved towards tighter screening of proposed investments from China. The US government has also begun to impose controls on the export of certain critical technologies and to discuss with some of its allies the possibility that they might take similar measures.[45] The effectiveness of restrictions on both investments and exports would be greatly enhanced if they were implemented on a multilateral basis.

The evolving structure of the global economy has left the democracies susceptible to coercion by Beijing. In its narrower form, this problem is a result of the fact that production of some critical materials and manufactured goods has come to be heavily concentrated within China. The COVID pandemic illuminated the risks of depending on a single, potentially uncooperative or even hostile source for the drugs and protective gear needed to cope with a mass medical emergency. Sudden loss of access to an assortment of chemicals, minerals, electronic components, and other parts could also disrupt economies in peacetime and complicate efforts to increase production of arms and military equipment in the event of a crisis or war. To mitigate these risks, democratic governments need to identify potential bottlenecks and then use tax incentives and other inducements to encourage the diversification of supply chains away from China. Instead of pursuing the chimerical goal of autarky, the democracies should work together to build networks in which productive capacity is distributed among groups of trusted partners.[46]

The extent to which other countries, or influential firms and sectors within them, have become dependent on the expanding Chinese market as a source of demand for their goods and services has created opportunities for a more generalized form of economic coercion. Beijing's increasingly frequent and brazen wielding of market access as a weapon is clearly intended both to punish the targeted countries or companies and to intimidate others. In the near term, the democracies should respond by working together to create mechanisms for collective economic defense. Operating on the principle that "an attack on one is an attack on all," these would commit members to retaliate for acts of economic aggression by imposing tariffs and sanctions on China and offering assistance to its intended victim.[47]

In the longer run, the only sure way of reducing Beijing's leverage will be to reduce dependence on China as a market as well as a production base. Given the potential for near-term profits, even companies that know they will eventually be squeezed out and displaced by government-backed domestic competitors will resist making such a transition.[48] If Xi Jinping's dual-circulation strategy works as it is intended to do, however, they may eventually have little choice. In the meantime, democratic governments should deploy a mix of regulations, legal restrictions, and economic inducements to encourage adjustment and help bring the interests of Western-based companies into closer alignment with the national interests of their home countries.

Economic historian Benn Steil suggests that the democracies have reached a juncture similar to the one they faced at the start of the Cold War. Having tried and failed to build an inclusive "One World" system, they must now return to the second-best solution of a global economy divided into liberal and illiberal spheres. As Steil explains,

> [C]ontinuation down a One World path while China persists in distorting the global economy and orchestrating its dominance of strategic technologies will only heighten economic dislocation, political polarization, and security risks. If China, like the Soviet Union in 1947, rejects the basic American vision of a liberal order, then the United States must be prepared to initiate a shift to a Two Worlds model.[49]

Beijing's attitudes on this point are no longer in question. In response, the advanced industrial democracies should initiate what Steil describes as "an escalating quarantining of Chinese firms and industries that persist in either illegal activities . . . or unfair trade practices" while simultaneously seeking to construct "a new multilateral trade regime, populated by nations that meet basic standards for respecting fair and open markets."[50] Such a grouping would not decouple its members entirely from China, but it would put them in a better position to protect their economies against Beijing's predatory practices. Reducing remaining barriers with one another, while raising them with China, will also divert some trade, increasing commerce among the democracies relative to their trade with China.[51]

Here, as in every other aspect of their economic policies, the United States and its allies must now be concerned with *relative* as well as *absolute* gains. Their goal should be not simply to grow richer from year to year, but also to maintain the widest possible advantage in total economic output over China, thereby making it easier for them to preserve a favorable balance of power. They can do this by accelerating their own growth, by slowing China's or, most likely, by some combination of the two. The CCP has always regarded economic policy as a tool for enhancing China's power relative to that of the United States and its allies. The democracies no longer have the luxury of ignoring this fact, proudly proclaiming their faith in "the magic of the marketplace," and refusing to respond in kind.

Counterbalancing

Within the US government, concern over China's rise has tended to focus on the shifting balance of military power in East Asia. Only in the last several years has awareness grown that the challenge is global rather than purely regional and that it extends across every domain – economic, diplomatic, and ideological, as well as military. Still, the fact remains that the military balance, and the problem of deterring coercion or aggression in what is now referred to as the Indo-Pacific, are of vital importance. Indeed, over the course of the coming decade, regional military developments could play a decisive role in shaping the future course of the overall competition with China.

Thirty years of assiduous investment in A2/AD capabilities have brought PLA planners to the point where they may believe that, if necessary, they could fight and win a short conventional war in the Western Pacific, either destroying America's forward-based forces and bases in a preemptive attack, or deterring the United States from intervening as they dispatch a local opponent.[52] Miscalculation on this score could easily lead to a wider war, perhaps resulting in the use of nuclear weapons. On the other hand, if Beijing succeeds in achieving a quick victory, it could alter the balance of power in the region and the world, radically and almost overnight.

Taiwan is the most obvious near-term target for Chinese aggression, and the risk there appears to be growing.[53] Despite the fact that its commitment has always been ambiguous, US failure to defend the island would damage the credibility of its other security guarantees and weaken its regional alliances, perhaps fatally. Taiwan's absorption by the mainland could put Beijing in possession of some of the high-end manufacturing capacity it still needs to close the technology gap with the United States.[54] Success would also be a major step forward in China's ongoing efforts to exert control over the waters and airspace within the so-called "first island chain" that runs from Japan down through the South China Sea.[55] For these reasons, the notion that Washington could somehow improve its position by preemptively abandoning Taiwan is strategically absurd as well as morally repugnant.[56] Like Berlin during the Cold War, Taiwan may be difficult to defend, but it would be dangerous to let go.

Even without making dramatic and risky moves, China may be able to achieve its objectives by continuing to advance incrementally: tilting the military balance further in its favor, deepening doubts about Washington's security guarantees, and eroding the foundations of its alliances. If it succeeds eventually in displacing the United States as the preponderant power in the Indo-Pacific, Beijing will be able both to dictate terms to its democratic maritime neighbors and to devote more resources to the pursuit of its global ambitions. This will be more difficult if it continues to encounter stubborn resistance closer to home.

The immediate task confronting US and allied strategists is therefore to shore up the regional military balance, bolstering deterrence and reducing the likelihood that, even in a crisis, China's leaders could reasonably conclude that they stood to gain by using force. This is partly a matter of military deployments and planning. After over a decade of discussion, Washington needs to reduce substantially its activities in other parts of the world and concentrate a greater portion of its military effort in the Indo-Pacific. Together with its partners, the United States must also do more to reduce the susceptibility of its forward-based forces to attack, including by defending and dispersing ports and airfields, and investing in more resilient command, control, and surveillance systems.[57] Washington and its partners can further erode Beijing's confidence in its ability to achieve a rapid victory by building an allied network of sensors and A2/AD weapons. Mobile anti-ship missile launchers deployed to many small islands in the Western Pacific would be less vulnerable to preemption and could help keep the PLA navy bottled up, denying it access to the open oceans beyond the first island chain.[58]

Deterrence also depends on using diplomacy and political messaging to send credible signals of resolve. The more certain China's leaders are that any attempt to alter the status quo by using threats or force would be met with effective, broad-based opposition, the less likely they will be to act. A public statement by Japan and the European Union affirming the "importance of peace and stability across the Taiwan Strait" does nothing directly to affect the military balance, but it does suggest to Beijing that the costs of aggression would extend beyond damage to its relations with the United States.[59] In the same way, the occasional cruise by Canadian, French, or British warships makes clear that extra-regional powers also have a strong interest in preserving freedom of navigation through the South China Sea.[60]

Somewhat more concretely, the newly revived US–Japan–Australia–India "quad" demonstrates the participants' belief that they face a common strategic challenge and provides a foundation on which to build more substantial cooperation in military planning, joint exercises, and intelligence sharing.[61] A loosely coordinated network of similar groupings of varying size and overlapping membership could make a significant contribution to deterrence even though, at least for the moment, it would fall well short of being an "Asian NATO." Beijing should be under no illusion that it can divide, conquer, and bully its way to regional dominance. The harder it pushes, the stiffer and more unified the resistance it must encounter.

On the other side of the diplomatic equation, the United States and its allies should continue to look for ways to pry Russia away from China and pull it closer to the West. Although the prospects are not promising at present, in the long run the goal should be to deprive Beijing of its most capable strategic partner, reducing the risk that Moscow might open a diversionary second front in Europe during a conflict in Asia, and denying China the luxury of a secure continental rear area and a reliable source of overland energy supply.[62]

Peaceful, status quo democracies are easily tempted by the belief that they can preserve their security through purely defensive measures. Unfortunately, in an era of high-speed, three-dimensional warfare, hunkering down behind a Maginot Line is rarely a winning strategy. Potential aggressors are more likely to be deterred if they believe they will suffer costly punishment, instead of simply being rebuffed. Offensive capabilities may also be necessary in order to reshape an ongoing peacetime military competition, pushing it in directions that are more favorable and sustainable for the nation or coalition trying to fend off an aggressive, revisionist opponent.

Counterbalancing China's growing strength will require offensive as well as defensive measures. For example, by building on their already substantial capabilities in surface and undersea warfare, the United States and its partners can highlight the threat that they might respond to aggression by imposing a crippling maritime blockade on China. In addition to contributing to deterrence, concern over this possibility could reinforce Beijing's inclination to spend money on uneconomical overland energy pipelines and transportation infrastructure. Defending against a possible naval blockade would also require greater investment in anti-submarine warfare, an expensive and challenging mission in which China's navy has comparatively little experience. Similarly, if PLA planners know that long-range conventional precision strikes on US and allied forces and bases will be met with retaliation in kind against targets on their own soil, they may be less prone to attack in the first place. The presence of this threat will also tend to encourage greater expenditure on air and missile defenses, possibly diverting funds that might otherwise go to further expand China's own offensive arsenal. Where they can, the United States and its allies should invest in capabilities that bolster deterrence, while at the same time helping to redirect a greater portion of China's finite resources towards activities that are less threatening to them and away from those that are more so.

Because China's ability to project military power far from its shores remains limited, it has thus far had to rely primarily on economic and political instruments in order to extend its global reach. As will be discussed below, the democracies must counter these activities selectively and by using similar tools of their own. For now it is sufficient to note that, in addition to creating opportunities to strengthen its geopolitical position relative to the democracies, Beijing's attempts to expand its presence in parts of the global South are also likely to saddle it with new burdens and to generate new vulnerabilities.

Building the types of aircraft, naval vessels, communications systems, and logistical networks necessary to project power on a global scale will be extremely expensive, creating a set of sizable budgetary demands and potentially forcing trade-offs with the more regionally focused portions of China's military buildup. Distant bases and power projection forces operating far from home will also be difficult and expensive to defend in the event of conflict.[63] More generally, some of China's infrastructure investments and other activities in the developing world are certain to prove wasteful, creating a further drain on national resources. Beijing's deepening involvement could also provoke a backlash in some places, possibly impelling it to come to the defense of friendly regimes or drawing it into costly counter-insurgencies. From their studies of the experience of other great powers, China's strategists are well aware of the dangers of overextension, but that does not mean that they will necessarily be able to avoid them.

On the other hand, US and allied defense planners have good reason to be concerned about some of Beijing's activities, especially along the "maritime silk road" portion of its Belt and Road Initiative. If its SOEs gain control of more of the world's major ports and build more "dual-use" air and naval facilities adjacent to key chokepoints, China may be better able to secure its own supply lines in a crisis while selectively disrupting global commerce, coercing other governments, and impeding their efforts to respond.[64] Should the PLA gain access to ports and airbases on the west coast of Africa or in Latin America, it could compel the United States to keep more of its forces closer to home, further tipping the balance in the Western Pacific.[65] Likewise, an island base in the South Pacific would put Chinese forces within range of the main sea lines of communication between the United States, Australia, and New Zealand.[66] From a military perspective, some places matter more than others. The democracies cannot oppose every one of China's overseas ventures, nor should they try. But they must be attentive to these dangers as they prioritize their responses to its push for an expanded global presence.

Waging "discursive struggle"

The CCP wants nothing more than to avoid an open ideological rivalry with the West; or rather, to be precise, it wants nothing more than to discourage the United States and its partners from engaging it forcefully and explicitly on ideological grounds. For its part, the CCP has no doubt that it is locked in what its theorists now describe as a "discursive struggle": a battle of narratives through which it hopes to diminish the moral stature and global influence of the liberal democracies while enhancing its own. The Party's aim here, as in everything else it does, is to preserve itself and perpetuate its rule.

To achieve these ends, the regime has mounted a massive, well-funded, multi-dimensional campaign targeted primarily, not at the democracies themselves, but rather at the people of the developing world, as well as their own population. Among the Party's major themes, as we have seen, is the assertion that "so-called universal values" are, in fact, Western values ill suited to non-Western societies, on which they have occasionally been forced, with disastrous consequences. Since the global financial crisis, Beijing has also articulated an increasingly blunt critique of the performance of the democracies in every respect: the management of their economies, the alleged dysfunction of their political systems, and, most recently, their handling of the pandemic. Finally, under Xi Jinping, the CCP has dropped its long-standing diffidence regarding the existence of a "China model." Beijing now boasts that its distinctive methods for maintaining political stability and fostering economic growth do indeed have broader applicability and should be a source of inspiration, especially for people in the developing world.

The West won the Cold War, not because it had better propaganda, but because it had a better system, a set of institutions and practices that generated increasing material prosperity, while at the same time protecting citizens from the arbitrary exercise of state power and permitting them to practice their faiths, express their opinions, and choose their leaders. At moments of crisis and collective self-doubt, the democracies always managed to find figures who could articulate the ideals on which their societies were founded. Without visible evidence of success, however, even the most impassioned defense would have begun to ring hollow. Today, too, the West needs leaders who believe in and can explain the virtues of liberal democracy, but it also must demonstrate that, despite its imperfections, the system still works, and that it is practically as well as morally superior to the alternatives.

While recent events have given the democracies ample grounds for introspection, the urgency of the external challenge they now face means that they cannot afford to wallow in solipsism and self-doubt. As they work to address their shortcomings, the democracies must also take the offensive in the ideological portion of their "systemic rivalry" with China. For starters, the CCP's presentation of itself as a sterling success story and a model for others to follow deserves to be rigorously deconstructed. The nation's economic transformation, while deeply impressive, was made possible by the poorly paid labor of politically powerless workers and peasants, the vast majority of whom remain at the bottom of a highly unequal society.[67] Decades of rapid growth have left the air, water, and soil laden with contaminants, causing hundreds of thousands of premature deaths, and creating what experts have described as a full-scale environmental health crisis.[68]

China's initial economic miracle was the product of a variety of unique factors, including the sheer size of its workforce and its ability to attract massive quantities of foreign capital, that will be difficult or impossible for other developing countries to replicate. Even the regime's leaders acknowledge that their growth model is no longer adequate and they clearly fear that, unlike Japan and South Korea, China will fall into the middle-income trap, getting old before it can get rich.[69] Xi Jinping's plan for avoiding this fate without allowing economic or political liberalization involves a high-stakes bet on state-directed technology promotion that may well fail. Beijing's self-congratulatory claims that its economic system is superior, that its continued rise and eventual dominance are inevitable, and that it provides a model that others should follow are, at best, premature.

The political stability that the CCP advertises as one of its signature achievements has been maintained by a system that is both brutally repressive and extraordinarily corrupt. China's leaders live well but they also live in perpetual fear of internal unrest and feel compelled to invest ever-increasing sums in preparing to deal with domestic disorder, monitoring their population, and crushing any hint of dissent. The regime's insecurity is manifest in its furious attempts to intimidate and silence foreign critics of its barbarous abuse of its Uighur minority, its obliteration of any remnants of political freedom in Hong Kong, and its evident mishandling of the early stages of the COVID-19 pandemic. The democracies need to keep a spotlight on how Beijing treats people who have the misfortune to live under its control. Doing so will provoke vitriol rather than any positive change in policy, but both its deeds and its defense of them can help to illuminate the true, ugly face of the CCP regime.

As regards the developing world, the appeal of the China model is more a matter of practice than theory. Along with a critique of the West that has resonance in many places, Beijing is not pushing a coherent doctrine but rather offering the example of its own success, the prospect of investment and other forms of material support to those willing to follow its lead, and a set of policies that promise to help other illiberal regimes stay in power.

The CCP's reliance on elites and "elite capture" is both a strength and a potential weakness of its approach to cultivating influence in developing countries. Rather than trying to win the hearts and minds of an entire population, Beijing may be able to get what it wants by persuading (or bribing) a few key figures. On the other hand, in countries that retain some semblance of a free press and functioning democratic institutions, backroom deals and high-level corruption can come undone when exposed to public scrutiny or if there is a change in leadership. For these reasons, it is important that Western governments continue to fund programs that strengthen the rule of law and encourage free and fair elections. Private foundations and NGOs should also provide support and training for the independent journalists, environmentalists, and civil society groups that have been able to expose the underside of China's activities. Where local governments lack the necessary expertise, outside consultants can help them evaluate the terms of proposed investments to avoid becoming victims of "debt trap diplomacy."[70] As always, transparency and openness provide the best defense against manipulation and malign influence.

Instead of simply criticizing what Beijing is doing in the developing world, the democracies must have something positive to offer. The United States and its partners need to continue to work with international institutions and private investors to offer funding on transparent, reasonable terms for infrastructure projects that are environmentally sound, serve real needs, and are built with local labor.[71] In addition to countering the most obvious manifestations of China's BRI, it will be important to compete with some of the quieter and subtler aspects of its influence-building campaign. Beijing is working to shape the attitudes of a rising generation of elites by organizing professional training programs and awarding scholarships to thousands of students from BRI countries.[72] Western governments need to renew their commitment to offering parallel programs of their own.

The CCP's exquisite sensitivity to criticism and ideological challenge, and its obvious lack of confidence in its own legitimacy, signal a source of vulnerability that the democracies cannot afford to ignore. Always alert to the threat of "peaceful evolution," the Party has constructed a multi-layered defensive system that will be very difficult to penetrate. Beijing has spared no expense in tightening and strengthening a network of technical barriers designed to block inflows of unwanted information. Perhaps more important, the regime has engineered and injected into its people a powerful concoction of patriotic ideas and symbols designed to inoculate them against ideological contamination. Even if dangerous notions somehow slip through the cracks, this last line of defense is meant to render them harmless.

Accurately gauging opinion in a society as thoroughly monitored and repressed as China's is obviously impossible, but it would not be surprising if nationalist and even pro-regime sentiments were widely held, perhaps especially among the young. Cracking this carapace will not be easy, but the democracies still need to try. One way of doing this is to remain as open as possible to ordinary Chinese citizens who want to study, work, or live in the West. Even if some of these people are unimpressed or even repulsed by what they see, not all will be, and some of those with favorable impressions of open societies will carry their positive impressions with them when they return home.

While it would be desirable, if possible, to win converts to liberalism simply by singing its praises, the more immediate goal must be a negative one: to increase the pressure that the CCP regime feels from within to address its own domestic failings by heightening awareness of them among its citizens. Towards this end, the democracies should continue to work at ways of getting through (or over) China's "Great Firewall."[73] The goal should not be to pump in Western critiques of the CCP regime, but rather to amplify critical Chinese voices and increase the availability of accurate information about official corruption, environmental pollution, poor working conditions, unfair treatment of ordinary citizens, rural poverty, income inequality, government mismanagement, wasteful overseas investments, and the Party's ongoing attempts to whitewash its own history.

Like any other nation, China's resources are limited and, in an era of slower growth, they will likely be more constrained than in the past. From a strategic standpoint, it would be better if the CCP regime had to devote more of them to dealing with domestic discontent – either by spending still more on internal security or, preferably, by addressing the genuine needs of the Chinese people – than pursuing its external objectives.

Conclusion

Three times in the past century, the democracies, led by the United States, tried without success to create an inclusive, globe-spanning international system comprised of liberal states and operating on liberal principles. When Woodrow Wilson's revolutionary vision collided with reality after the close of World War I, America recoiled into isolation, leaving the democratic world divided, weak, and incapable of deterring fascist aggression. As World War II drew to a close and the wartime alliance with the Soviet Union broke down, Franklin Roosevelt's efforts to revive the Wilsonian dream also ended in disappointment. This time, however, the democracies were able to regroup, joining together to create a partial, rather than a truly global, liberal system that grew strong and prosperous enough eventually to win the Cold War.

Although it has taken too long for many to acknowledge, it is now obvious that three decades of earnest efforts to complete construction of a new, all-encompassing order by stretching the boundaries of the old, partial system have also ended in failure. Trying to incorporate the major illiberal powers ended up making them stronger, but it did not induce them to reform their domestic systems or to abandon their revisionist ambitions. And it has put them in a position to weaken the democracies from within and to corrode what were supposed to have been the institutional and normative foundations of a global liberal system.

Today the democracies face a choice: repeat the mistakes of the 1920s and 1930s or relearn the lessons of the 1940s and 1950s. If they fall out among themselves and, in particular, if the United States succumbs again to the isolationist temptation, the democratic world will be left fragmented and weakened, the illiberal powers will be further emboldened, and the dangers of subversion, coercion, and open conflict will continue to grow. Instead the United States and its democratic partners must redraw the perimeters and strengthen the boundaries of a geographically limited liberal international sub-system, falling back to a more defensible position from which they can better promote their interests and protect their common values.

The architects of engagement got China wrong because they underestimated the skill and tenacity of the CCP. But they were not wrong to insist that universal values exist and that all people, including China's citizens, are entitled to enjoy the rights and freedoms that flow from them. Nor were they wrong in believing that a more liberal system of government would be better for the Chinese people and for the peace, prosperity, and freedom of the entire world. That is still the case and democratic leaders should not shrink from saying so, lest they appear through their silence to have accepted the inevitability of perpetual CCP rule.

Notes

Introduction

1 I will use the terms "West" and "liberal democracies" interchangeably. Once confined to the trans-Atlantic zone, liberal democracies can now be found in every region of the world. These are countries with popularly elected governments whose powers are restrained by the rule of law and which are committed to protecting the civil rights of all their citizens.

2 Joint Communication to the European Parliament, the European Council, and the Council, "EU–China – A Strategic Outlook," March 12, 2019, p. 1.

Chapter 1 *The Origins of Engagement*

1 James Mann, *About Face: A History of America's Curious Relationship with China, from Nixon to Clinton* (New York: Knopf, 1998), pp. 35–6.

2 Aaron L. Friedberg, *A Contest for Supremacy: China, America, and the Struggle for Mastery in Asia* (New York: W.W. Norton, 2011), pp. 74–85.

3 Bernard Gwertzman, "Reagan Decides to Relax Curbs on China Trade," *New York Times*, June 6, 1981.

4 Hugo Meijer, *Trading with the Enemy: The Making of US Export Control Policy toward the People's Republic of China* (New York: Oxford University Press, 2016), p. 70.

5 Ibid., pp. 76–9.

6 Ibid., p. 60.

7 Department of State, "US Export Controls and China," *DISAM Journal* (Winter 1989/90), pp. 57–8.

8 Harry Harding, *A Fragile Relationship: The United States and China since 1972* (Washington, DC: Brookings Institution Press, 1992), p. 367.

9 Mann, *About Face*, pp. 104–5.

10 Xin-zhu J. Chen, "China and the US Trade Embargo, 1950–1972," *American Journal of Chinese Studies*, vol. 13, no. 2 (October 2006), pp. 169–86.

11 Don Oberdorfer, "Trade Benefits for China Are Approved by Carter," *Washington Post*, October 24, 1979.

12 Harding, *A Fragile Relationship*, pp. 364 and 366.

13 Both cited in Hal Brands, *Making the Unipolar Moment: US Foreign Policy and*

the Rise of the Post-Cold War Order (New York: Oxford University Press, 2016), p. 218.

14 Richard M. Nixon, "Asia after Vietnam," *Foreign Affairs*, vol. 46, no. 1 (October 1967), pp. 121–2.

15 Mann, *About Face*, p. 236.

16 Ibid., p. 147.

17 Harding, *A Fragile Relationship*, p. 363.

18 Brands, *Making the Unipolar Moment*, p. 359.

19 Meijer, *Trading with the Enemy*, p. 68.

20 Report of The Commission on Integrated Long-Term Strategy, *Discriminate Deterrence* (Washington, DC: US Government Printing Office, January 1988), p. 6.

21 See G. John Ikenberry, *After Victory: Institutions, Strategic Restraint, and the Rebuilding of Order after Major Wars* (Princeton: Princeton University Press, 2001), pp. 117–62.

22 Henry A. Kissinger, *Diplomacy* (New York: Simon & Schuster, 1994), pp. 44 and 30.

23 Henry A. Kissinger, *World Order* (New York: Penguin Books, 2014), p. 269.

24 From the text of the Atlantic Charter, a joint declaration by Roosevelt and British Prime Minister Winston Churchill, and a subsequent unilateral statement by Roosevelt on the first anniversary of the Charter. "The Atlantic Charter: Declaration of Principles Issued by the President of the United States and the Prime Minister of the United Kingdom," August 14, 1941.

25 Arnold Beichman, "Roosevelt's Failure at Yalta," *Humanitas*, vol. XVI, no. 1 (2003), p. 104.

26 "NSC 68: United States Objectives and Programs for National Security," April 14, 1950, in Thomas H. Etzold and John Lewis Gaddis, eds., *Containment: Documents on American Policy and Strategy, 1945–1950* (New York: Columbia University Press, 1978), p. 389.

27 Brands, *Making the Unipolar Moment*, p. 278.

28 George H.W. Bush, "Address before a Joint Session of the Congress on the State of the Union," January 29, 1991.

29 Brands, *Making the Unipolar Moment*, p. 325.

30 Thomas L. Friedman, "Baker Spells Out US Approach: Alliances and 'Democratic Peace,'" *New York Times*, April 22, 1992.

31 Anthony Lake, "From Containment to Enlargement," September 21, 1993. In Alvin Z. Rubenstein, Albina Shayevich, and Boris Zlotnikov, eds., *The Clinton Foreign Policy Reader: Presidential Speeches with Commentary* (Armonk, NY: M.E. Sharpe, 2000), pp. 21–2.

32 Ibid.

33 Ibid., p. 22.

34 Francis Fukuyama, "The End of History," *The National Interest*, no. 16 (Summer 1989), pp. 3–18.

35 Michael Beschloss and Strobe Talbott, *At the Highest Levels: The Inside Story of the End of the Cold War* (New York: Little Brown, 1993), p. 17.

36 Samuel P. Huntington, *The Third Wave: Democratization in the Late Twentieth Century* (Norman: University of Oklahoma Press, 1991), p. 26.

37 Ibid., pp. 15–16.

38 Jeffry A. Frieden, *Global Capitalism: Its Fall and Rise in the Twentieth Century* (New York: Norton, 2006), p. 398.

39 Ibid., p. 376.

40 John Williamson, "A Short History of the Washington Consensus," Institute for International Economics, September 2004.

41 Brands, *Making the Unipolar Moment*, pp. 213.

42 Robert Gilpin, *The Challenge of Global Capitalism: The World Economy in the 21st Century* (Princeton: Princeton University Press, 2000), p. 52.

43 Frieden, *Global Capitalism*, pp. 278–90.

44 Ibid., pp. 394–412; "Rates on Overseas Calls Decline," *New York Times*, May 19, 1982.

45 Theodore Levitt, "The Globalization of Markets," *Harvard Business Review*, May/June 1983, p. 93.

46 Frieden, *Global Capitalism*, p. 378.

47 Ronald Findlay and Kevin H. O'Rourke, *Power and Plenty: Trade. War, and the World Economy in the Second Millennium* (Princeton: Princeton University Press, 2007), p. 499.

48 Ibid., pp. 496–526.

49 Richard Baldwin, *The Great Convergence: Information Technology and the New Globalization* (Cambridge, MA: Harvard University Press, 2016), p. 132.

50 Ibid., p. 142.

51 Ibid., pp. 79–110.

52 Harding, *A Fragile Relationship*, p. 364.

53 James P. Walsh, ErPing Wang, and Katherine R. Xin, "Same Bed, Different Dreams: Working Relationships in Sino-American Joint Ventures," *Journal of World Business*, vol. 34, no. 1 (1999), pp. 69–93.

54 Robert L. Suettinger, *Beyond Tiananmen: The Politics of US–China Relations, 1989–2000* (Washington, DC: Brookings Institution Press, 2003), pp. 117–22.

55 Peter Behr, "Major US Companies Lobbying Clinton to Renew China's Trade Privileges," *Washington Post*, May 6, 1994.

56 Ho-fung Hung, "The Periphery in the Making of Globalization: The China Lobby and the Reversal of Clinton's China Trade Policy, 1993–1994," *Review of International Political Economy*, vol. 28, no. 4 (2020), p. 1017.
57 David M. Lampton, "America's China Policy in the Age of the Finance Minister: Clinton Ends Linkage," *The China Quarterly*, no. 139 (September 1994), p. 606.
58 David M. Lampton, *Same Bed, Different Dreams: Managing US–China Relations* (Berkeley: University of California Press, 2001), p. 380.
59 Harding, *A Fragile Relationship*, p. 368.
60 Hung, "The Periphery in the Making of Globalization," p. 14.
61 Neil Thomas, "For Company and for Country: Boeing and US–China Relations," *MacroPolo*, February 26, 2019.
62 William Warwick, "A Review of AT&T's Business History in China: The Memorandum of Understanding in Context," *Telecommunications Policy*, vol. 18, no. 3 (April 1994), pp. 265, 268–9.
63 Amy Harmon and David Holley, "GM Announces It Will Assemble Trucks in China," *Los Angeles Times*, January 16, 1992.
64 Suettinger, *Beyond Tiananmen*, p. 145.
65 Barry Naughton, *Growing Out of the Plan: Chinese Economic Reform, 1978–1993* (New York: Cambridge University Press, 1995), p. 304.
66 Mann, *About Face*, p. 285.
67 Suettinger, *Beyond Tiananmen*, p. 145.
68 Mann, *About Face*, p. 284.
69 Nicholas D. Kristof, "Foreign Investors Pouring into China," *New York Times*, June 15, 1992.
70 Quoted in Bob Davis and Lingling Wei, *Superpower Showdown: How the Battle between Trump and Xi Threatens a New Cold War* (New York: HarperCollins, 2020), pp. 56–7.
71 Mann, *About Face*, p. 123.
72 Samuel Wagreich, "Lobbying by Proxy: A Study of China's Lobbying Practices in the United States 1979–2010 and the Implications for FARA," *Journal of Politics and Society*, no. 24 (2013), pp. 130–60.
73 Joseph Weisskopf, "Backbone of the New China Lobby: US Firms," *Washington Post*, June 14, 1993.
74 Ann Scott Tyson, "China Uses US Firms to Lobby," *Christian Science Monitor*, May 9, 1994.
75 Lampton, "America's China Policy in the Age of the Finance Minister," p. 612.
76 Mann, *About Face*, pp. 292–3.
77 Quoted in Philip C. Saunders, "Supping with a Long Spoon: Dependence and

Interdependence in Sino-American Relations," *Pacific Review*, no. 93 (January 2000), p. 78.

78 "Press Conference of the President," May 26, 1994.

79 Joyce Barnathan, "China's Gates Swing Open," Bloomberg, June 13, 1994.

Chapter 2 Rationales and Expectations

1 Henry Kissinger, *On China* (New York: Penguin, 2011), p. 284.

2 Jeffrey A. Engel, *When the World Seemed New: George H.W. Bush and the End of the Cold War* (New York: Houghton Mifflin Harcourt, 2017), p. 197.

3 Quoted in Harding, *A Fragile Relationship*, p. 227.

4 George Bush and Brent Scowcroft, *A World Transformed* (New York: Vintage, 1998), pp. 104 and 102.

5 Testimony of Deputy Secretary of State Lawrence Eagleburger, Hearing before the Senate Committee on Foreign Relations, *US Policy Toward China*, 101st Congress, 2nd session (Washington, DC: US Government Printing Office, 1990), p. 15.

6 Ibid., p. 14.

7 Mann, *About Face*, p. 227.

8 Testimony of Deputy Secretary of State Lawrence Eagleburger, p. 14.

9 Suettinger, *Beyond Tiananmen*, pp. 171–4, 266–71, 322, and 335

10 White House, *A National Security Strategy of Engagement and Enlargement* (Washington, DC: White House, 1995), p. 29.

11 White House, *A National Security Strategy for a New Century* (Washington, DC: White House, 1998), p. 44.

12 White House, *A National Security Strategy for a Global Age* (Washington, DC: White House, 2000), p. 64.

13 White House, *A National Security Strategy for a New Century*, p. 45.

14 "Remarks by the President in Address on China and the National Interest," Voice of America, Washington, DC, October 24, 1997.

15 See Alastair Iain Johnston, "Is China a Status Quo Power?" *International Security*, vol. 27, no. 4 (Spring 2003), pp. 5–56. Johnston's answer to the question raised in his title was a cautious, conditional "yes." Although acknowledging that things could change in the future, he concluded that "it is not clear that describing China as a revisionist or non-status quo state is accurate at this moment in history" (p. 6).

16 G. John Ikenberry, "The Rise of China and the Future of the West: Can the Liberal System Survive?" *Foreign Affairs*, vol. 87, no. 1 (January/February 2008), p. 24.

17 Testimony of Under Secretary of State for Political Affairs Peter Tarnoff,

Hearing before the House International Relations Committee Subcommittee on Asia and the Pacific, Subcommittee on International Economic Policy and Trade, *China and MFN*, 104th Congress, 2nd session (Washington, DC: US Government Printing Office, 1996).

18 See Alastair Iain Johnston, *Social States: China in International Relations, 1980–2000* (Princeton: Princeton University Press, 2008).

19 "President Clinton Press Conference on Human Rights in China, 1994," May 26, 1994.

20 White House, *A National Security Strategy for a Global Age*, p. 50.

21 Robert B. Zoellick, Remarks to National Committee on US–China Relations, "Whither China: From Membership to Responsibility?" September 21, 2005.

22 Nicholas Lardy, *Markets over Mao: The Rise of Private Business in China* (Washington, DC: Peterson Institute for International Economics, 2014).

23 "Statement by Press Secretary Fitzwater on the Renewal of Most-Favored-Nation Trade Status for China," May 24, 1990.

24 "Statement by Press Secretary Fitzwater on Continuation of China's Most-Favored-Nation Trade Status," June 2, 1992.

25 "President Clinton Press Conference on Human Rights in China, 1994."

26 Statement of Ambassador Charlene Barshefsky, Deputy United States Trade Representative, on Trade Policy toward China, Hearing before the Subcommittee on Trade of the Committee on Ways and Means, House of Representatives, *HR 4590, United States–China Act of 1994*, 103rd Congress, 2nd Session (Washington, DC: US Government Printing Office, 1994), p. 109.

27 "Remarks by the President in Address on China and the National Interest."

28 Bill Clinton, "Statement on the Decision to Extend Normal Trade Relations Status with China, June 3, 1999," in *Public Papers of the Presidents of the United States: William J. Clinton, 1999, Book I – January 1 to June 30, 1999* (Washington, DC: Government Printing Office, 2000), p. 874.

29 United States Census Bureau, "Foreign Trade: Trade in Goods with China" (*https://www.census.gov/foreign-trade/balance/c5700.html*).

30 Charlene Barshefsky, Foreign Affairs Briefing to the National Conference of Editorial Writers at the US Department of State, "US–China Trade Relations," US Department of State, March 10, 2000.

31 "Full Text of Clinton's Speech on China Trade Bill," Johns Hopkins School of Advanced International Studies, Washington, DC, March 8, 2000.

32 Bill Clinton, "Opening Remarks at a Roundtable Discussion in Akron on Permanent Normal Trade Relations with China, Akron, OH, May 12, 2000," in *Public Papers of the Presidents of the United States: William J. Clinton, 2000,*

Book I – January 1 to June 26, 2000 (Washington, DC: Government Printing Office, 2001), p. 919.

33 "Full Text of Clinton's Speech on China Trade Bill."

34 "Remarks by the President in Foreign Policy Speech," Mayflower Hotel, Washington, DC, April 7, 1999.

35 "Opening Remarks at a Roundtable Discussion in Akron on Permanent Normal Trade Relations with China."

36 Bill Clinton, "Remarks on House of Representatives Action on Permanent Normal Trade Relations with China, May 24, 2000," in *Public Papers of the Presidents of the United States: William J. Clinton, 2000, Book I – January 1 to June 26, 2000*, p. 1018.

37 Statement of the Honorable Lawrence H. Summers, Secretary, US Department of the Treasury, Hearing before the Committee on Ways and Means, House of Representatives, *Accession of China to the WTO*, 106th Congress, 2nd Session (Washington, DC: US Government Printing Office, 2001), pp. 25–6.

38 Statement of Ambassador Charlene Barshefsky, United States Trade Representative. Ibid., pp. 48–9.

39 President Bill Clinton, "Expanding Trade, Projecting Values: Why I'll Fight to Make China's Trade Status Permanent," *The New Democrat*, January 1, 2000.

40 "Full Text of Clinton's Speech on China Trade Bill."

41 "Statement by Press Secretary Fitzwater on the Renewal of Most-Favored-Nation Trade Status for China."

42 Bill Clinton, "Statement on Permanent Normal Trade Relations with China," April 11, 2000," in *Public Papers of the Presidents of the United States: William J. Clinton, 2000, Book I – January 1 to June 26, 2000*, p. 676.

43 Barshefsky, "US–China Trade Relations."

44 Gregory C. Chow, "The Impact of Joining WTO on China's Economic, Legal and Political Institutions," International Conference on Greater China and the WTO, March 22–4, 2001.

45 "Full Text of Clinton's Speech on China Trade Bill."

46 Joseph Fewsmith, "The Political and Social Implications of China's Accession to the WTO," *The China Quarterly*, no. 167 (September 2001), p. 575.

47 "Remarks by Samuel R. Berger, Assistant to the President for National Security Affairs on China," Woodrow Wilson International Center for Scholars, Washington, DC, February 2, 2000.

48 "Full Text of Clinton's Speech on China Trade Bill."

49 Fewsmith, "The Political and Social Implications of China's Accession to the WTO," pp. 574–5.

50 Nicholas R. Lardy, "Permanent Normal Trade Relations for China," *Brookings Policy Brief*, no. 58, May 2000, p. 7.

51 "Remarks by Samuel R. Berger, Assistant to the President for National Security Affairs on China."

52 Testimony of Treasury Secretary Lawrence Summers, Hearing before the Committee on Banking and Financial Services, House of Representatives, *Permanent Normal Trade Relations for China (PNTR)*, 106th Congress, 2nd session (Washington, DC: US Government Printing Office, 2000), p. 174.

53 "Written Responses to Questions Submitted by Xinhua News Agency of China," February 16, 1989.

54 Bush and Scowcroft, *A World Transformed*, p. 98.

55 "The President's News Conference," June 5, 1989.

56 Ibid.

57 "Remarks at the Yale University Commencement Ceremony in New Haven, Connecticut," May 27, 1991.

58 Huntington, *The Third Wave*, pp. 59–72.

59 Henry S. Rowen, "The Short March: China's Road to Democracy," *The National Interest*, no. 45 (Fall 1996), pp. 61–70.

60 Bill Bradley, "Trade, the Real Engine of Democracy," *New York Times*, May 25, 1994.

61 Testimony of Howard H. Lange, Acting Deputy Assistant Secretary of State for East Asian and Pacific Affairs, Hearing before the Subcommittee on Trade of the Committee on Ways and Means, House of Representatives, *The Future of United States–China Trade Relations and the Possible Accession of China to the World Trade Organization*, 105th Congress, 1st session (Washington, DC: US Government Printing Office, 1999), p. 41.

62 White House, *A National Security Strategy of Engagement and Enlargement* (Washington, DC: White House, 1996), p. 40.

63 "President Clinton Press Conference on Human Rights in China, 1994."

64 Letter from Wendy R. Sherman, Assistant Secretary of State for Legislative Affairs to Representative Sam M. Gibbons, Acting Chairman, Hearing before the Subcommittee on Trade of the Committee on Ways and Means, House of Representatives, *HR 4590, United States–China Act of 1994*, 103rd Congress, 2nd Session (Washington, DC: US Government Printing Office, 1994), p. 88.

65 See Michael Bernhard, "Civil Society and Democratic Transition in East Central Europe," *Political Science Quarterly*, vol. 108, no. 2 (Summer 2003), pp. 307–26.

66 Andrew J. Nathan, "Authoritarian Resilience," *Journal of Democracy*, vol. 14, no. 1 (January 2003), p. 6.

67 Huntington, *The Third Wave*, p. 63.

68 Andrew J. Nathan, "Even Our Caution Must be Hedged," *Journal of Democracy*, vol. 9, no. 2 (January 1998), pp. 61–2.

69 George Gilboy and Eric Heginbotham, "China's Coming Transformation," *Foreign Affairs*, vol. 8, no. 4 (July/August 2001), p. 28.

70 For a guarded but optimistic assessment see Minxin Pei, "Is China Democratizing?" *Foreign Affairs*, vol. 77, no. 1 (January/February 1998), pp. 68–82.

71 Testimony of Catharin E. Dalpino, "Supporting Political Liberalization in China: The Role of the United States," Before the Subcommittee on International Operations and Human Rights of the Committee on International Relations, US House of Representatives, March 7, 2001.

72 "Remarks by the President on US–China Relations in the 21st Century," National Geographic Society, Washington, DC, June 11, 1998.

73 "Remarks by the President in Foreign Policy Speech."

74 "Remarks by Samuel R. Berger, Assistant to the President for National Security Affairs on China."

75 Ibid.

76 Statement of the Honorable Lawrence H. Summers, p. 26.

77 "Full Text of Clinton's Speech on China Trade Bill."

78 "Remarks by the President in Address on China and the National Interest."

79 "Remarks by the President in Foreign Policy Speech."

80 "Full Text of Clinton's Speech on China Trade Bill."

81 James Mann, *The China Fantasy: How Our Leaders Explain Away Chinese Repression* (New York: Viking Press, 2007).

82 George W. Bush, "A Distinctly American Internationalism," Ronald Reagan Presidential Library, Simi Valley, California, November 19, 1999.

83 George W. Bush, "Remarks to the Los Angeles World Affairs Council," Los Angeles, California, May 29, 2001.

Chapter 3 Politics: "The Party Leads Everything"

1 Qiang Zhai, "1959: Preventing Peaceful Evolution," *China Heritage Quarterly*, no. 18 (June 2009).

2 George J. Church, "China: Old Wounds Deng Xiaoping," *Time*, January 6, 1986.

3 Stein Ringen, *The Perfect Dictatorship: China in the 21st Century* (Hong Kong: Hong Kong University Press, 2016), p. 2.

4 Leszek Kolakowski, *Main Currents of Marxism, Volume 2: The Golden Age* (New York: Oxford University Press, 1981), p. 508.

5 Robert Service, *Comrades! A History of World Communism* (Cambridge, MA: Harvard University Press, 2007), p. 9.

6 Franz Schurmann, *Ideology and Organization in Communist China* (Berkeley: University of California Press, 1968), p. 24.

7 Neil Harding, *Leninism* (Durham, NC: Duke University Press, 1996), p. 5.

8 Ezra F. Vogel, *Deng Xiaoping and the Transformation of China* (Cambridge, MA: Harvard University Press, 2011), p. 585.

9 Ibid., p. 262.

10 Hu and Zhao served as General Secretary of the CCP from 1982 to 1987 and from 1987 to 1989, respectively.

11 Minxin Pei, *China's Trapped Transition: The Limits of Developmental Autocracy* (Cambridge, MA: Harvard University Press, 2006), p. 55.

12 Ibid., p. 47.

13 Merle Goldman, *Sowing the Seeds of Democracy in China: Political Reform in the Deng Xiaoping Era* (Cambridge, MA: Harvard University Press, 1994), p. 17.

14 Vogel, *Deng Xiaoping*, p. 590.

15 Goldman, *Sowing the Seeds of Democracy in China*, p. 256.

16 Minxin Pei, *From Reform to Revolution: The Demise of Communism in China and the Soviet Union* (Cambridge, MA: Harvard University Press, 1994), p. 173.

17 Andrew J. Nathan, "China's Political Trajectory: What Are the Chinese Saying?" in Cheng Li, ed., *China's Changing Political Landscape: Prospects for Democracy* (Washington, DC: Brookings Institution Press, 2008), p. 37.

18 Pei, *China's Trapped Transition*, p. 57.

19 Ibid., p. 56.

20 Excerpts from this memo are translated in Andrew J. Nathan and Perry Link, eds., *The Tiananmen Papers* (New York: Public Affairs, 2002), pp. 338–48. Quote from p. 338.

21 David Shambaugh, *China's Communist Party: Atrophy and Adaptation* (Washington, DC: Woodrow Wilson Center Press, 2008), p. 43.

22 Ibid., p. 43.

23 Ibid., p. 45.

24 Julian Gewirtz, *Unlikely Partners: Chinese Reformers, Western Economists, and the Making of Global China* (Cambridge, MA: Harvard University Press, 2017), p. 233.

25 Ibid., p. 135.

26 See Shambaugh, *China's Communist Party*, pp. 41–86.

27 Joseph Fewsmith, *China since Tiananmen: The Politics of Transition* (New York: Cambridge University Press, 2001), p. 33.

28 Vogel, *Deng Xiaoping*, p. 667.

29 Gewirtz, *Unlikely Partners*, p. 240.

30 Minxin Pei, "Beijing's Social Contract Is Starting to Fray," Carnegie Endowment for International Peace, June 7, 2004.

31 Pei, *China's Trapped Transition*, p. 82.

32 Richard Baum, "The Limits of Consultative Leninism," in Mark Mohr, ed., *China and Democracy: A Contradiction in Terms?* (Washington, DC: Woodrow Wilson Center for Scholars, 2006), p. 15.

33 See Yuhua Wang and Carl Minzner, "The Rise of the Chinese Security State," *The China Quarterly*, vol. 222 (June 2015), pp. 339–59.

34 Willy Wo-Lap Lam, *China after Deng Xiaoping: The Power Struggle in Beijing since Tiananmen* (Singapore: John Wiley & Sons, 1995), pp. 257–8.

35 Ibid., p. 155.

36 Pei, *China's Trapped Transition*, pp. 90–1.

37 Gewirtz, *Unlikely Partners*, p. 12.

38 Vogel, *Deng Xiaoping*, p. 589.

39 Fewsmith, *China since Tiananmen*, p. 9.

40 Zheng Wang, *Never Forget National Humiliation: Historical Memory in Chinese Politics and Foreign Relations* (New York: Columbia University Press, 2012), p. 96.

41 Ibid., pp. 71–117.

42 A.M. Rosenthal, "On My Mind: Here We Go Again," *New York Times*, April 9, 1993.

43 Susan Shirk, *China: Fragile Superpower* (New York: Oxford University Press, 2007), p. 57.

44 Baum, "The Limits of Consultative Leninism," p. 15.

45 Timothy R. Heath, *China's New Governing Party Paradigm: Political Renewal and the Pursuit of National Rejuvention* (New York: Ashgate Publishing, 2014), p. 21.

46 Ibid., pp. 20–4.

47 See Bruce J. Dickson, *The Dictator's Dilemma: The Chinese Communist Party's Strategy for Survival* (New York: Oxford University Press, 2016), pp. 164–213.

48 Ibid., p. 135.

49 See Joseph Fewsmith, *The Logic and Limits of Political Reform in China* (New York: Cambridge University Press, 2013).

50 Elizabeth C. Economy, *The Third Revolution: Xi Jinping and the New Chinese State* (New York: Oxford University Press, 2018), pp. 65–8.

51 Baum, "The Limits of Consultative Leninism."

52 Steve Tsang, "Consultative Leninism: China's New Political Framework," *Journal of Contemporary China*, vol. 18, no. 2 (November 2009), pp. 865–80. Quotes from pp. 866 and 868.

53 Frank N. Pieke, "The Communist Party and Social Management in China," *China Information*, vol. 26, no. 2 (2012), pp. 149–65.

54 Baum, "The Limits of Consultative Leninism," p. 13.

55 Kellee S. Tsai, *Capitalism without Democracy: The Private Sector in Contemporary China* (Ithaca, NY: Cornell University Press, 2007), p. 64.

56 Archive, "China's Official Media Tout Jiang Zemin's Leadership – 2002-07-22," voanews.com, October 29, 2009.

57 Heath, *China's New Governing Party Paradigm*, p. 39.

58 Ibid., p. 41.

59 Ibid., p. 46.

60 Shambaugh, *China's Communist Party*, pp. 115–19.

61 Ibid., p. 124.

62 Ibid., p. 126.

63 Ibid., pp. 128–30.

64 Ibid., p. 115.

65 Jessica Chen Weiss, *Powerful Patriots: Nationalist Protest in China's Foreign Relations* (New York: Oxford University Press, 2014), pp. 42–81, 127–59.

66 Nicholas D. Kristof, "The Tiananmen Victory," *New York Times*, June 2, 2004.

67 Gilboy and Heginbotham, "China's Coming Transformation," p. 26.

68 Thomas A. Metzger, "Will China Democratize? Sources of Resistance," *Journal of Democracy*, vol. 9, no. 1 (January 1998), p. 18.

69 David Shambaugh, *China's Future* (Cambridge: Polity, 2016), p. 99.

70 Shambaugh, *China's Communist Party*, p. 92.

71 Perry Link, "China's Charter 08," *New York Review of Books*, January 15, 2009.

72 Jonathan D. Pollack, "Unease from Afar," in Kenneth M. Pollack et al., *The Arab Awakening: America and the Transformation of the Middle East* (Washington, DC: Brookings Institution Press, 2011), p. 301.

73 Fewsmith, *The Logic and Limits of Political Reform in China*, pp. 26–7.

74 Carl Minzner, *End of an Era: How China's Authoritarian Revival Is Undermining Its Rise* (New York: Oxford University Press, 2018), p. 92.

75 Ibid., p. 80.

76 See John Garnaut, *The Rise and Fall of the House of Bo* (Canberra: Penguin Group, 2012).

77 Barbara Demick and Julie Makinen, "China May Struggle to Move beyond Bo Xilai Scandal," *Los Angeles Times*, September 28, 2012.

78 Willy Wo-Lap Lam, *The Fight for China's Future: Civil Society vs. the Chinese Communist Party* (New York: Routledge, 2020), p. 106.

79 Ibid., pp. 105–9.

80 Ibid., p. 112.

81 Economy, *The Third Revolution*, p. 66.

82 Shambaugh, *China's Communist Party*, pp. 107 and 91.

83 Ibid., p. 91.

84 Carl F. Minzner, "China's Turn against the Law," *American Journal of Comparative Law*, vol. 59 (2011), p. 948.

85 Fewsmith, *The Logic and Limits of Political Reform in China*, p. 107.

86 Joseph Fewsmith, "Political Reform Was Never on the Agenda," *China Leadership Monitor*, no. 34 (Winter 2011).

87 Pieke, "The Communist Party and Social Management in China," p. 159.

88 Adrian Zenz, "China's Domestic Security Spending: An Analysis of Available Data," *China Brief*, vol. 18, no. 4 (March 2018).

89 Christopher A. Ford, *China Looks at the West: Identity, Global Ambitions, and the Future of Sino-American Relations* (Lexington: University of Kentucky Press, 2015), pp. 339–44.

90 Dickson, *The Dictator's Dilemma*, pp. 39–42 and 127–35.

91 James Fallows, "Arab Spring, Chinese Winter," *The Atlantic* (September 2011).

92 Economy, *The Third Revolution*, pp. 70–1.

93 See Gary King, Jennifer Pan, and Margaret E. Roberts, "How Censorship in China Allows Government Criticism But Prevents Collective Expression," *American Political Science Review*, vol. 107, no. 2 (May 2013), pp. 1–18.

94 Zenz, "China's Domestic Security Spending."

95 François Bougon, *Inside the Mind of Xi Jinping* (London: Hurst and Co., 2018), p. 5; Michal Bogusz and Jakub Jakóbowski, *The Chinese Communist Party and Its State: Xi Jinping's Conservative Turn* (Warsaw: Centre for Eastern Studies, 2020), p. 70.

96 "Looking Back at 'China's Lost Decade,'" dw.com, March 13, 2013.

97 Bogusz and Jakóbowski, *The Chinese Communist Party and Its State*, p. 74.

98 "Xi's 'New Normal' Theory," China.org.cn., November 10, 2014.

99 Bougon, *Inside the Mind of Xi Jinping*, p. 5.

100 Larry Diamond, "China and East Asian Democracy: The Coming Wave," *Journal of Democracy*, vol. 23, no. 1 (January 2012), p. 6.

101 Andrew J. Nathan, "China at the Tipping Point? Foreseeing the Unforeseeable," *Journal of Democracy*, vol. 24, no. 1 (January 2013), p. 20.

102 See David Cohen and Peter Martin, "A Mandate, Not a Putsch: The Secret of Xi's Success," *China Brief*, vol. 15, no. 3 (February 2015).

103 Brendan Forde, "China's 'Mass Line' Campaign," *The Diplomat*, September 9, 2013.

104 Jerome Doyon, "The End of the Road for Xi's Mass Line Campaign: An Assessment," *China Brief*, vol. 14, no. 20 (October 2014).

105 Forde, "China's 'Mass Line' Campaign."

106 Simon Denyer, "Command and Control: China's Communist Party Extends Reach into Foreign Companies," *Washington Post*, January 28, 2018.

107 "Cells to 'Guide' NGOs in Beijing Clampdown," *Straits Times*, September 30, 2015.

108 Nis Grünberg and Katja Drinhausen, "The Party Leads on Everything: China's Changing Governance in Xi Jinping's New Era," *Merics China Monitor*, September 24, 2019.

109 Chris Buckley, "Xi Jinping Is China's 'Core' Leader: Here's What It Means," *New York Times*, October 30, 2016.

110 James Mulvenon, "Xi Jinping Has a Cool New Nickname: 'Commander-in-Chief,'" *China Leadership Monitor*, no. 51 (Fall 2016).

111 Chris Buckley and Keith Bradsher, "China Moves to Let Xi Stay in Power by Abolishing Term Limit," *New York Times*, February 25, 2018.

112 Jerome A. Cohen, "Xi Jinping Amends China's Constitution," *Lawfare*, March 7, 2018.

113 Joseph Torigian, "The Shadow of Deng Xiaoping on Chinese Elite Politics," *War on the Rocks*, January 30, 2017.

114 See Brantly Womack, "Xi Jinping and Continuing Political Reform in China," *Journal of Chinese Political Science*, no. 22 (2017), p. 398; Chun Han Wong, "For China's Leaders, Age Cap Is But a Moving Number," *Wall Street Journal*, November 1, 2016.

115 Torigian, "The Shadow of Deng Xiaoping on Chinese Elite Politics."

116 Shaun Shieh, "The Chinese State and Overseas NGOs: From Regulatory Ambiguity to the Overseas NGO Law," *Nonprofit Policy Forum*, vol. 9, no. 1 (2018).

117 Andrew Jacobs and Chris Buckley, "China Targeting Rights Lawyers in Crackdown," *New York Times*, July 22, 2015.

118 Carl Minzner, "After the Fourth Plenum: What Direction for Law in China?" *China Brief*, vol. 14, no. 22 (November 2014).

119 Rogier Creemers, "The Pivot in Chinese Cybergovernance," *China Perspectives*, no. 4 (2015), pp. 5–13.

120 See Katja Drinhausen and Vincent Brussee, "China's Social Credit System in 2021: From Fragmentation towards Integration," *Merics China Monitor*, March 3, 2021.

121 Shai Oster, "China Tries Its Hand at Pre-Crime: Beijing Wants to Identify Subversives before They Strike," Bloomberg, March 3, 2016.

122 See John Pomfret, "China's Leader Attacks His Greatest Threat," The Atlantic (January 2021).

123 See Adrian Zenz, "'Wash Brains, Cleanse Hearts': Evidence from Chinese Government Documents about the Nature and Extent of Xinjiang's Extrajudicial Internment Campaign," *Journal of Political Risk*, vol. 7, no. 11 (November 2019).

124 "Document 9: A ChinaFile Translation," *ChinaFile*, November 8, 2013.

125 Ibid.

126 Quoted in Tanner Greer, "Xi Jinping in Translation: China's Guiding Ideology," *Palladium*, May 31, 2019.

127 Heike Holbig, "The 19th Party Congress: Its Place in History," in "China's 'New Era' with Xi Jinping characteristics," European Council on Foreign Relations, December 15, 2017.

128 Greer, "Xi Jinping in Translation."

129 "His Own Words: The 14 Principles of 'Xi Jinping Thought,'" BBC Monitoring, October 16, 2017.

130 Greer, "Xi Jinping in Translation"; Willy Wo-Lap Lam, "What Is Xi Jinping Thought?" *China Brief*, vol. 17, no. 2 (September 2017).

131 Heike Holbig, "Ideology after the End of Ideology: China and the Quest for Autocratic Legitimation," *Democratization*, vol. 20, no. 1 (2013), pp. 75–6.

132 T.H. Jiang and Shaun O'Dwyer, "The Universal Ambitions of China's Illiberal Confucian Scholars," *Palladium*, September 26, 2019.

133 Ying Miao, "Romanticising the Past: Core Socialist Values and the China Dream as Legitimisation Strategy," *Journal of Current Chinese Affairs* (January 2021), pp. 1–23.

134 Carl Minzner, "Old Wine in an Ancient Bottle: Changes in Chinese State Ideology," *China Brief*, vol. 14, no. 6 (March 2014).

135 Miao, "Romanticising the Past," pp. 11–12.

136 "Xi Jinping's 19 August Speech Revealed (Translation)?" *China Copyright and Media*, November 12, 2013.

137 Jacqueline Newmyer Deal, "China's Nationalist Heritage," *National Interest*, no. 123 (January/February 2013), pp. 44–53.

138 Zheng Wang, "The Chinese Dream: Concept and Context," *Journal of Chinese Politics*, no. 19 (2014), p. 9.

139 William A. Callahan, "Identity and Security in China: The Negative Soft Power of the China Dream," *Politics*, vol. 35, no. 3–4 (2015), p. 223.

140 Ringen, *The Perfect Dictatorship*, pp. 176–7.

141 The one possible exception to this rule is the Kuomintang or Chinese Nationalist Party of Taiwan. See Bruce J. Dickson, "China's Democratization and the Taiwan Experience," *Asian Survey*, vol. 38, no. 4 (April 1998), pp. 349–64.

142 Graeme Gill, "Personal Dominance and the Collective Principle: Individual Legitimacy in Marxist-Leninist Systems," in T.H. Rigby and Ferenc Fehér, eds., *Political Legitimation in Communist States* (London: Macmillan, 1982), pp. 94–109.

143 Robert C. Tucker, ed., *The Lenin Anthology* (New York: W.W. Norton, 1975), p. xxxviii.

Chapter 4 Economics: "A Bird in a Cage"

1 See, for example, "China's Economic Reforms Have Stalled. Why?" *Wall Street Journal*, February 16, 2016; Tetsushi Takahashi, "40 Years after Opening Up, China Is Going Backward," *Nikkei Asia*, March 20, 2018.

2 Nicholas R. Lardy, *The State Strikes Back: The End of Economic Reform in China?* (Washington, DC: Peterson Institute for International Economics, 2019).

3 This section draws on the discussion in Charles W. Boustany, Jr. and Aaron L. Friedberg, *Answering China's Economic Challenge: Preserving Power, Enhancing Prosperity* NBR Special Report #76 (February 2019), pp. 6–17.

4 Christian Caryl, *Strange Rebels: 1979 and the Birth of the 21st Century* (New York: Basic Books, 2014), p. 124.

5 Barry Naughton, "China's Economy from 'Enlivening' to 'Steerage,'" in Jacques deLisle and Avery Goldstein, eds., *To Get Rich Is Glorious: Challenges Facing China's Economic Reform and Opening at Forty* (Washington, DC: Brookings Institution Press, 2019), pp. 31–2.

6 Naughton, *Growing Out of the Plan*, p. 63.

7 Vogel, *Deng Xiaoping*, pp. 359–61.

8 Ibid., pp. 426–8.

9 See Gewirtz, *Unlikely Partners*.

10 Naughton, *Growing Out of the Plan*, p. 59.

11 Ibid., pp. 59–169.

12 Yasheng Huang, *Capitalism with Chinese Characteristics: Entrepreneurship and the State* (New York: Cambridge University Press, 2008), p. 112.

13 Barry Naughton, *The Chinese Economy: Transitions and Growth* (Cambridge, MA: MIT Press, 2007), p. 144.

14 Huang, *Capitalism with Chinese Characteristics*, pp. 112 and 102.

15 Ibid., p. xvii.

16 Barry Naughton, "A Political Economy of China's Economic Transition," in Loren Brandt and Thomas Rawski, eds., *China's Great Economic Transformation* (Cambridge: Cambridge University Press, 2008), p. 99.

17 Naughton, *The Chinese Economy*, pp. 101–2.

18 Pei, *From Reform to Revolution*, pp. 68–9.

19 Naughton, *Growing Out of the Plan*, p. 247.

20 András Székely-Doby, "Why Have Chinese Reforms Come to a Halt? The Political Economic Logic of Unfinished Transformation," *Europe-Asia Studies*, vol. 70, no. 2 (March 2018), p. 285.

21 For various attempts by Chinese analysts to measure CNP, see Michael Pillsbury, *China Debates the Future Security Environment* (Washington, DC: National Defense University Press, 2000), pp. 203–58.

22 Huang, *Capitalism with Chinese Characteristics*, p. 42.

23 Naughton, *The Chinese Economy*, pp. 430–4.

24 Nicholas R. Lardy, "Financial Repression in China," *Peterson Institute for International Economics Policy Brief*, September 2008.

25 Harry G. Broadman, "The Business(es) of the Chinese State," *The World Economy*, vol. 24, no. 7 (July 2001), p. 849.

26 Andrew Batson, "The State Never Retreats," *DeepChina*, October 1, 2020, p. 7.

27 Huang, *Capitalism with Chinese Characteristics*, p. 113.

28 "China: Foreign Direct Investment, Percent of GDP," TheGlobalEconomy. com (*https://www.theglobaleconomy.com/China/Foreign_Direct_Investment/*).

29 Huang, *Capitalism with Chinese Characteristics*, p. 124.

30 Eduardo Porter, "The Promise of Today's Factory Jobs," *New York Times*, April 3, 2012, and European Parliamentary Research Service Blog, "Global Manufacturing Exports and China's Share," March 25, 2014.

31 "China: Trade Balance, Percent of GDP," TheGlobalEconomy.com (*https://www.theglobaleconomy.com/China/Trade_balance/*).

32 Anne-Marie Brady, *Marketing Dictatorship: Propaganda and Thought Work in Contemporary China* (Lanham, MD: Rowman & Littlefield, 2008), p. 170.

33 Dong Zhang and Owen Freestone, "China's Unfinished State-Owned Enterprise Reforms," *Economic Roundup*, no. 2 (2013).

34 Andrew Batson, "Zhu Rongji Nostalgia and Li Peng's Legacy," *Andrew Batson's Blog*, August 31, 2020.

35 Sarah Eaton, *The Advance of the State in Contemporary China: State–Market Relations in the Reform Era* (New York: Cambridge University Press, 2016), p. 46.

36 Ibid.

37 Willy Wo-Lap Lam, *The Era of Jiang Zemin* (Singapore: Prentice Hall, 1999), pp. 369–70.

38 Richard McGregor, *The Party: The Secret World of China's Communist Rulers* (New York: Harper, 2010), p. 43.

39 Banning Garrett, "China Faces, Debates, the Contradictions of Globalization," *Asian Survey*, vol. 41, no. 3 (May/June 2001), p. 409.

40 Joseph Fewsmith, "China and the WTO: The Politics behind the Agreement," *NBR Analysis*, vol. 10, no. 5, November 1999.

41 Quoted in Thomas G. Moore, "China and Globalization," *Asian Perspective*, vol. 23, no. 4 (1999), p. 91.

42 See AEGIS Europe, "10 Commitments China Made When It Joined the WTO and Has Not Respected" (*https://static1.squarespace.com/static/5537b2 fbe4b0e49a1e30c01c/t/568f7bc51c1210296715af19/1452243910341/The+10 +WTO+Committments+of+China.pdf*).

43 Nicholas R. Lardy, "Issues in China's WTO Accession," testimony before the US–China Economic and Security Review Commission, May 9, 2001.

44 Thomas Rawski, "China Reform Watch: Turning Point Looming," *China Perspectives*, no. 38 (November/December 2001), p. 31.

45 See Justin R. Pierce and Peter K. Schott, "The Surprisingly Swift Decline of US Manufacturing Employment," *The American Economic Review*, vol. 106, no. 7 (July 2016), pp. 1632–62.

46 Stewart Paterson, *China, Trade and Power: Why the West's Economic Engagement Has Failed* (London: London Publishing Partnership, 2018), p. 48.

47 Ibid., pp. 33–53.

48 Ibid., pp. 41–3.

49 "China: Trade Balance, Percent of GDP."

50 David Orsmond, "China's Economic Choices," *Lowy Institute Analyses*, December 17, 2019.

51 Tom Holland, "Wen and Now: China's Economy Is Still 'Unsustainable,'" *South China Morning Post*, April 10, 2017.

52 Willy Wo-Lap Lam, *Chinese Politics in the Hu Jintao Era: New Leaders, New Challenges* (Armonk, NY: M.E. Sharpe, 2006), p. 254.

53 Feng Wang, "China's Population Destiny: The Looming Crisis," Brookings, September 30, 2010.

54 See Aaron L. Friedberg, *"Going Out": China's Pursuit of Natural Resources and the Implications for the PRC's Grand Strategy* (Seattle, WA: National Bureau of Asian Research, 2006), pp. 21–2.

55 "China: Government Debt," GlobalEconomy.com (*https://www.theglobalecon omy.com/China/Government_debt/*).

56 Orsmond, "China's Economic Choices."

57 David Dollar, "China's Economic Problems (and Ours)," *The Milken Institute Review*, 3rd quarter (2005), p. 50.

58 See Edward S. Steinfeld, *Playing Our Game: Why China's Rise Doesn't Threaten the West* (New York: Oxford University Press, 2010), pp. 70–119.

59 James McGregor, *China's Drive for "Indigenous Innovation": A Web of Industrial Policies* (Washington, DC: US Chamber of Commerce, 2010), p. 28.

60 John Lee, *Will China Fail? The Limits and Contradictions of Market Socialism* (Sydney: Centre for Independent Studies, 2009), pp. 94–5.

61 Garrett, "China Faces, Debates, the Contradictions of Globalization," p. 420.

62 Barry Naughton, "Strengthening the Center, and Premier Wen Jiabao," *China Leadership Monitor*, no. 21 (Summer 2007).

63 Nicholas R. Lardy, "China: Toward a Consumption-Driven Growth Path," *Policy Briefs in International Economics*, no. PB06-6, October 2006.

64 Batson, "The State Never Retreats," p. 14.

65 Lee, *Will China Fail?*, p. 84.

66 Rawski, "China Reform Watch," p. 31.

67 Batson, "The State Never Retreats," p. 15.

68 Rawski, "China Reform Watch," p. 32.

69 Joo-Youn Jung, "Retreat of the State? Restructuring the Chinese Central Bureaucracies in the Era of Economic Globalization," *The China Review*, vol. 8, no. 1 (Spring 2008), p. 118.

70 Regarding the State-Owned Assets Supervision and Administration Commiss-ion (SASAC) and the National Development and Reform Commission (NDRC), see Mark Wu, "The 'China Inc.' Challenge to Global Trade Governance," *Harvard International Law Journal*, vol. 57, no. 2 (Spring 2016), p. 277.

71 McGregor, *China's Drive for "Indigenous Innovation,"* p. 6.

72 Cong Cau, Richard P. Suttmeier, and Denis Fred Simon, "China's 15-Year Science and Technology Plan," *Physics Today* (December 2006), pp. 39–40.

73 Wen Jiabao quoted in McGregor, *China's Drive for "Indigenous Innovation,"* p. 4.

74 State Council of the People's Republic of China, "The National Medium- and Long-Term Program for Science and Technology Development (2006–2020): An Outline"(February 2006), p. 3.

75 McGregor, *China's Drive for "Indigenous Innovation,"* p. 4.

76 *The IP Commission Report* (Seattle, WA: National Bureau of Asian Research, 2013), pp. 17 and 1.

77 Barry Naughton, "China's Economic Policy Today: The New State Activism," *Eurasian Geography and Economics*, vol. 52, no. 3 (May 2011), p. 320.

78 Ibid., p. 324.

79 Tai Ming Cheung et al., *Planning for Innovation: Understanding China's Plans for Technological, Energy, Industrial, and Defense Development* (San Diego, CA: Institute on Global Conflict and Cooperation, 2016), pp. 35–7.

80 Naughton, "China's Economic Policy Today," p. 321.

81 McGregor, *China's Drive for "Indigenous Innovation,"* pp. 20–30.

82 Chen Ling and Barry Naughton, "An Institutionalized Policy-Making Mechanism: China's Return to Techno-Industrial Policy," *Research Policy*, no. 45 (2016), p. 2147.

83 Sebastian Heilmann and Lea Shih, "The Rise of Industrial Policy in China, 1978–2012," Harvard-Yenching Institute Working Paper Series (2013), p. 21.

84 See Jeremy Goldkorn, "Why Did So Many Foreigners Believe That Xi Would Be a Reformer?" *SupChina*, December 23, 2019.

85 The measures necessary to avoid this fate were discussed in a jointly authored report: World Bank and the Development Research Center of the State Council, People's Republic of China, *China 2030: Building a Modern, Harmonious, and Creative Society* (Washington, DC: World Bank, 2013).

86 See Jamil Anderlini and Ed Crooks, "China's Labour Pool Begins to Drain," *Financial Times*, January 18, 2013.

87 "China Pledges 'Decisive' Role for Markets in Reform Push," *Reuters*, November 12, 2013.

88 Arthur Kroeber, "Reform of Prices, Not Ownership," in Scott Kennedy, ed., *State and Market in Contemporary China* (Washington, DC: Center for Strategic and International Studies, 2016), p. 5.

89 Peter Martin, "Why Patchy Progress on China's Economic Reforms Is Inevitable," in ibid., p. 10.

90 See Barry Naughton, "Supply-Side Structural Reform: Policy-Makers Look for a Way Out," *China Leadership Monitor*, no. 49 (Winter 2016); Sean O'Connor, "SOE Megamergers Signal New Direction in China's Economic Policy," US–China Economic and Security Review Commission, Staff Research Report, May 24, 2018.

91 See Barry Naughton, "The Financialisation of the State Sector in China," *East Asian Policy*, vol. 11, no. 2 (2019), pp. 46–60.

92 Amir Guluzade, "The Role of China's State-Owned Companies Explained," *World Economic Forum*, May 7, 2019.

93 Margaret Pearson, Meg Rithmire, and Kellee S. Tsai, "Party-State Capitalism in China," Harvard Business School, Working Paper 21-065, 2020; Tanner

Brown, "What China's History of Reining in Business Executives Means for Ant's IPO," *Barron's*, November 6, 2020.

94 "Xi Jinping's Assault on Tech Will Change China's Trajectory," *The Economist*, August 14, 2021.

95 Jude Blanchette, "From 'China Inc.' to 'CCP Inc.': A New Paradigm for Chinese State Capitalism," *China Leadership Monitor*, no. 26 (Winter 2020).

96 "President Xi's Speech on Science, Technology Published," *ChinaDaily*, June 2, 2016.

97 September 2013 speech to the Politburo quoted in Greg Levesque, "Testimony before the US–China Economic and Security Review Commission Hearing on What Keeps Xi Up at Night: Beijing's Internal and External Challenges," 116th Congress, 1st session (Washington, DC: US Government Publishing Office, 2019), p. 120.

98 See US Chamber of Commerce, *Made in China 2025: Global Ambitions Built on Local Protections* (2017); European Union Chamber of Commerce in China, *China Manufacturing: Putting Industrial Policy Ahead of Market Forces* (2017).

99 Levesque, "Testimony before the US–China Economic and Security Review Commission," pp. 121–2.

100 Barry Naughton, *The Rise of China's Industrial Policy 1978 to 2020* (Mexico City: Universidad Nacional Autónoma de México, 2020), p. 72.

101 Levesque, "Testimony before the US–China Economic and Security Review Commission," p. 122.

102 Pearson et al., "Party-State Capitalism in China," p. 15.

103 Naughton, *The Rise of China's Industrial Policy*, p. 82.

104 Levesque, "Testimony before the US–China Economic and Security Review Commission," p. 123.

105 See Richard A. Bitzinger, "China's Shift from Civil–Military Integration to Military–Civil Fusion," *Asia Policy*, vol. 16, no. 1 (January 2021), pp. 5–24.

106 PRC Ministry of Science and Technology, "The 13th Five-Year Special Plan for Science and Technology Military–Civil Fusion Development." Translated by the Georgetown Center for Security and Emerging Technology, August 24, 2017.

107 Kate O'Keefe and Jeremy Page, "China Taps Its Private Sector to Boost Its Military, Raising Alarms," *Wall Street Journal*, September 25, 2019.

108 See the detailed critique of Chinese policies in Office of the United States Trade Representative, *Findings of the Investigation into China's Acts, Policies,*

and Practices Related to Technology Transfer, Intellectual Property, and Innovation Under Section 301 of the Trade Act of 1974 (Washington, DC: Executive Office of the President, 2018).

109 Bob Davis, "US Enlists Allies to Counter China's Technology Push," *Wall Street Journal*, February 28, 2021.

110 Chris Buckley and Steven Lee Myers, "China's Leaders Vow Tech 'Self-Reliance,' Military Power and Economic Recovery," *New York Times*, October 29, 2020; Adam Segal, "Seizing Core Technologies," *China Leadership Monitor*, no. 60 (Summer 2019).

111 World Bank, World Integrated Trade Solution, "China Trade Balance, Exports and Imports by Country and Region 2017" (*https://wits.worldbank.org/ CountryProfile/en/Country/CHN/Year/2017/TradeFlow/EXPIMP/Partner/all*).

112 Professor Jin Canrong of Renmin University quoted in Aaron L. Friedberg, "Globalisation and Chinese Grand Strategy," *Survival*, vol. 60, no. 1 (February/ March 2018), p. 31.

113 "Xi Jinping: Speech at the Forum of Experts in Economic and Social Fields," *Teller Report*, August 24, 2020.

114 Alicia Garcia-Herrero, "Why China's 'Dual Circulation' Plan Is Bad News for Everyone Else," *NikkeiAsia*, September 17, 2020.

115 Jude Blanchette and Andrew Polk, "Dual Circulation and China's New Hedged Integration Strategy," *CSIS Commentary*, August 24, 2020.

116 Julian Gewirtz, "The Chinese Reassessment of Interdependence," *China Leadership Monitor*, no. 64 (Summer 2020).

117 "Xi Jinping: Speech at the Forum of Experts in Economic and Social Fields."

118 Viviana Zhu, "China's Dual Circulation Economy," Institut Montaigne, *China Trends* (October 2020).

119 Xi Jinping, "Certain Major Issues for Our National Medium- to Long-Term Economic and Social Development Strategy." Translated by Georgetown Center for Security and Emerging Technology, November 10, 2020.

120 James Crabtree, "China's Radical New Vision of Globalization," *NOEMA*, December 10, 2020.

121 Xu Bin, "Dual Circulation, Consumption Stimulation or Regional Economic Integration . . . Which is the Way Forward for China's Economy in 2021?" *CEIBS Research*, January 15, 2021.

122 Gao Cheng quoted in Friedberg, "Globalisation and Chinese Grand Strategy," pp. 32–3.

123 Li Wei, Xu Jin, and Gao Cheng, quoted in ibid., p. 33.

124 Nadège Rolland, *China's Eurasian Century? Political and Strategic Implications*

of the Belt and Road Initiative (Seattle, WA: National Bureau of Asian Research, 2017), p. 96.

125 Crabtree, "China's Radical New Vision of Globalization."

126 H.R. McMaster, "How China Sees the World," *The Atlantic* (May 2020).

127 Michael Pettis, "The Problems with China's 'Dual Circulation' Economic Model," *Financial Times*, August 25, 2020.

Chapter 5 Strategy: "The Great Rejuvenation of the Chinese Nation"

1 Samuel P. Huntington, *The Clash of Civilizations and the Remaking of World Order* (New York: Simon & Schuster, 1996), p. 229.

2 Orville Schell and John Delury, *Wealth and Power: China's Long March to the Twenty-First Century* (New York: Random House, 2013), p. 387.

3 This concept and its implications for strategy are discussed in François Jullien, *A Treatise on Efficacy: Between Western and Chinese Thinking* (Honolulu: University of Hawaii Press, 2004), pp. 15–31.

4 Ren Xiao, "The International Relations Theoretical Discourse in China: A Preliminary Analysis," Sigur Center Asia Papers Number 9, Sigur Center for Asian Studies, Washington, DC, 2000, p. 3.

5 Huan Xiang quoted in Pillsbury, *China Debates the Future Security Environment*, p. 11.

6 April 1990 memo quoted in Michael Yahuda, "Deng Xiaoping: The Statesman," *The China Quarterly*, no. 135 (September 1993), p. 564.

7 Philip C. Saunders, "China's America Watchers: Changing Attitudes towards the United States," *The China Quarterly*, no. 161 (March 2000), p. 47.

8 Ibid.

9 Final report of a December 1993 symposium of high-level civilian and military leaders, quoted in Allen S. Whiting, "The PLA and China's Threat Perception," *The China Quarterly*, no. 146 (June 1996), p. 608.

10 Lam, *China after Deng Xiaoping*, pp. 140–1.

11 Ibid.

12 Pillsbury, *China Debates the Future Security Environment*, pp. 97–9.

13 Biwu Zhang, "Chinese Perceptions of American Power, 1991–2004," *Asian Survey*, vol. 45, no. 5 (September/October 2005), pp. 678–9.

14 Ren, "The International Relations Theoretical Discourse in China," p. 8.

15 Yahuda, "Deng Xiaoping," p. 564.

16 Dingding Chen and Jianwei Wang, "Lying Low No More? China's New Thinking on the Tao Guang Yang Hui Strategy," *China: An International Journal*, vol. 9, no. 2 (September 2011), p. 197.

17 Yahuda, "Deng Xiaoping," p. 564.

18 John W. Garver, *China's Quest: The History of the Foreign Relations of the People's Republic of China* (New York: Oxford University Press, 2016), pp. 493–7.

19 See Bates Gill, *Rising Star: China's New Security Diplomacy* (Washington, DC: Brookings, Institution Press 2007), pp. 74–103. Quote from p. 99.

20 Aaron L. Friedberg, *Beyond Air–Sea Battle: The Debate over US Military Strategy in Asia* (London: International Institute for Strategic Studies, 2014), pp. 15–44.

21 Pillsbury, *China Debates the Future Security Environment*, pp. 3–61.

22 Wang Jisi quoted in Yong Deng, "Hegemon on the Offensive: Chinese Perspectives on US Global Strategy," *Political Science Quarterly*, vol. 116, no. 3 (Autumn 2001), p. 346.

23 Gilbert Rozman, *Chinese Strategic Thought toward Asia* (New York: Palgrave Macmillan, 2010), p. 73.

24 See US Department of Defense, "US Security Strategy for the East Asia-Pacific Region," February 28, 1995.

25 Deng, "Hegemon on the Offensive," p. 349.

26 Zong Hairen, "Responding to the 'Two States Theory,'" *Chinese Law and Government*, vol. 35, no. 2 (March/April 2002), p. 24. Zong Hairen is the pseudonym of an aide to Zhu Rongji who arranged for his notes on high-level meetings to be translated and published in the West.

27 Deng, "Hegemon on the Offensive," p. 351.

28 David Shambaugh, *Modernizing China's Military: Progress, Problems, and Prospects* (Berkeley: University of California Press, 2002), pp. 3–4.

29 Andrew S. Erickson, *Chinese Anti-Ship Ballistic Missile (ASBM) Development: Drivers, Trajectories and Strategic Implications* (Washington, DC: Jamestown Foundation, 2013), p. 31.

30 See Rush Doshi, *The Long Game: China's Grand Strategy to Displace American Order* (New York: Oxford University Press, 2021), pp. 73–80.

31 Suettinger, *Beyond Tiananmen*, p. 322.

32 Garver, *China's Quest*, pp. 542–52.

33 David Shambaugh, "China Engages Asia: Reshaping the Regional Order," *International Security*, vol. 29, no. 1 (Winter 2004–5), p. 70; Gill, *Rising Star*, p. 27.

34 David M. Finkelstein, "China's New Security Concept," in Stephen J. Flannagan and Michael E. Marti, eds., *The People's Liberation Army and China in Transition* (Washington, DC: National Defense University Press, 2003), pp. 198–9.

35 Shirk, *China: Fragile Superpower*, p. 118.

36 Gill, *Rising Star*, p. 29.

37 Wu Xinbo, "Integration on the Basis of Strength: China's Impact on East Asian Security," Stanford University, Asia Pacific Research Center, February 1998, p. 10.

38 Finkelstein, "China's New Security Concept," p. 200.

39 David M. Finkelstein, "China Reconsiders Its National Security: The Great 'Peace and Development' Debate of 1999," Center for Naval Analyses, Arlington, VA, December 2000, pp. i–ii.

40 Zong Hairen, "The Bombing of China's Embassy in Yugoslavia," *Chinese Government and Politics*, vol. 35, no. 1 (January/February 2002), p. 75.

41 Shirk, *China: Fragile Superpower*, p. 193. The author reports having heard this story from a number of PLA officers.

42 Shambaugh, *Modernizing China's Military*, p. 185.

43 Quoted in Friedberg, *A Contest for Supremacy*, p. 98.

44 Prepared Statement of George J. Tenet, Director of Central Intelligence, Hearing before the Select Committee on Intelligence, *Current and Projected National Security Threats to the United States*, 106th Congress, 2nd session (Washington, DC: US Government Printing Office, 2000), p. 18.

45 Prepared Statement of J. Stapleton Roy, Assistant Secretary of State for Intelligence and Research, ibid., p. 7.

46 Jim Mann, "US Starting to View China as Potential Enemy," *Los Angeles Times*, April 16, 1995.

47 Rozman, *Chinese Strategic Thought toward Asia*, p. 115.

48 Andrew J. Nathan and Bruce Gilley, *China's New Rulers: The Secret Files* (New York: New York Review of Books, 2003), p. 236.

49 Wen Jiabao quoted in ibid., p. 236.

50 Ni Shixiong and Zhuang Jianzhong, "Bushi zhengfu dui Hua xin zhanlüe yu Zhongguo dui guan xin zhanlüe chutan" [A Preliminary Analysis of the Bush Administration's New China Strategy and China's Responding New Strategy], *Meiguo wenti yanjiu* [American Issues Analysis/Fudan American Review] (2002), p. 22.

51 Jin Tao, "Relations among Major Powers after '9.11'," *International Strategic Studies*, no. 4 (June 2002), p. 36.

52 Cui Liru, "China's 'Period of Historic Opportunities,'" *China–US Focus*, February 1, 2018.

53 Liu Jianfei, "Zhongguo minzhu zhengzhi jianshe yu Zhong Mei guanxi" [The Building of China's Democratic Politics and Sino-US Relations], *Zhanlüe yu guanli* [Strategy and Management], vol. 2 (2003).

54 Liu Huaqiu, Director of the State Council Foreign Affairs Office, quoted in Friedberg, *A Contest for Supremacy*, p. 151.

55 Evan S. Medeiros and M. Taylor Fravel, "China's New Diplomacy," *Foreign Affairs*, vol. 82, no. 6 (November/December 2003), pp. 22–35.

56 See Bonnie S. Glaser and Evan S. Medeiros, "The Changing Ecology of Foreign Policy-Making in China: The Ascension and Demise of the Theory of 'Peaceful Rise,'" *The China Quarterly*, no. 190 (June 2007), pp. 291–310.

57 William A. Callahan, "China's Strategic Futures," *Asian Survey*, vol. 52, no. 4 (July/August 2012), p. 624.

58 See Nina Silove, "The Pivot before the Pivot: US Strategy to Preserve the Power Balance in Asia," *International Security*, vol. 40, no. 4 (Spring 2016), pp. 45–88.

59 Friedberg, *Beyond Air–Sea Battle*, pp. 26–38.

60 Paul Schwartz, "Evolution of Sino-Russian Defense Cooperation since the Cold War," ASAN Forum (June 2014).

61 David E. Sanger, "US Would Defend Taiwan, Bush Says," *New York Times*, April 26, 2001.

62 See "US–China Counterterrorism Cooperation: Issues for US Policy," Congressional Research Service, RL33001, July 15, 2010.

63 Jacques deLisle, "9/11 and US--China Relations," Foreign Policy Research Institute, September 2011.

64 Xu Jian, "Yatai xingshi bianhua de si da qushi" [Four Main Trends in Changes in the Asia-Pacific Situation], *Liaowang* [Outlook], no. 41, October 10, 2005.

65 Qiu Danyang, "Zhongguo–Dongmeng ziyou maoyi: Zhongguo heping jueqi de diyuan jingji xue sikao" [China–ASEAN Free Trade Agreement: Examining China's Peaceful Rise from a Geoeconomic Perspective], *Dangdai Yatai* [Contemporary Asia-Pacific], no. 1 (2005).

66 Shi Yinhong, "Yilake zhanzheng yu Zong Mei guanxi taishi" [The Iraq War and Sino-US Relations], *Xiandai guoji guanxi* [Contemporary International Relations], no. 5 (2007).

67 Fu Menzhi, "Guoji zhengzhi jingji xingshi zhengzai jingli jubian" [International Politics and Economy Undergoing Great Changes], *Xiandai guoji guanxi* [Contemporary International Relations], no. 9 (2008).

68 Pan Zhongqi, "Cong 'suishi' dao 'moushi': youguan Zhongguo jinyubu heping fazhan de zhanlüe sikao" [From 'Trend-Follower' to 'Trend-Maker': Reflections on China's Further Peaceful Development Strategy], *Shijie jingji yu zhengzhi* [World Economy and Politics], no. 2 (2010).

69 Chen and Wang, "Lying Low No More?" pp. 195–216; Liu Mingfu, *The China Dream: Great Power Thinking and Strategic Posture in the Post-American Era* (New York: CN Times Books, 2015), p. 117.

70 Dai Bingguo, "Adhere to the Path of Peaceful Development," Xinhua, December 6, 2010. For an overview of this debate, see Yan Xuetong, "From Keeping a Low Profile to Striving for Achievement," *The Chinese Journal of International Politics*, vol. 7, no. 2 (2014), pp. 153–84.

71 Chen and Wang, "Lying Low No More?" p. 212.

72 Rush Doshi characterizes these changes in language as "momentous," and they did open the door to more assertive policies. But their full implications would not emerge until after Hu left office. Doshi, *The Long Game*, p. 160.

73 Work report of the 2012 18th Party Congress quoted in Michael D. Swaine, "Chinese Views and Commentary on Periphery Diplomacy," *China Leadership Monitor*, no. 44 (Summer 2014).

74 Suisheng Zhao, "Chinese Foreign Policy as a Rising Power to Find Its Rightful Place," *Perceptions*, vol. 18, no. 1 (Spring 2013), pp. 114–15. On the role of PLA "hawks" in this process, see Andrew Chubb, "Propaganda Not Policy: Explaining the PLA's 'Hawkish Faction' (Part One)," *China Brief*, vol. 13, no. 15 (July 2013) and "Propaganda Not Policy: Explaining the PLA's 'Hawkish Faction' (Part Two)," *China Brief*, vol. 13, no. 15 (August 2013).

75 Michael McDevitt, "The Origin and Evolution of the Rebalance," in Hugo Mejer, ed., *Origins and Evolution of the US Rebalance toward Asia: Diplomatic, Military, and Economic Dimensions* (New York: Palgrave Macmillan, 2015), pp. 31–54.

76 Yuan Peng, "Zhongguo zhanlüe jiyu qi bing wei zhongjie" [China's Period of Strategic Opportunity Is Far from Over], *People's Daily Overseas Edition*, July 30, 2012.

77 For the argument that China suffers from "great power autism," see Edward N. Luttwak, *The Rise of China vs. the Logic of Strategy* (Cambridge, MA: Harvard University Press, 2012).

78 "Zhongguo guoji zhanlüe huanjing zai pingheng" [Rebalancing China's International Strategic Environment], *Xuexi shibao* [Study Times], January 17, 2011.

79 Cheng Yue, "Zhongguo dangqian huanjing ji yingdui" [China's Current Environment and Counter-responses], *Xiandai guoji guanxi* [Contemporary International Relations], no. 11 (2010).

80 "Xi Pledges 'Great Renewal of Chinese Nation,'" Xinhua, November 29, 2012.

81 Bonnie S. Glaser and Deep Pal, "Is China's Charm Offensive Dead?" *China Brief*, vol. 14, no. 15 (July 2014).

82 Yan, "From Keeping a Low Profile to Striving for Achievement," p. 160.

83 See Zheng Wang, "The Chinese Dream: Concept and Context," *Journal of Chinese Political Science*, no. 19 (2014), pp. 1–13.

84 Shi Yinhong, "The Latest Transfer in China's Foreign Strategy: From 'Military Strategy' to 'Economic Strategy,'" *China International Relations*, vol. 25, no. 2 (March/April 2015), p. 52.

85 Quoted in Daniel Tobin, "World Class: The Logic of China's Strategy and Global Military Ambitions," in Roy Kamphausen, David Lai, and Tiffany Ma, eds., *Securing the China Dream: The PLA's Role in a Time of Reform and Change* (Seattle, WA: National Bureau of Asian Research, 2020), pp. 16–17.

86 Zhang Lu, "Meiguo chong fan Yatai shifou yi zai ezhi Zhongguo" [Is the US Return to the Asia-Pacific Intended to Contain China?], *Zhongguo Qinnianbao* [China Youth Daily], July 20, 2012.

87 Philip Rucker, "At US–China Shirtsleeves Summit, Formalities and Suspicions Abound," *Washington Post*, June 9, 2013.

88 On the origins of the concept, see Paul Mancinelli, "Conceptualizing 'New Type Great Power Relations': The Sino-Russian Model," *China Brief*, vol. 14, no. 9 (May 2014).

89 Cui Tiankai quoted in Michael S. Chase, "China's Search for a 'New Type of Great Power Relationship,'" *China Brief*, vol. 12, no. 17 (September 2012).

90 Chris Buckley, "China Leader Affirms Policy on Islands," *New York Times*, January 29, 2013; Timothy Heath, "The 'Holistic Security Concept': The Securitization of Policy and Increasing Risk of Militarized Crisis," *China Brief* vol. 15, no. 12 (June 2015).

91 See "The Asia-Pacific Maritime Security Strategy: Achieving US National Security Objectives in a Changing Environment," Department of Defense, August 2015, p. 15.

92 Josh Gerstein, "White House: China, Japan Squabble over 'Bunch of Rocks,'" *Politico*, January 21, 2011.

93 Jeff M. Smith, "Innocent Mistake," foreignaffairs.com, December 3, 2015.

94 "South China Sea: Obama Urges Beijing to Abide by Ruling," BBC News, September 3, 2016.

95 Jeremy Page, Carol E. Lee, and Gordon Lubold, "China's President Pledges No Militarization in Disputed Island," *Wall Street Journal*, September 25, 2015.

96 See Michael D. Swaine, "Chinese Views and Commentary on Periphery Diplomacy," *China Leadership Monitor*, no. 44 (Summer 2014); Timothy Heath, "China's Big Diplomacy Shift," *The Diplomat*, December 22, 2014.

97 David Bradley, "A 'New Situation': China's Evolving Assessment of Its Security Environment," *China Brief*, vol. 14, no. 15 (July 2014).

98 Chen Xiangyang, "Zhongguo heping fazhan san da tiaozhan yu duice"

[Three Major Challenges Facing China's Peaceful Development and Counter-measures], *Liaowang* [Outlook], no. 5 (2014).

99 Quotes from professors Jin Canrong and Wang Jisi in the report of a closed-door symposium of civilian researchers and strategists: Zhan Shiming, "Zhongguo de 'xijin' wenti: Yanpan yu sikao" [China's "Marching Westward" Topic: Assessment and Analysis], *Xiya Feizhou* [West Asia and Africa], no. 2 (2013).

100 Li Chenyang, "Zhongguo zai zhoubian diqu de mou pian buju" [China's Overall Layout for the Periphery Region], *Shijie zhishi* [World Affairs] no. 18 (2014).

101 Guo Shuyong, "'Zhoubian shi shouyao,' dang yi quyu zhili youxian" ["Periphery Is the Most Important," Regional Governance Should Be Prioritized], *Huanqiu Shibao* [Global Times], February 11, 2015.

102 Ma Xiaolin quoted in Zhan, "China's 'Marching Westward' Topic."

103 Yan Xuetong, "Zhengti de 'zhoubian' bi Meiguo geng zhongyao" [The Whole "Periphery" Is More Important Than the United States], *Huanqiu Shibao* [Global Times], January 15, 2015.

104 Wang Sheng and Luo Xiao, "Guoji tixi zhuanxing yu Zhongguo zhoubian waijiao zhi bian: Cong weiwen dao weiquan" [The Transformation of the International System and Changes in China's Periphery Diplomacy: From Maintaining Stability to Safeguarding Rights], *Xiandai guoji guanxi* [Contemporary International Relations], no. 1 (2013).

105 Wu Zhicheng, "Strategic Planning for Its Neighboring Diplomacy," *China International Relations*, vol. 25, no. 2 (March/April 2015), p. 63.

106 Shi, "The Latest Transfer in China's Foreign Strategy," p. 52.

107 The definitive study of OBOR/BRI is Rolland, *China's Eurasian Century?*

108 Song Guoyou, "Sichouzhilu jingjidai 'duichong' TPP" [Silk Road Economic Belt "Hedges against" TPP], *Guoji xianqu daobao* [International Herald Tribune], September 16, 2013.

109 Doshi, *The Long Game*, pp. 159–82.

110 Senior diplomats Yang Jiechi and Fu Ying quoted in Nadège Rolland, "Beijing's Vision for a Reshaped International Order," *China Brief*, vol. 18, no. 3 (February 2018).

111 Timothy R. Heath, "China and the US Alliance System," *The Diplomat*, June 11, 2014.

112 Xi Jinping, "New Asian Security Concept for New Progress in Security Cooperation," Remarks at the Fourth Summit of the Conference on Interaction and Confidence Building Measures in Asia, Shanghai Expo Center, May 21, 2014.

113 "Full Text of Hu Jintao's Report at 18th Party Congress," November 27, 2012.

114 Wu Jianmin, president emeritus of China's Foreign Affairs University, quoted in "China Wants Closer Relations But Not G2 – Official," Reuters, May 1, 2009.

115 Nadège Rolland, *China's Vision for a New World Order*, NBR Special Report #83 (January 2020), pp. 14–15.

116 Fu Ying, "2014: A Turning Point in the Global Order," *Chinese International Relations*, vol. 25, no. 2 (March/April 2015), p. 2.

117 Yuan Peng, "Quanqiu da bianju yu shijie xin zhixu" [Great Global Changes and the New World Order], *Xiandai guoji guanxi* [Contemporary International Relations], no. 10 (2016).

118 "Xi Calls for Reforms on Global Governance," Xinhua, September 29, 2016.

119 Helene Cooper, "US Defense Secretary Supports Trade Deal with Asia," *New York Times*, April 6, 2015.

120 Da Wei, "Sino-US Relations: Strategic Consensus and Stability Framework," *China International Relations*, vol. 25, no. 4 (July/August 2015), p. 77.

121 Early Chinese assessments are analyzed in François Godement, Camille Boullenois, Jiakun Jack Zhang, Melanie Hart, Blaine Johnson, and Earl Wang, "The Trump Opportunity: Chinese Perceptions of the US Administration," European Council on Foreign Relations, June 20, 2018.

122 Julian Gewirtz, "China Thinks America Is Losing," *Foreign Affairs*, vol. 99, no. 6 (November/December 2020), pp. 62–72.

123 The origins and significance of this term are discussed in Doshi, *The Long Game*, pp. 265–71.

124 Wu Baiyi, "American Illness," *China–US Focus*, June 17, 2020.

125 Chen Xiangyang, "China Advances as the US Retreats," *China–US Focus*, January 23, 2018.

126 Jude Blanchette, "Beijing's visions of American decline," *Politico*, March 11, 2021.

127 Jin Canrong quoted in Doshi, *The Long Game*, p. 271.

128 Yuan Peng, "The COVID-19 Pandemic and Changes Unseen in a Century," *China International Relations*, vol. 30, no. 4 (July/August 2020), p. 2.

129 Xi Jinping, "Secure a Decisive Victory in Building a Moderately Prosperous Society in All Respects and Strive for the Great Success of Socialism with Chinese Characteristics for a New Era," delivered at the 19th National Congress of the Communist Party of China, October 18, 2017, p. 9.

130 Ibid., p. 25.

131 Ibid., p. 24.

132 Ibid., pp. 48–9.

133 Ibid., p. 4.
134 Ibid., p. 9.
135 Ibid., p. 54.
136 Ibid., p. 9.
137 Greer, "Xi Jinping in Translation."
138 Daniel Tobin, Testimony before the US–China Economic and Security Review Commission, "How Xi Jinping's 'New Era' Should Have Ended US Debate on Beijing's Ambitions," March 13, 2020, p. 6.
139 "Commentary: Milestone Congress Points to New Era for China, the World," Xinhua, October 24, 2017.
140 Nadège Rolland, "Examining China's 'Community of Common Destiny,'" Power 3.0, January 23, 2018.
141 Elizabeth C. Economy, "Yes, Virginia, China Is Exporting Its Model," Asia Unbound, December 11, 2019. For evidence that Chinese strategists have been actively considering how best to disseminate their model in Africa, see Nadège Rolland, "A New Great Game? Situating Africa in China's Strategic Thinking," NBR Special Report #91, June 2021, pp. 21–4.
142 Alexander Sullivan and Kristine Lee, People's Republic of the United Nations (Washington, DC: Center for a New American Security, 2019), p. 6.
143 Yaroslav Trofimov, Drew Hinshaw, and Katie O'Keeffe, "How China Is Taking Over International Organizations, One Vote at a Time," Wall Street Journal, September 29, 2020.
144 Melanie Hart and Blaine Johnson, Mapping China's Global Governance Ambitions (Washington, DC: Center for American Progress, 2019), p. 20.
145 Anna Gross and Mahumita Murgia, "China and Huawei Propose Reinvention of the Internet," Financial Times, March 27, 2020.
146 Rolland, China's Vision for a New World Order, pp. 44–7.
147 Ibid., pp. 7–13.
148 Andrea Worden, "China at the UN Human Rights Council: Conjuring a 'Community of Shared Future for Humankind'?" in Nadège Rolland, ed., An Emerging China-Centric Order: China's Vision for a New World Order in Practice (Seattle, WA: National Bureau of Asian Research, 2020), p. 35.
149 Yi Edward Yang, "China's Strategic Narratives in Global Governance Reform under Xi Jinping," Journal of Contemporary China, vol. 30 (2021), pp. 299–313.
150 Mareike Ohlberg, "Boosting the Party's Voice: China's Quest for Global Ideological Dominance," Merics China Monitor, July 21, 2016.
151 Tanner Greer, "China's Plans to Win Control of the Global Order," Tablet, May 17, 2020.

152 Rolland, *China's Vision for a New World Order*, p. 49.

153 Hsu Szu-chien, Anne-Marie Brady, and J. Michael Cole, "Introduction," in Hsu Szu-Chien and J. Michael Cole, eds., *Insidious Power: How China Undermines Global Democracy* (Manchester: Camphor Press, 2020), p. xxxix.

154 Anne-Marie Brady, "Magic Weapons: China's Political Influence Activities under Xi Jinping," Woodrow Wilson Center, September 18, 2017.

155 Clive Hamilton, *Silent Invasion: China's Influence in Australia* (Melbourne: Hardie Grant, 2018).

156 Audrye Wong, "China's Economic Statecraft under Xi Jinping," Brookings, January 22, 2019.

157 Sui-Lee Wee and Keith Bradsher, "Why Are China's Consumers Threatening to Boycott H&M and Other Brands?" *New York Times*, April 6, 2021.

158 Keith Zhai and Yew Lun Tian, "In China, a Young Diplomat Rises as Aggressive Foreign Policy Takes Root," Reuters, March 31, 2020.

159 Andrew Small and Dhruva Jaishankar, "'For Our Enemies We Have Shotguns: Explaining China's New Assertiveness," *War on the Rocks*, July 20, 2020.

160 Chris Buckley, "'The East is Rising': Xi Maps Out China's Post-COVID Ascent," *New York Times*, March 3, 2021.

Chapter 6 Getting China Right

1 James Green, "In Defense of Diplomacy with China," *ChinaFile*, September 10, 2020.

2 Alastair Iain Johnston, "The Failures of the 'Failure of Engagement' with China," *Washington Quarterly*, vol. 42, no. 2 (Summer 2019), p. 103.

3 Neil Thomas, "Matters of Record: Relitigating Engagement with China," *MacroPolo*, September 3, 2019.

4 Johnston, "The Failures of the 'Failure of Engagement' with China," p. 110.

5 Robert Zoellick, "The China Challenge," *National Interest*, February 14, 2020.

6 Thomas, "Matters of Record: Relitigating Engagement with China."

7 See Andrew S. Erickson and Gabriel Collins, "Competition with China Can Save the Planet," *Foreign Affairs*, vol. 100, no. 3 (May/June 2021), pp. 136–49.

8 For an overview of recent research on this issue, see Scott Lincicome, "Testing the 'China Shock': Was Normalizing Trade with China a Mistake?" *Cato Institute Policy Analysis*, no. 895, July 8, 2020.

9 Green, "In Defense of Diplomacy with China."

10 Ibid.

11 Johnston, "The Failures of the 'Failure of Engagement' with China," p. 110.

12 See the discussion of counterfactuals in James B. Steinberg, "What Went Wrong? US–China Relations from Tiananmen to Trump," *Texas National Security Review*, vol. 3, no. 1 (Winter 2019/20), pp. 119–33.

13 This paragraph is derived from Aaron L. Friedberg, "Competing with China," *Survival*, vol. 60, no. 3 (June/July 2018), p. 15.

14 Mann, *The China Fantasy*, pp. 29–47.

15 Larry Diamond and Orville Schell, eds., *China's Influence and American Institutions* (Stanford: Hoover Institution Press, 2019).

16 These developments are vividly recounted in Josh Rogin, *Chaos under Heaven: Trump, Xi, and the Battle for the 21st Century* (New York: Houghton Mifflin Harcourt, 2021).

17 Laura Silver, Kat Devlin, and Christine Huang, "Most Americans Support Tough Stance toward China on Human Rights, Economic Issues," Pew Research Center, Washington, DC, March 4, 2021.

18 Michael Martina, "Biden to Hammer Trump's 'Tough Talk, Weak Action' on China, Top Adviser Says," Reuters, May 12, 2020.

19 Nick Wadhams, "What Biden Said about China in His First Speech to Congress," Bloomberg, April 18, 2021.

20 Alex Leary and Bob Davis, "Biden's China Policy Is Emerging – and It Looks a Lot Like Trump's," *Wall Street Journal*, June 10, 2021.

21 Laura Silver, Kat Devlin, and Christine Huang, "Unfavorable Views of China Reach Historic Highs in Many Countries," Pew Research Center, Washington, DC, October 6, 2020, p. 9.

22 Mann, *The China Fantasy*, p. 29.

23 John Feng, "China Chides 'Cold War Mentality' as Antony Blinken Bolsters Anti-Beijing Alliance," *Newsweek*, March 16, 2021.

24 Thomas Christensen, "There Will Not Be a New Cold War," foreignaffairs .com, March 24, 2021.

25 Andrew Bacevich, "We Don't Need a New Cold War with China," *Los Angeles Times*, April 18, 2021.

26 See Michael Pillsbury, "The Sixteen Fears: China's Strategic Psychology," *Survival*, vol. 54, no. 5 (October/November 2012), pp. 149–82.

27 Shawn Donnan and Katrina Manson, "Beijing Warns US against Trying to Contain China's Rise," *Financial Times*, October 30, 2017.

28 Finbarr Bermingham, "You Can't Contain China: Former US Trade Chief Robert Zoellick Warns Donald Trump," *South China Morning Post*, January 14, 2019.

29 Hugh White, "The Costs of Containing China," *EastAsiaForum*, January 9, 2019.

30 "Xi Challenges US Global Leadership, Warns against Decoupling," Bloomberg, April 20, 2021.

31 Henry Farrell and Abraham Newman, "The Folly of Decoupling from China," foreignaffairs.com, June 3, 2020.

32 "European Chamber Decoupling Report Launch. Decoupling: Severed Ties and Patchwork Globalisation," January 14, 2021.

33 For an attempt to calculate the costs of a 25% tariff on all two-way trade, see a report by the Rhodium Group and the US Chamber of Commerce, *Understanding US–China Decoupling: Macro-Trends and Industry Impacts*, February 2021.

34 Roxanne Liu and Lew Lun Tian, "Xi Says Chinese People Will Never Agree with Any Who Attempt to Impose Will on China," Reuters, September 3, 2020.

35 "Xi Says Party Can't Be Split from Masses in Rebuke to US," Bloomberg, September 3, 2020.

36 See, for example, Graham Allison and Fred Hu, "An Unsentimental China Policy," foreignaffairs.com, February 18, 2021.

37 "NSC 68: United States Objectives and Programs for National Security," April 14, 1950, in Etzold and Gaddis, eds., *Containment*, p. 389.

38 Together with Australia, Canada, Chile, Japan, and New Zealand, the CPTPP includes two countries that Freedom House rates as "unfree" (Vietnam and Brunei) and four described as "partly free" (Singapore, Peru, Mexico, and Malaysia). India is also rated as "partly free." Freedom House, "Countries and Territories" (*https://freedomhouse.org/countries/freedom-world/scores*).

39 Winston S. Churchill, *The Gathering Storm* (New York: Houghton Mifflin, 1948), p. 18.

40 Tom O'Connor, "China Says 'Biggest Threat to US Is US Itself' as Bill to Fund Competition Passes," *Newsweek*, June 9, 2021.

41 Jeff D. Colgan and Robert O. Keohane, "The Liberal Order Is Rigged," *Foreign Affairs*, vol. 96, no. 3 (May/June 2017), pp. 40, 43.

42 *Global Times* quoted in Sadanand Dhume, "It's Not Bigotry to Tell the Truth about China," *Wall Street Journal*, April 1, 2021.

43 See Charles W. Boustany, Jr. and Aaron L. Friedberg, *Partial Disengagement: A New US Strategy for Economic Competition with China*, NBR Special Report #82 (November 2019).

44 James Manyika, William H. McRaven, and Adam Segal, "Innovation and National Security: Keeping Our Edge," Council on Foreign Relations, Independent Task Force, no. 77 (2019).

45 "US to Look at More Restrictions on Tech Exports to China," Reuters, February 10, 2021.

46 Charles Edel, "Democracies Need Alliances to Secure Vital Supply Chains," *The Strategist*, May 6, 2020; Chad P. Brown and Douglas A. Irwin, "Why Does Everyone Suddenly Care about Supply Chains?" *New York Times*, October 14, 2021.

47 Anthony Vinci, "Like NATO But for Economic Warfare: How to Stop China from Imposing Its Values," *The Atlantic* (August 2020).

48 "Foreigners Rush inside the Great Wall," *The Economist*, June 12, 2021.

49 Benn Steil, "Models for a Post-COVID US Foreign Economic Policy," in Hal Brands and Frank Gavin, Jr., eds., *COVID-19 and World Order* (Baltimore, MD: Johns Hopkins University Press, 2020), p. 200.

50 Ibid.

51 Ashley Tellis, "The Geopolitics of the TTIP and the TPP," in Sanjaya Baru and Suvi Dogra, eds., *Power Shifts and New Blocs in the Global Trading System* (London: International Institute for Strategic Studies, 2015), pp. 93–119.

52 Ashley Townshend and Brendan Thomas-Noone with Matilda Steward, *Averting Crisis: American Strategy, Military Spending and Collective Defence in the Indo-Pacific* (Sydney: United States Study Centre, 2019), p. 2.

53 Helen Davidson, "China Could Invade Taiwan in Next Six Years, Top US Admiral Warns," *Guardian*, March 9, 2021.

54 "The Most Dangerous Place on Earth," *The Economist*, May 1, 2021.

55 Wendell Minnick, "Post-Invasion Nightmare: Taiwan Becomes America's Enemy," *National Interest*, January 21, 2019.

56 For the arguments in favor of a change in policy, see Charles L. Glaser, "Washington Is Avoiding the Tough Questions on Taiwan and China," foreig naffairs.com, April 28, 2021. Regarding the critical importance of defending Taiwan to sustaining the US position in Asia, see Bridge A. Colby, *The Strategy of Denial: American Defense in an Age of Great Power Conflict* (New Haven: Yale University Press, 2021).

57 Joe Gould, "Eyeing China, Indo-Pacific Command Seeks $27 billion Deterrence Fund," *DefenseNews*, March 1, 2021.

58 Felix K. Chang, "The Ryukyu Defense Line: Japan's Response to China's Push into the Pacific Ocean," Foreign Policy Research Institute, February 8, 2021.

59 Takuya Mizorogi, "Japan and EU Name Taiwan in Joint Statement for First Time," *NikkeiAsia*, May 28, 2021.

60 Ralph Jennings, "Western Countries Send Ships to South China Sea in Pushback against Beijing," voanews.com, February 22, 2021.

61 Sheila A. Smith, "The Quad in the Indo-Pacific: What to Know," cfr.org, May 27, 2021.

62 Richard J. Ellings, "The Strategic Context of China–Russia Relations," in Richard J. Ellings and Robert Sutter, eds., *Axis of Authoritarians: Implications of China–Russia Cooperation* (Seattle, WA: National Bureau of Asian Research, 2018), pp. 3–50.

63 See Toshi Yoshihara and Jack Bianchi, *Seizing on Weakness: Allied Strategy for Competing with China's Globalizing Military* (Washington, DC: Center for Strategic and Budgetary Assessments, 2021).

64 See Devin Thorne and Ben Spevack, *Harbored Ambitions: How China's Port Investments Are Strategically Reshaping the Indo-Pacific* (Washington, DC: C4ADS, 2017).

65 Lauren Giella, "US General Worried about China's Efforts to Establish Military Base on Africa's West Coast," *Newsweek*, May 6, 2021.

66 Steve Raaymakers, "China Expands Its Island-Building Strategy into the Pacific," *The Strategist*, September 11, 2020.

67 See Scott Rozelle and Natalie Hell, *Invisible China: How the Urban–Rural Divide Threatens China's Rise* (Chicago: University of Chicago Press, 2020).

68 See Yanzhong Huang, *Toxic Politics: China's Environmental Health Crisis and the Challenge to the Chinese State* (New York: Cambridge University Press, 2020).

69 Derek Scissors, "China's Economic 'Miracle' in Context," aei.org, August 26, 2019.

70 Ben Kesling and Jon Emont, "US Goes on the Offensive against China's Empire-Building Funding Plan," *Wall Street Journal*, April 9, 2019.

71 Steve Holland and Guy Falcounbridge, "G7 Rivals China with Grand Infrastructure Plan," Reuters, June 13, 2021.

72 Beth Daley, "China Has Been Transforming International Education to Become a Leading Host of Students," *The Conversation*, May 12, 2021.

73 Michael Schwille and Scott Fisher, "Satellite Internet Services – Fostering the Dictator's Dilemma?" *Small Wars Journal*, April 11, 2021.

Index